MW00851411

MEGA
PLANNING

RENEWALS 458-4574

DATE DUE

MAR 1 9			
GAYLORD			PRINTED IN U.S.A.

MEGA
PLANNING

**Practical
Tools
for
Organizational
Success**

Roger Kaufman

Sage Publications, Inc.
International Educational and Professional Publisher
Thousand Oaks ▪ London ▪ New Delhi

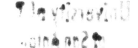

For information:

Sage Publications, Inc.
2455 Teller Road
Thousand Oaks, California 91320
E-mail: order@sagepub.com

Sage Publications Ltd.
6 Bonhill Street
London EC2A 4PU
United Kingdom

Sage Publications India Pvt. Ltd.
M-32 Market
Greater Kailash I
New Delhi 110 048 India

Printed in the United States of America

Library of Congress Cataloging-in-Publication Data

Kaufman, Roger A.

   Mega planning: Practical tools for organizational success / by
Roger Kaufman.
       p. cm.
   Includes bibliographical references and index.
   ISBN 0-7619-1324-6 (cloth: acid-free paper)
   ISBN 0-7619-1325-4 (pbk.: acid-free paper)
   1. Management. 2. Strategic planning. 3. Organizational
effectiveness. 4. Success in business. I. Title.
   HD31 .K3459 1999
   658.4'012--dc21   99-6731

00   01   02   03   04   05   06   7   6   5   4   3   2   1

Acquiring Editor:	Harry Briggs
Editorial Assistant:	MaryAnn Vail
Production Editor:	Sanford Robinson
Editorial Assistant:	Patricia Zeman / Nevair Kabakian
Copy Editor:	Joyce Kuhn
Typesetter/Designer:	Marion Warren
Indexer:	Mary Mortensen
Cover Designer:	Ravi Balasuriya

Contents

Acknowledgments

My continuing education has me noticing an increasing number of professionals who have found that there indeed must be formal linkages among what organizations use, do, produce, and deliver. They must also add value for external clients and society.

I wish to thank many of these professionals for helping me to continuously improve my ideas, formulations, and writings, including:

Ryan Watkins, Nova Southeastern University, and Doug Leigh, Office for Needs Assessment & Planning at Florida State University, who have not only critiqued my work and helped me think things through but have published articles and chapters with me on evolving concepts and related research and have also co-developed exercises, some of which are included in this book;

Leon Sims, Scott Schaffer, and John Parker, of Florida State University's Office for Needs Assessment & Planning;

The faculty and students of the Educational Research and Instructional Systems program at Florida State University;

William Swart, Professor of Engineering Management and Dean, College of Engineering & Technology, Old Dominion University;

Clients who provide the opportunity, platform, and feedback to subject all of this to continuous improvement;

Neil Crispo and Florida TaxWatch;

Larry Lipsitz, Editor of Educational Technology Publishers (who had the foresight and conviction to support the entire field and help develop it);

Members and staff of the International Society for Performance Improvement;

Joe Eckenrode and Technomic Publishers, who have provided a publishing forum for previous books;

American Society for Training and Development staff;

Sage Publications and Corwin Press, who have made several of my books available to a broad range of interested professionals. Of special note are Sage's Harry Briggs, who was early to commit to this book's predecessor, *Strategic Planning Plus,* and who is bringing this book to you, and Marquita Flemming, who first signed this book with faith in me and the topic;

Trish Dreher and Christin Hernet, who prepared many of the graphics and fought off computer viruses in the production drama, and Jean Van Dyke, who did final manuscript preparation.

The list of mentors would be very long indeed—so many have attempted to make me smarter than I really am—but I must include Leon Lessinger, Ted Blau, the late Harold Crosby and Bob Corrigan, Roger Addison, Sivasailam (Thiagi) Thiagarajan, Paula MacGillis, Steve Duncan, Dale Brethower, Don Triner, JC Fikes, Dave Feldman, Bob Gagne, Harold Greenwald, Joe Harless, Dale Lick, Ken Modesitt, Fred Nickles, Mariano Bernardez, Caesar Naples, Wess Roberts, Tom Tinney, Mel Stith, Steve Slepin, Jerry Herman, John Lombardi, Doug Zahn, Hugh Oakley-Browne, Peter Sharp, Jane McCann, Phil Hanford, Don Watts, Doug Hinchliffe, and Ronald Forbes, to name but a few. A very few.

But most central of all is my wife Jan, who has provided both the feedback and partnership that makes me more than I could possibly dream of being without her.

Introduction

An "Owner's Manual" for Benefiting From This Book

Let's get right to the point. Defining and then achieving sustained organizational success is possible. It relies on two basic elements:

1. *A societal value-added "frame of mind" or paradigm*: Your perspective about your organization, people, and our world; it is the "paradigm"[1] you use to understand reality
2. *Pragmatic and basic tools*

The Societal Value-Added Perspective and Frame of Mind

The required frame of mind, your guiding paradigm, is simple, straightforward, and sensible. It is to have a primary concern for adding value for external clients and society. From this societal value-added frame, everything one uses, does, produces, and delivers is linked to achieving positive societal results. This societal frame of reference, or paradigm, I call the *Mega* level of planning. Mega Planning has societal value added as its primary focus and perspective.

A central question that each and every organization should ask and answer is this:

If your organization is the solution, what's the problem?

This fundamental proposition is central to thinking and planning strategically: Mega Planning. It represents a shift from the usual focus only on oneself and one's organization to making certain you also add value to external clients and society. Yes, external clients and society. This basic question, directly or indirectly, will reappear throughout this book, for it keeps ends and means in perspective and better assures your success through making a useful contribution outside your organization where you and your clients live and work.

▓ An Overview of the Basic Concepts and Tools for Mega Planning

There are three basic tools, guides actually, that will be helpful to you as you define and achieve organizational success. I will define each in much greater detail later, but for our entry into Mega Planning and strategic thinking, here is the short introduction to these three guides:

Guide 1: Organizational Elements Model

The Organizational Elements Model (OEM) defines and links what any organization uses, does, produces, and delivers with external client and societal value added. For each Element, there is an associated level of planning. Successful planning links and relates all of the Organizational Elements, for each organization has external clients for which it must add value. Measurable value.

Here, in Table I.1[2] are the Organizational Elements along with the levels of planning to which each relates.

Guide 2: Six-Step Problem-Solving Model

A six-step problem-solving model, shown in Figure I.1, includes (1.0) identifying problems based on needs, (2.0) determining detailed solution requirements and identifying (but not yet selecting) solution alternatives, (3.0) selecting solutions from among alternatives, (4.0) implementation, (5.0) evaluation, and (6.0) continuous improvement (at each and every step).

Each time you want to identify problems and opportunities and systematically get from current results and consequences to desired ones, use the six-step process.

Guide 3: Six Critical Success Factors

Figure I.2 shows the six critical success factors (CSFs)[3] that set the vital framework of this book and for Mega Planning. Unlike conventional "critical success factors," these are factors for successful planning, not just for the things that an organization must get done to meet its mission. These are for Mega Planning, regardless of the type or size of the organization.

To be successful—to do and apply Mega Planning—you have to realize that yesterday's methods and results often are not appropriate for tomorrow. Most planning experts agree that the past is only prologue, and tomorrow must be crafted through new patterns of perspectives, tools, and results.[4] The tools and concepts for meeting the new realities of society, organizations, and people are linked to each of the six CSFs.

TABLE I.1 The Three Levels of Planning, and a Brief Description of Each

Name of the Organizational Element	*Name of the Level of Planning and Focus*	*Brief Description*
Outcomes	Mega	Results and their consequences for external clients and society
Outputs	Macro	The results an organization can or does deliver outside itself
Products	Micro	The building-block results produced within the organization
Processes	Process	The ways, means, activities, procedures, and methods used internally
Inputs	Input	The human, physical, and financial resources an organization can or does use

NOTE: These elements are also useful for defining the basic questions every organization must ask and answer as provided in Figure I.2.

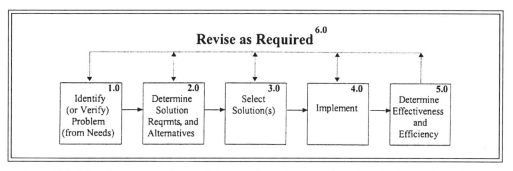

Figure I.1. The six-step problem-solving process: A process for identifying and resolving problems (and identifying opportunities).

The first five chapters are devoted to detailing one or more of the CSFs. Provided in these chapters are the basic concepts and rational for each area as well as the appropriate tools for achieving each, such tools as *needs assessment, needs analysis, costs-consequences analysis, system analysis, quality management/continuous improvement, evaluation,* and *methods-means analysis.*

The details and how-to's for each of the three guides are also provided. There are a number of applications for the guides. They should be considered as forming an integrated set of tools—like a fabric—instead of only each one on its own.[5]

In order to apply the guides and concepts provided early in the book, a Mega Planning framework is provided later. This framework, in turn, has three phases: Scoping, Planning, and

---

CRITICAL SUCCESS FACTOR 1
USE NEW AND WIDER BOUNDARIES FOR THINKING, PLANNING, DOING, AND EVALUATING/
CONTINUOUSLY IMPROVING: MOVE OUT OF TODAY'S COMFORT ZONES.

CRITICAL SUCCESS FACTOR 2
DIFFERENTIATE BETWEEN ENDS AND MEANS—FOCUS ON "WHAT" (Mega/Outcomes, Macro/Outputs,
Micro/Products) BEFORE "HOW."

CRITICAL SUCCESS FACTOR 3
USE ALL THREE LEVELS OF PLANNING AND RESULTS
(Mega/Outcomes, Macro/Outputs, and Micro/Products).

CRITICAL SUCCESS FACTOR 4
PREPARE OBJECTIVES—INCLUDING IDEAL VISION AND MISSION OBJECTIVES—THAT HAVE
MEASURES OF HOW YOU WILL KNOW WHEN YOU HAVE ARRIVED
(Mission statement plus success criteria).

CRITICAL SUCCESS FACTOR 5
DEFINE "NEED" AS A GAP IN RESULTS
(not as insufficient levels of resources, means, or methods).

CRITICAL SUCCESS FACTOR 6
USE AN IDEAL VISION AS THE UNDERLYING BASIS
FOR PLANNING (don't be limited to your organization).

Figure I.2. The six critical success factors for Mega-level strategic planning (and strategic thinking).

Implementation/Continuous Improvement. From this framework, specific tools and methods are provided to do Mega Planning. It is not complex, really. If you simply use the three guides, you will be able to put it all together.

When doing Mega planning, you and your associates will ask and answer the questions shown in Figure I.3.

A "yes" to all questions will lead you toward Mega Planning and allow you to prove that you have added value, something that is becoming increasingly important. These questions relate to Guide 1. It defines each Organizational Element in terms of its label and the question each addresses.

Use these guides throughout this book, for they provide the conceptual structure. They are Mega Planning guides.

Mega Planning is proactive. Many approaches to organizational improvement wait for problems to happen and then scramble to respond. Of course, like true love, the course of organizational success hardly every runs smoothly. But there is a temptation to react to problems and never take the time to plan so that surprises are fewer and success is defined—before problems

?	Do you commit to deliver organizational contributions that have positive impacts for society? (**MEGA**/Outcomes)
?	Do you commit to deliver organizational contributions that have the quality required by your external partners? (**MACRO**/Outputs)
?	Do you commit to produce internal results that have the quality required by your internal partners? (**MICRO**/Products)
?	Do you commit to have efficient internal products, programs, projects, and activities? (**PROCESSES**)
?	Do you commit to create and ensure the quality and appropriateness of the human, capital, and physical resources available? (**INPUTS**)
?	Do you commit to deliver (a) products, activities, methods, and procedures that have positive value and worth, and (b) the results and accomplishments defined by our objectives? (**EVALUATION/CONTINUOUS IMPROVEMENT**)

Figure I.3. The basic questions every organization must ask and answer.

spring up—and then systematically achieved. Figure I.4 provides a job aid to consider any time you start organizational planning.

Major Topics of This Book

Here are some of the major topics to be covered. And these will also be related one to the others, with applications provided for each. The topics are popular and important, but often, in the conventional literature, they are not precisely defined and usually not interrelated:

- *Strategic thinking:* An approach to any and all improvement with a primary focus on societal value added.[6]
- *Strategic planning plus:* Another name for Mega planning. It is strategic planning that incorporates strategic thinking and links everything that is used, done, produced, and delivered to Mega: to societal value added.[7]
- *Quality management:* The important and useful process, built on the insights and contributions of Deming and Juran, that involves the continuous improvement of what organizations use, do, and produce. It is often termed Total Quality Management (TQM).
- *Quality management plus:* A process for continuous improvement (or TQM) that includes societal (Mega) value added to the array of ends and means to be improved.
- *Needs assessment:* The identification of *needs* as gaps between current and required results (not gaps in resources or inputs or processes) and placing those needs in priority order on the basis of the costs to meet the needs as compared to the costs to ignore them.[8]
- *Needs analysis:* Based on the needs assessment that identified *needs* (in terms of gaps between current and desired/required results), *needs analysis* diagnoses the causes for the gaps in results and then identifies possible ways and means (but not selecting them) to meet the needs, that is, close the gaps in results.[9]

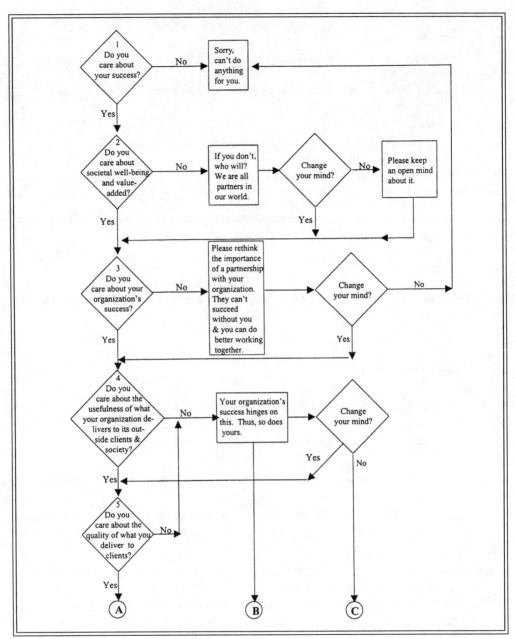

Figures I.4a, b, c. An algorithm for choosing what to accomplish before electing to attempt to make things better.

- *Benchmarking:* Comparing one's processes and results with a standard, usually the processes of another organization, in order to improve one's own procedures and results.

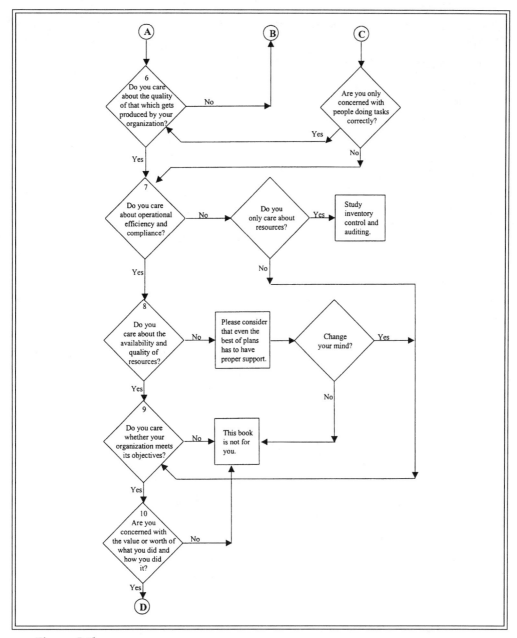

Figure I.4b.

- *Reengineering:* An improvement process that asks "If this current process, procedure, activity, method, unit, and or operation did not exist, would we create it? And if we did re-create it, would it be exactly as it now is?" Reengineering questions can and should be

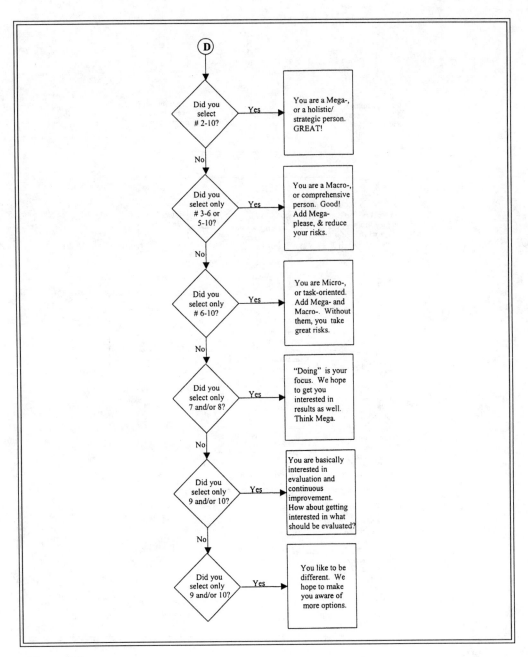

Figure I.4c.

answered about organizational means, and ends as well as for entire organizations and for communities and societies.

- *Continuous improvement/evaluation:* Evaluation compares results with intentions. *Continuous improvement* uses evaluation data to constantly and consistently improve. Both are reactive in that they build on data and existing systems.[10] Data should be used for improving and fixing, never for blaming.

- *Value added:* The measurable increase of the value and worth of any resource and/or process/methods/activities in terms of results that happen as a consequences of that resource and/or process/methods/activities being applied. This calculation is often called *costs-consequences analysis.* Based on what you give, and what you get back, indicators are derived for estimating value added. Your organization has to add value to all, both inside and outside the organization. Calculating this type of return-on-investment is central to proving worth.

- *Two bottom lines:* There are two ways of measuring value added: a *conventional bottom line,* such as a quarterly profit-and-loss sheet or refunding of a public agency, and a *societal bottom line,* which indicates value added to external clients and society.[11]

Each of these terms and concepts will be defined, related, and have applications provided. Now let's turn to the six CSFs and provide you with brief examples of each. The extent to which you and your organization incorporates all six CSFs is the extent to which you will define and achieve success.

The Six Critical Success Factors[12]

Each of these six CSFs (Guide 3) forms the basis of a chapter following this Introduction. To get a feel for the frame of mind (or paradigm) that Mega Planning requires, let's look at each CSF in brief.

Critical Success Factor 1. Use new and wider boundaries for thinking, planning, doing, and evaluating/continuously improving. Move out of today's comfort zones.

Look around our world. There is evidence just about everywhere that tomorrow is not a linear projection—a straight-line function—of yesterday and today, such as car manufacturers that squander their dominant client base by shoving unacceptable vehicles into the market or airlines that focus on shareholder value and ignore customer value. A lot of "conventional paradigm" organizations are "history," as noted by futurist Alvin Toffler in his early classic *The Third Wave* and his more recent *War and Anti-War.*[13] An increasing number of credible authors have been and continue telling us that the past is, at best, prologue and not a harbinger of what the future will be. In fact, old paradigms can be so deceptive that Tom Peters suggests that "organizational forgetting" must become conventional culture.[14]

Chapter 1 provides the "new realities" for future Mega Planning and success: the bases for applying CSF 1. Times have changed, and anyone who doesn't also change appropriately is risking failure. It is vital to use new and wider boundaries for thinking, planning, doing, and delivering. Doing so will require getting out of current comfort zones. Not doing so will likely deliver failure.[15]

Critical Success Factor 2: Differentiate between ends and means. Focus on "what" (Mega/Outcomes, Macro/Outputs, Micro/Products) before "how."[16]

People, especially in our U.S. culture, are "doing-type people." We hate delay and detest not swinging right into action. We want to get going. In this dash to doing, we often jump right into *solutions*—means—before we know the results—ends—we must deliver. Writing and using measurable performance objectives is something upon which almost all performance improvement authors agree. Objectives correctly focus on ends and not methods, means, or resources.[17] Ends, the "what," sensibly should be identified and defined before we select "how" to get from where we are to our destinations. If we don't base our solutions, methods, resources, and interventions on the basis of what results we are to achieve, what do we have in mind to make the selections of means, resources, or activities?

Focusing on means, processes, and activities are usually more comfortable as a starting place for conventional performance improvement initiatives. Doing so can be seductive but dangerous. For example, imagine that you are in a novel area and then are provided with a new automobile, keys in the ignition, and fully fueled, but there are no maps for navigation toward where to head or to guide your journey after you start out. This situation would be similar if, for any organization and performance improvement initiative, you were provided process tools and techniques without a clear map that included a definite destination identified (along with a statement of why you want to get to the destination in the first place). Also, one risk for starting a performance improvement journey with means and processes that there is no way of knowing whether your trip is taking you toward a useful destination or the criteria for telling you if you were making progress.[18]

It is vital that successful planning focuses first on results—useful performance in measurable terms—for setting its purposes, measuring progress, and providing continuous improvement toward the important results, and for determining what to keep, what to fix, and what to abandon.

Chapter 2 provides the concepts and tools for focusing on useful ends before deciding "how" to get things done. It also sets the stage for the next two related CSFs (3 and 4).

Critical Success Factor 3: Use all three levels of planning and results.

As I noted in CSF 2 (above), it is vital to prepare all objectives that focus only on ends, never on means or resources. As will be seen in later chapters, there are three levels each of planning and results, shown in Table I.2, that are important to target and link.

Chapter 2 discusses and defines the three levels of planning (Mega, Macro, Micro) and the three levels of results (Outcomes, Outputs, Products)[19] and how to assure that there is strategic, tactical, and operational alignment among what you and your organization use, do, produce, deliver, and the value added for external clients.

Critical Success Factor 4: Prepare objectives—including those for the Ideal Vision and mission objective—that have indicators of how you will know when you have arrived (mission statement plus success criteria).

TABLE I.2 Levels of Planning and Results That Should Be Linked During Planning, Doing, and Evaluation and Continuous Improvement

Primary Client and Beneficiary	*Level of Planning*	*Level of Result*
Society and external clients	Mega	Outcomes
The organization itself	Macro	Outputs
Individuals and small groups	Micro	Products

It is vital to state, precisely and rigorously, where you are headed and how to tell when you have arrived.[20] Statements of objectives must be in performance terms so that one can plan how best to get there, how to measure progress toward the end, and how to note progress toward it.[21]

Objectives, at all levels of planning, activity, and results, are absolutely vital. And as will be noted later, everything is measurable, so don't kid yourself into thinking you can dismiss important results as being "intangible" or "nonmeasurable." It is only sensible and rational to make a commitment to measurable purposes and destinations. Increasingly, organizations throughout the world are focusing on Mega-level results.[22]

Chapter 2 presents the concepts and tools for the required levels of precision and rigor, at all organizational levels of planning and doing, to make you successful.

Critical Success Factor 5: Define "need" as a gap between current and desired results (not as insufficient levels of resources, means, or methods).

Conventional English-language usage would have us employ the common world "need" as a verb (or in a verb sense) to identify means, methods, activities, and actions and/or resources we desire or intend to use.[23] Terms such as "need to," "need for," "needing," and "needed" are common, conventional, and destructive to useful planning. What? Semantic quibbling? Absolutely not.

As hard as it is to change our own behavior (and most of us who want others to change seem to resist it the most ourselves!) it is central to useful planning to distinguish between ends and means, noted as CSF 2. To do reasonable and justifiable planning, we have to (1) focus on ends and not means and thus (2) use "need" as a noun. Need, for the sake of useful and successful planning is used only as a noun, as a gap between current and desired results.

In Chapter 3, if we use need as a noun, we will be able to not only justify useful objectives but what we do and deliver on the basis of costs-consequences analysis. We will be able to justify everything we use, do, produce, and deliver. It is the only sensible way we can demonstrate value added. It really is. Also provided are the tools for needs assessment and needs analysis: what they are and how to do them.

Critical Success Factor 6: Use an Ideal Vision as the underlying basis for all planning and doing (don't be limited to your own organization).

Here is another area that requires some change from the conventional ways of doing planning. Again, we have to buck the conventional wisdom.

An Ideal Vision is never prepared for an organization but, rather, identifies the kind of world we want to help create for tomorrow's child. From this societal-linked Ideal Vision, each organization can identify what part or parts of the Ideal Vision it commits to deliver and move ever closer toward. If we base all planning and doing on an Ideal Vision of the kind of society we want for future generations, we can achieve "strategic alignment" for what we use, do, produce, deliver, and the external payoffs for Outputs.

But we have to change some paradigms, change some old habits. Even, as Peters suggests, "forget" processes and paradigms that will hamper our success.[24] Get out of our current comfort zones. Chapter 6 identifies the nature and characteristics of an Ideal Vision, defines what they are, and how to both derive and use them.

The balance of this book takes you from tools and concepts to application and continued success. Each chapter is intended to build on the previous ones, so please read and use them sequentially for moving ahead into the "whats," "whys," and "hows" of Mega Planning. Your objective and critical thought and actions will be the vital elements in achieving personal and organizational success.

Ready? Let's start.

Note: General references for Mega Planning (and strategic thinking) by authors cited in the Notes sections are combined in the Bibliography at the end of the book. Cited works and related readings in that section with a • in front of them are basic to Mega Planning.

EXERCISES

Everyone in every organization should be adding value to the organization and external clients and society. To calibrate what value you and your organization contribute, answer the following questions:

1. How do you now add value to
   a. yourself?
   b. your group?
   c. your organization?
   d. your external clients?
   e. society?

2. How do you know? What data can you use to justify your answers?

3. What could you do to add value to
   a. yourself?
   b. your group?
   c. your organization?

       d. your external clients?

       e. society?

    4. How will you know when you have added value? What data and evidence will be required?

Notes

1. The work of Thomas Kuhn for the "hard sciences" and the work of Joel Barker, who relates Kuhn's findings to the social sciences, provide the definitions for my use of "paradigm."

2. In each chapter and section, figures and tables are identified with the chapter number first (e.g., Figure 2.3 is the third figure in Chapter 2).

3. Please realize that, unlike many other presentations of critical success factors, these relate to any organization and should be generalized to any organization, public or private. Most "critical success factors" discussed in the management literature refer to organization-specific factors related to a unique business. The CSFs discussed here apply to any organization and so are "above" any organization-specific factors.

4. Most planning experts now agree. I first proposed using a societal frame of reference as the primary focus for individuals and organizations in 1968 and 1969 (which brought alarm and suspicion on the part of many "old paradigm" thinkers). But I have recently been joined in this call for such new paradigms by many future-oriented thinkers including (but not limited to) those noted in this Introduction. This shift in thinking to new paradigms—frames of reference that are radically different from the "conventional wisdom"—are sprouting as Joel Barker suggested that they would when seen by the "paradigm pioneers" of our world. Please review the references in the Bibliography that are noted with a • before them, for these particularly focus on new paradigms for Mega Planning and are fundamental to the major thrusts of, and suggestions in, this book.

5. Of course, each one is valuable, but used together they are even more powerful.

6. I will continue to note that a focus on societal value added is termed "Mega"-level planning. I do this not to be annoying but simply because it is so central to Mega Planning and personal and organizational success. It is this societal focus, in measurable terms, that is unique to strategic planning plus.

7. Later, I further define the Organizational Elements Model (OEM)—Guide 1—as the basis for linking what any organization uses, does, produces, and delivers with societal value added. Contemporary strategic planning models do not yet incorporate societal payoffs, or Mega-level results and consequences.

8. This is different from the conventional usage of *need* and *needs assessment* because it has a primary focus on gaps in results and not gaps in resources and methods-means.

9. It is important to realize that many improvement approaches prematurely start with "analysis." *Analysis* is the process of "breaking the parts of a system into its components and identifying what each part contributes and how it interacts with the others." *Assessment* comes before analysis and identifies what should be analyzed in the first place. Assessment identifies what parts of the system there are (and should be) in order to identify the value and worth of the elements in order to identify gaps between current and desired results (needs) in order to meet the needs.

10. I prefer using the label *continuous improvement* because it does not carry the conventional "baggage" of poorly done evaluations that use performance data for blaming. *Continuous improvement* uses data for fixing and improvement and never for blaming.

11. The *societal bottom line* is indicated in the Mega level of results (termed Outcomes): value added for external clients and society.

12. Some of the organizational examples in this book are "anonymous." Although I have worked almost worldwide with many major organizations, both public and private, I often do not use their names in cases-in-point because most organizations prefer not to have their situation made public. Some are in very

competitive environments and do not want to share their status. Others have not taken advice (although they often wish they had). Finally, others have learned, continued to learn, and simply want to get on with their continuous improvement.

13. See Toffler's interview with Peter Schwartz in an interview in the November 1993 issue of *Wired*. In this interview, Toffler suggests that the failure to pay attention and respond to changed realities, such as the "information age," is a "failure in imagination." Instead, most people seem to rely on experts who are usually trapped in old paradigms themselves. He points to some consensus assessment techniques, such as Delphi studies, that build on old paradigms instead of imagining new ones.

14. Peters (1997).

15. Peters (1997) states that it is easier to kill an organization than it is to change it.

16. It might seem as if there are a bunch of new words—jargon—flowing at you now. And there are. Please be patient. Each will be defined, justified, and related to the others. The distinctions are important.

17. Bob Mager set the original standard for measurable objectives. Later, Tom Gilbert made the important distinction between behavior and performance (between actions and consequences). Recently, some "Constructivists" have had objections to writing objectives because they claim it cuts down on creativity and imposes the planners' values on the clients. This view, I believe, is not useful. For a detailed discussion of Constructivism, see the analysis by David Gruender (1996).

18. Jan Kaufman provided this insight.

19. It is interesting and curious that in the popular literature *all* results tend to be called "outcomes." This failure to distinguish among three levels of results blurs the importance of identifying and linking all three levels in planning, doing, and evaluating/continuous improvement.

20. An important contribution of strategic planning at the Mega level is that objectives can be linked to justifiable purposes. Not only should one have objectives that state "where you are headed and how you will know when you have arrived," they should also be justified on the basis of "why you want to get to where you are headed." Although it is true that objectives only deal with measurable destinations, useful strategic planning adds the reasons why objectives should be attained.

21. Note that this CSF also relates to CSF 2.

22. Kaufman, Watkins, Triner, and Stith (1998).

23. Because most dictionaries provide common usage, not necessarily correct usage, they note that "need" is used as a noun as well as a verb. This dual conventional usage doesn't mean that it is useful. Much of this book depends on a shift in paradigms about "need." The shift is to use it only as a noun and *never* as a verb or in a verb sense.

24. Tom Peters (1997) suggests that "organizational forgetting" can be a vital element in success. He notes that the successful organization will "forget" the conventional wisdom of the past—erase it from the corporate reality—in order to use new thinking. Good advice.

1

The New Realities for Organizations, Society, and Planning

Changing Paradigms

This chapter focuses on Critical Success Factor 1. It provides the rationale for recognizing and putting the new realities to work for you and your organization:

> *Critical Success Factor 1:* **Use new and wider boundaries for thinking, planning, doing, and evaluating/continuously improving. Move out of today's comfort zones.**

Change or die. It is almost boring to say it, but it is still true: Times have changed. And they will continue to change. You can be the master of change or the victim of it. As modern management experts (such as Tom Peters) note, "Change or die." That presents a dire alternative. It *is* reality.

Why would one opt to stay in their comfort zones and only tinker with cosmetic change and not assure their continuation and success? Which do you choose?

Paradigms and choice. Behind choice is the paradigm one uses. Paradigms determine what we see, think, use, and do. A paradigm is

> *the framework and ground rules one uses to filter reality and understand the world around them.*[1]

We have paradigms for everything: for ourselves, book authors, family, politicians, professors, society, and business. Paradigms are useful if they are based on reality. They are dangerous if they do not provide us with reality filters that will help us make successful choices. As Barker[2] points out, sometimes our old paradigms will get us into trouble because we will not see opportunities but, rather, threats.[3] Figure 1.1 shows that paradigms are the boundaries, patterns, and ground rules we use to understand and filter reality. In that figure is an example of how a simple proposition of 1 + 1 = ? can be differently interpreted depending on one's paradigm.

Choice. We don't often consciously realize it, but choice is a part of our lives. And our choices determine our future. Choosing to change, and what to change to is central to defining and achieving success. Fortunately, the answers to the question of what to change to—and why—is known and available. And what we now know about change and success—even though the process might seem quite different from the old conventional wisdom—is much better than using a ouija board or consulting a soothsayer. Or tinkering around the edges of change. Or following old paradigms about organizations, people, change, and reality.

There are some important insights and tools to guide us. We can stay comfortable and look for increased efficiency, or we can choose to create a better future. This is a matter of choice, pure and simple. Choice.[4]

▨ Old Paradigm Thinking

Let's look at some Old Realities that were considered sound advice in the past:[5]

"First we do the analysis of problems and then solve them."

"A day's work for a day's pay."

"We deal with problems one at a time."

"Academics don't know the 'real world.'"

"Stocks have reached what looks like a permanently high plateau."
                                            —Irving Fisher, Professor of Economics,
                                            Yale University, 1929

"Everything that can be invented has been invented."
                                            —Charles H. Duell,
                                            Commissioner, U.S. Office of Patents, 1899

"If I had thought about it, I wouldn't have done the experiment.
The literature was full of examples that said you can't do this."
                                            —Spencer Silver on the work that led to the unique
                                            adhesives for 3M "Post-it" notepads

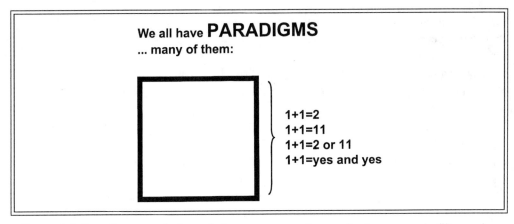

Figure 1.1. Paradigms are the boundaries, patterns, and ground rules we use to filter and understand external reality. Also shown are several different results for a basic math question depending upon one's paradigm about it.

"Louis Pasteur's theory of germs is ridiculous fiction."
> —Pierre Pachet, Professor of Physiology
> at Toulouse, 1872

"640K ought to be enough for anybody."
> —Bill Gates, 1981

"Heavier-than-air flying machines are impossible."
> —Lord Kelvin, president of the Royal Society, 1895

"I think there is a world market for maybe five computers."
> —Thomas Watson, chairman of IBM, 1943

"There is no reason anyone would want a computer in their home."
> —Ken Olson, president, chairman, and founder of
> Digital Equipment Corporation, 1977

Most organizations and their associates choose to stay with the "tried and true" and repeat thinking and actions that are contrary to the new realities. Talk with today's workers. Regardless of their level in the company, most agree not to "rock the boat" or question the prevailing culture or paradigms.[6] This can be very bad for one's corporate health, not to mention one's own survival. They choose to tinker and not consider shifting from the old or current paradigms. And that choice has led to disaster in the past.

Once conventional wisdom, now destructive paradigms. Why are these "Old Wisdom"? Just scan them. This sample of what most people once believed was "reality" varies from the "old saw" that academics don't know the real world (whatever "the real world" is) to the linear lock-step thinking of taking on problems one at a time instead of realizing that reality is about wholes and a system, not splinters and parts. Other old "realities" seem to outlive their usefulness, such as thinking and acting in terms of "work and pay" as a basic paradigm instead of acting in terms of productive contribution and return on investment . . . they pay people for time on the job and not on the basis of value added.[7]

Why not first analyze a problem and then solve it? Easy. Things happen so rapidly in the external world that one must assess, analyze, and act almost in a seamless and concurrent manner, for there is often no time to do detailed data collection and analysis: simultaneity of problem identification/problem resolution is a new reality for all to deal with.

These "Old Paradigm Wisdom" items once guided people in their homes, in the marketplace, and in organizations. Although they seem mostly silly now, they were taken very seriously then. Computer "giants" did not see the potential of the computer and left it to start-ups such as Apple and other "niche" players to bring the digital computer into common use both at home and at the office.[8]

Can we afford not to change our paradigms, or at least question the existing ones, rather than blindly pursuing the conventional wisdom of the day?

▓ Some New Realities

But what might be the realities—new realities—that will help guide us as we define and seek organizational success? Following are some that are increasingly supported from the literature and acute observers of our changing world.[9]

As you review these, please not only consider each of them only on their own merit but also at the same time see them as a woven fabric, a tapestry of realities that can and should guide us as we do realistic and useful planning.

Don't expect to be comfortable with them at first. Most provide an alternative that often flies in the face of conventional wisdom and conventional practice.

- Tomorrow is not a linear projection of yesterday.
- You can't solve today's problems with the same paradigms and tools that created them.
- Reality is not divided into disciplines, courses, departments, sections, agencies, laws, policies, or issues.
- Useful change has to add value for all internal and external partners.
- Ask "If my organization is the solution, what's the problem?"
- There are two "bottom lines" for any organization: conventional and societal.
- Today's capitalism is not one of money or things but of knowledge and information (quote by Drucker, 1993).
- Doing societal good is no longer a corporate option, it is a must (quote by Popcorn, 1991).

- If you can't predict the future, create it (quote by Drucker, 1993).
- Think globally as you act locally.
- Operate as if you intend to put your organization out of business through success.
- Don't be the best of the best—be the only one who does what you do (attributed to Jerry Garcia, the late singer with the rock group Grateful Dead).
- It is easier to kill an organization that it is to change it (quote by Peters, 1997).

Let's take a closer look at some of these.

Tomorrow is not a linear projection of yesterday.[10]

What worked yesterday will not necessarily work today. Or tomorrow. The world changes suddenly, and if we only "react" we will always be struggling to catch up. We cannot depend on the tools, concepts, and approaches that worked yesterday. "You must crawl before you walk" is old paradigm thinking. The world is not conveniently incremental and what happens and what works is not a gradual and smooth transition from yesterday to today to tomorrow. Frequently, the changes are in large, often very large, steps. And often what was useful yesterday will get us into trouble today. Look at the changing nature of the human dietary requirements, how market regulating initiatives such as deregulation worked a bit—with partial results—yesterday but hampers us today, and how harassment and discrimination so usual in the past is illegal as well as counterproductive now.

The former undisputed computer champion IBM had to be hauled back from the ashes because it used old paradigms. They believed that mainframe computers were required, whereas the changing world of their clients knew it was all about networking and individual workstations. No amount of selling could change that reality. They were very efficient but turning out something that few people wanted.

The dominant auto manufacturer in the United States in the 1940s and '50s, General Motors, had one brand that was the most pre-sold automobile in the world. Everyone's dad and mom seemed to have a Chevrolet, and it was only "natural" that the children would get one as well. But the executives let that advantage slip away to competition that noted the changed realities of the marketplace and purchased cars on the basis of other factors such as comfort and styling that the dominant brand assumed was the same as yesterday. Following organizational comfort, GM management and other conventional organizations face the requirement to change from a "splintering" of its divisions and operations[11] without an overall mission that adds values to external clients and society. Its fortunes have reflected old paradigms of thinking about how an organization should operate rather than how to link everything that an organization uses, does, produces, and delivers to societal good.[12]

Sometimes we fail to see what "reality" actually is. For example, what about being financially successful as individuals. Contrary to popular opinion, the "millionaire next door"[13] is likely to be frugal, drive an older used car, and live well below his or her means. The old paradigm—new imported cars, big house, great imported clothes, private schools—does not really describe the new wealthy, who more than likely live in your neighborhood, own their own business, dress and act modestly, and save for their future.

You can't solve today's problems with the same paradigms and tools that created them.[14]

We have learned lots and lots of tools in our business schools, colleges of public administration, and colleges of education: systems analysis, needs analysis[15], task analysis, instructional systems design, conventional "strategic planning,"[16] and strategic management, to name a few. But many of these tools were derived from a different and older world, and might not serve us well today—no matter how competent we are with them.[17]

One popular corporate "quick fix" is to solve every problem with training. It turns out that training is not always the best way to resolve a performance problem. In fact, if one starts problem solving with training (and its associated conventional wisdom tool of "training needs assessment") one will be wrong 80% to 90% of the time[18]—unbelievably bad odds, but a gamble that is taken often because it is the "paradigm de jour."

Just because the conventional tools are there doesn't mean they will serve you well. First, make certain that the tools you choose to use are responsive to the new realities.

Reality is not divided into disciplines, courses, departments, sections, agencies, laws, policies, or issues.

Think about it for a minute. Our university and high school courses were about disciplines. We learned English, algebra, Spanish, history, and biology all as discrete topics.

What didn't we learn in school? How to select from the menu of courses and content based on a situation confronting us and how to integrate and bundle the information from each discipline. We were trapped into a "splinter" curriculum, and only the hardiest among us were able to sort these pieces out. Yet, the conventional wisdom is that we divide things into "god given" disciplines. And we deliver these in discrete courses. Nonsense.

What happens in curriculum when we splinter it—divide it into discrete courses or topics—is seen in Figure 1.2. It shows the usual curriculum organization where disciplines are designed, developed, delivered, and evaluated in "splinters." By embedding the various courses into an overall box that represents the combined and integrated knowledge and information relative to our future world, survival and contribution in it, we see some interesting things. For one thing, what happens to the "blank spaces" in the overall, holistic knowledge base required to be self-sufficient and self-reliant in tomorrow's world? Do the sum of the individual subject areas (or issues or policies, for that matter) equal the whole? This splintering is very destructive to our individual and collective future. It lulls us into thinking that splinters, taken together, will deliver the whole. Not true.

And the beat goes on. Our organizations are divided into departments (as are our universities and public schools), sections, and even agencies. The same splintering occurs for organizations, departments, and operations. Figure 1.3 shows the effects of splintering what applied to entire organizations.

Ever look at that convenient fiction called an "organization chart"? Know anyone who operationally uses it and its hierarchies? Few do. What most people do is pull out the organization

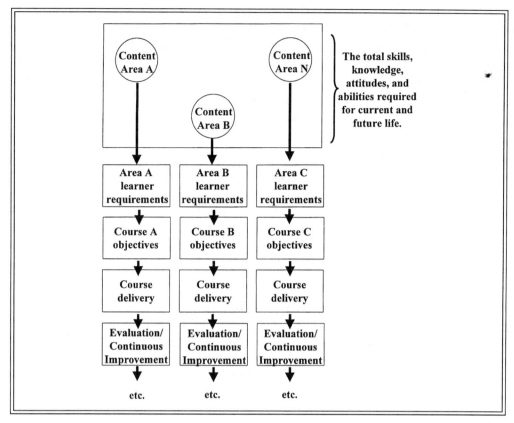

Figure 1.2. By dividing and delivering curriculum and learning sequences into disciplines, or content areas, we don't include the "blank spaces" of what education or training should deliver and accomplish.

chart to show visitors, but they themselves operate on the basis of knowing who to call and when, regardless of their level or position on the chart—the "informal organization." Conventional wisdom is wrong again. In fact, a more functional organization chart would be a circular pattern with external clients and society in the center.

Also equally conventional, and also wrong, is that laws, policies, and issues are the unit of analysis for public and private organizations, such as I noted earlier when discussing courses and curriculum. If you are sensitive enough to realize that organizations—all organizations—are means to societal ends, then one realizes that the laws, policies, and issues are simply splinters of the societal whole: old paradigms that lead to splintered efforts and results.

For as long as any of us can remember, sociologists have been telling us that "the whole is more than the sum of its parts." They were and are correct. The literature (from Von Bertalanffy to Senge and from Churchman to me) continues this theme.

Organizations, societies, communities, and families are all systems, and each time we attempt to break them into "splinters" for the ease of analysis, we lose the whole. People are more

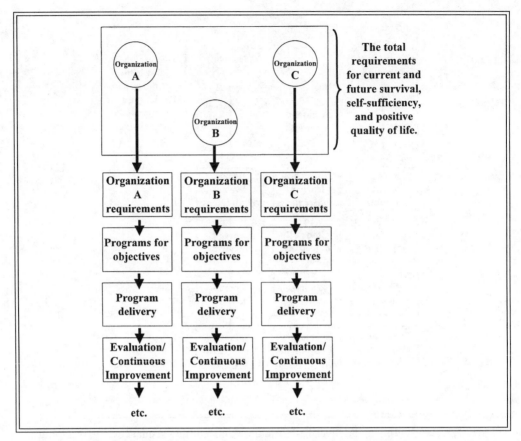

Figure 1.3. By dividing and delivering organizational objectives in response to specific issues, we don't include the "blank spaces" of what organizations and markets should deliver and accomplish. There is no synergy, and the system is not always responsive to the people whose lives cut across many organizations (who live in the topmost portion of the figure).

than the sum of their parts (splinters), as are organizations. System planning, a concept I have attempted to further, looks at wholes, not just parts. These organization "wholes" must also be seen as part of a larger system: society. Strategic thinking focuses first on the Mega.

There are two "bottom lines" for any organization: conventional and societal.[19]

The old paradigm is for organizations to focus only on the quarterly profit-and-loss sheet and not also focus on societal value added. The new reality is a simple concept. Every organization that expects to survive has external clients. And each organization operates in society. If one does not add value to external clients and society, they will be replaced.

Many organizations have failed or faltered because they only looked at the conventional bottom line: the quarterly profit-and-loss sheet and the quarterly dividends. Ford's Pinto automobile program, even after fire/injury/crash problems surfaced, felt that perhaps it was more cost-efficient to not recall and change the design problem than it was to pay potential lawsuits. But people didn't trust the automobile or the manufacturer for years to come because as consumers they were personally more interested in the "societal bottom line" and their safety. Ford has changed dramatically from that old paradigm. On the other hand, Johnson & Johnson recalled Tylenol after a kook poisoned a batch on a shelf in the United States. Instead of passing it off as a one-shot problem (which it was), they instead opted to recall everything on the shelves, refund money, and develop a tamper-resistant package and a capsule that too was tamper-resistant. Their immediate profits went down (to nothing, actually) but soon they were back with market dominance and higher profits. Customers realized that the company cared more about them—the societal bottom line—than they cared about short-term, medium-term, and longer-term profits.

Today's capitalism is not one of money or things but of knowledge and information.[20]

According to Drucker,[21] the new "coin of the realm" is not money or things but knowledge and information.[22] This notes a shift of paradigm from the conventional zero-sum game (at the end of the day we add up the scores and note winners and losers, usually in dollar terms) to a win-win game. Why? Because when we get knowledge and information from elsewhere, not only do we get it and can use it, but the creator of the knowledge also keeps it as well. This means that the new capital is an inexhaustible resource. This dramatically changes the head-to-head/destroy the competition of old paradigm capitalism. And recall that Peter Drucker is the most articulate advocate of capitalism. The paradigm has shifted.

This fits quite well with another reality: We have shifted from an industrial, labor-intensive model to that of the information age. The new marketable commodity is knowledge and information, not lifting, moving, and sweating.

Doing societal good is no longer a corporate option, it is a must.

This Faith Popcorn (1990) quote is dramatic. It is also correct. If one doesn't add value for external clients and society, then there is no future for that individual and organization. (I discussed aspects of this earlier in the New Realities section on two bottom lines. Believe it.)

The Water Board of a major Australian city, in spite of several consultants urging management to focus on societal well-being and health (what I later define as the "Mega" level of thinking and planning) instead continued to focus on the conventional improvement approach to the individual performance improvement of employees. By continuing a conventional concern with splinters—individuals and small groups—of their complex operation, it resulted in their having to make their citizens boil their water twice in one year. The conventional approach was to make each employee efficient in one's own job instead of linking everything to external value added. The old paradigm, one of focusing on the parts and not on the whole, had poor consequences.

All organizations are means to societal ends and must make a contribution to external clients and society. If they don't, they will fade or die. Cigarette companies have come to that reality far too late to save their clients and their corporate futures. Automobile manufacturers are also realizing that safety is more than hype, it is a vital responsibility.[23]

Our democracy depends on all people adhering to a "social contract" that includes not harming oneself or others. A societal focus (called the Mega level of planning) is in keeping with our individual and collective social contracts.

This new reality links well with the earlier one of "two bottom lines." Again, this is an example of how these new realities are really a tapestry, not just single threads.

If you can't predict the future, create it.

Again, Peter Drucker shows us the way. Instead of "being competitive," which is a loser's game because one has to wait until the competition does something and then hustle to catch up (being reactive is very time consuming and inefficient), Drucker advises us to define the future and then go ahead and create it. How refreshing—and how different from the conventional wisdom.

This new reality urges us to define the kind of world we want to create for tomorrow's child, and further, state that in measurable terms (later I define this in Chapter 4 when Ideal Visions are presented), and then go ahead and create the future. Sound advice. Very sound.

Think globally as you act locally.

This is a page taken directly from environmentalists. Although most activities, efforts, and resources are at the "micro" or operational level, everything one uses, does, produces, and delivers must be focused on adding value to external clients and society. Most of our time and effort will be spent on using resources and on our activities. However, unless we link everything to societal and external client value added, we will miss making a necessary contribution within and outside the organization.

Operate as if you intend to put your organization out of business through success.

"What? Put myself out of business? You can't be serious!" But I am. If you don't intend to put yourself out of business through success, your competitors will. If you don't intend to be responsive and responsible for adding value to clients, your opposition will.[24]

One inspiring example comes from the Florida Department of Corrections and its then Secretary Harold K. Singletary in the late 1990s. After a needs assessment workshop, Singletary and his staff worked from an Ideal Vision—what kind of world they wanted to help create for tomorrow's Florida and for tomorrow's child. The associates of the Department of Corrections came up with an operating mission objective:

Put the Florida Department of Corrections out of business through success. Reduce recidivism to zero and work with other agencies and agents to create a society where no one had to go to jail.[25]

They committed, on a working basis, to put themselves out of business through success. It not only made organizational sense, it also made societal sense.

The charitable U. S. organization, the March of Dimes, was founded in 1938 and first went on a crusade to put a stop to polio. It did in 1955. Then, in 1958 it changed its mission to birth defects and is now attacking this mission with the same intention of putting itself out of business through success.

Tallahassee, Florida, dermatologist Armand Cognetta, Jr., really hates melanomas and the deaths that usually follow their discovery. Even though there are precise methods for identifying them once they are in "full bloom," once they get to that level they are almost always fatal. Noting that dermatology would be a relaxed specialty if it weren't for cancer, Cognetta wanted to put himself out of the cancer business. Making a conceptual leap from a dog's ability to smell corpses under a lake, he asked himself if dogs couldn't "sniff out" melanomas under the surface of the skin.[26] Teaming with an animal trainer, he found out that dogs could sense melanomas before they were clearly observable on the surface and is well on his way to helping dermatologists "get out of the cancer death business."

Whether you are a prison system or make computers, fighting a crippling disease or overcoming an injustice, it is creative and productive to think about how you might be replaced. If you don't do it, others will seek to accomplish that reality.

Don't be the best of the best—be the only one who does what you do.

When Jerry Garcia (of Grateful Dead fame) suggested this, some eyebrows were raised. But he was (and is) correct. If you are the only person or organization that does and delivers what you do, you are unique. And ahead of the pack. Instead of playing "catch up," you are setting the direction and pace. You are the leader, not the follower. One indicator of being the only one who does what you do (and delivers) is to see if others choose to benchmark you.

It is easier to kill an organization than it is to change it.

Tom Peters[27] suggests this. It is disconcerting. Why do people resist change? If they identify and deal with the "new realities," there is a simple choice: change or die.[28]

Change is often the most uncomfortable thing that you can ask anyone to endure. The "comfort zones" we languish in are tempting. But we are foolish if we don't take into account the new realities.

Corporate culture may be defined as "how we do things around here." Corporate culture can inspire everyone to achieve and contribute, or it may focus everyone on doing things that are not productive. Let's see.

The Studebaker Company, in earlier days an automobile innovator, squandered its market by making old-paradigm choices.[29] Its managerial decisions created a corporate culture of no change. This proved difficult to overcome when it had to become, once more, innovative. It was this no-change culture that hastened the firm's demise. When Studebaker ended production in 1967, it had not introduced an all-new sedan since the 1953 model year. By contrast, the standard-size Ford sedan had undergone 10 complete sheet metal changes in the same period.

Lakeside, California, dentist Robert Siegel wanted to find a way to relieve the intense pain of some patients. In the early 1970s, he worked with a novel technique called TMJ, which took a new approach to fixing pain through realigning the jaw to reduce intense pressure. He was derided by most of his fellow dentists and even accused by some of quackery. Now, after his death, TMJ is a standard dental practice much to the relief of many patients. Classical dentists didn't want to consider the viability of this new method for it didn't fit the conventional wisdom; they were out of their comfort zones.[30]

Change must add value for all internal and external partners.

We are in an interactive and interdependent world. There is no longer a zero-sum game.[31] All partners, associates, management, clients, and society must share in both the successes and failures of organizations. You cannot have a successful organization that doesn't have (a) outputs that are useful for external clients and society, (b) quality that makes clients satisfied and come back, and (c) associates who want that to happen. Adding value to one or two of these elements without adding to all will bring failure. Everyone must win, for everyone must make useful results happen.

In the world of the future, there can be no winners and losers. Strife and conflict—organizational and societal—stem from "winners and losers" being arbitrarily selected by others. Perhaps Japan's economic woes in the 1990s came about by their trying to keep all profits for themselves and not "leaving anything on the table" for others. Poverty, anywhere, is good for no one. Disease, hunger, and terror benefit nobody. Adding value for everyone within and outside the organization is a must, not an option.[32]

Consider the example of *Eastern Airlines.*[33] Conventional management wisdom back in 1989 had it that now-bankrupt Eastern Airlines simply had a labor-management block and that to get competitive management they had to cut labor costs. Doggedly, the CEO started brutally cutting costs, selling off Eastern's assets, and focusing on costs rather than value added to employees, management, external clients, and society. Eastern failed to include its employees as full partners in adding value to shareholders along with employees, managers, and clients. Instead, it focused almost exclusively on one dimension: cutting costs. The machinist union, also using old paradigms, employed tactics to extract raises for some of its employees without looking at adding value to all other partners. They worked "to rule," called in minute problems to the government in order to delay flights, enlisted competitor companies' employees to walk the picket lines with them (perhaps ignoring the possibility that these same "friends" on the line wanted Eastern to go out of business so theirs would get more business), and refused to rethink a pay scale that was the envy of workers in their industry. All of this old-paradigm thinking resulted in a hostile set of employees, intractable executives, and dissatisfied customers. The company quickly went under. There were no winners. What might have happened to this formerly great company if it had included all of its partners and worked to add value for all?

In the case of *Delta,* shortly after winning the 1998 Airline of the Year award, this giant southeastern U.S.-based airline decided to optimize shareholder value. By doggedly attacking costs and restricting decision making by line supervisors, its other partners (including customers) are being squeezed and left out of the equation. In the wake of this emphasis on "shareholder value," a number of critical newspaper articles and reports have been written about Delta's dramatic reduction in and elimination of in-flight food and services. The airline is also accused of overbooking flights at a significantly higher rate than other airlines. Will these policy changes and Delta's not making certain that all partners benefit from any change affect its success in the future? Time will tell if there are any mid- and long-term penalties for ignoring the new realities.

If you look at the *Fortune* 500 list of organizations from 10 years ago and compare that with the current one, you will note that a lot of organizations are missing. Each of the demoted or defunct organizations probably hired change consultants,[34] reorganized, restructured, and went through some superficial change exercises but never really rethought itself in terms of asking the basic question discussed next. Dealing with basic, not superficial, change is vital to organizational success.[35]

Ask "If my organization is the solution, what's the problem?"
A basic theme of Mega planning is to see yourself and your organization as a means to societal ends. By asking this question, you put means and ends into perspective and link what you use, do, produce, and deliver to adding value to external clients and society. You do Mega thinking.
How about some more "New Realities?"

- Change is so rapid that we don't have the luxury of linear response.
- Each person is a rapidly depreciating asset; . . . unless they are constantly growing they are becoming obsolete (quote by Peters, 1997).
- Compliance is nowhere near as important as competence.
- The new organizational structure is not one of hierarchies but, rather, networks.
- If it ain't broke, fix it—or better yet, blow it up and build new.
- Anything worth doing is worth doing poorly, at least at first.
- Organizational vitality is only as good as the vitality and competence of its people.
- The new professional: A towering competence at something; . . . they have value in the marketplace (Peters, 1997).
- Don't trust any solution that can fit on a bumper sticker.

What advice for a successful future can we get from these?

Compliance is nowhere near as important as competence.
Many organizational cultures talk about innovation and empowerment but reward compliance and "business as usual." If there is a basic missing element in effective change, it is that we encourage change and don't change the reward systems to support change. Examine your pay and incentive system and see if it doesn't focus on compliance and maintaining the status quo instead of on value added to all partners.

In a nuclear power meltdown at a U.S. site, everyone did their job, complied with the rules and regulations, and watched a disaster unfold. They were compliant, but their individual compliance did not add up to useful results.

A favorite union tactic is to "work to rule." For example, the border crossings from the United States to Canada have been known to freeze and create long lines of angry drivers and overheating cars as employees simply follow the rules. To the letter. If compliance can be that crippling, don't you think that a possible change to the current rules about compliance should be questioned and changed?

Failing to shift paradigms—frames of reference—can be lethal. One old paradigm myth about organizations is that to survive they must be "lean and mean." This often is implemented by trying to cut labor costs, which is single-issue thinking—like that of Eastern Airlines, "old" Apple Computer, and many others—that fails to take into account the whole array of important considerations, including the necessary partnerships among workers, external clients, management, and society.

Try to get along without any of these "clients," and trouble is sure to follow. Let's see.

The new organizational structure is not one of hierarchies but, rather, networks.

In an earlier New Reality, I noted that reality is not divided into disciplines, courses, departments, sections, agencies, laws, policies, and issues. We know that organizations don't operate as shown on organization charts and that successful ones use networks—relationships of trust and knowledge—that allow fluidity of operations and sharing toward a common purpose.

The military model of rigid hierarchies is better on paper than in reality. The Department of Defense of a major developed nation held a retreat[36] to identify what the New Realities meant for a stereotypically authoritarian organization such as theirs. They found that the basic responsibility of any supervisor, regardless of rank or status, is to mentor, not to order or dictate. Networks based on common purpose, trust, and empowerment are what will work.

If it ain't broke, fix it—or better yet, blow it up and build new.[37]

We have seen an era of all kinds of patches, repairs, quick fixes, and cosmetic change. Benchmarking, reengineering, and quality management are all useful tools that are usually applied incompletely or incorrectly.[38]

Simply improving efficiency will make one, as Drucker warns, get better and better at doing that which should not be done at all. Much misguided "quality management" is about process improvement that does not take the time to define (a) what results the process should deliver and (b) how the results are useful to internal and external clients. In addition, conventional and poorly conceived quality management often focuses more on compliance and data collection than it does on adding value. Thus, a good idea often fails for the wrong reason.

Ask the basic reengineering question "If this didn't exist, would we reinvent it? And if we reinvented it, would it be exactly as it now is?" We can and should pose this question to society, forms of government, and organizations as well as to operations.

If we simply follow old models and paradigms based on old realities, we find ourselves doing nonproductive things. One activity of faith in the 1980s and early 1990s was to see Japan as the model of economic development and a process to be copied, to be benchmarked. With arrogance and confidence in their new and superior status, the minister of commerce even wrote a book titled *The Japan That Can Say No* to tell the world that they were taking direction from no others. The world sent experts to learn "Japanese Management" and to benchmark their industries, paradigms, and methods. We copied them with the blind faith that they were right. Then, in the early 1990s they hit the economic wall. They did not leave "anything on the table" for other countries, peoples, and industries. The Japanese were firmly focused on the conventional bottom line and did not first focus on adding value to society. Old paradigms, not new ones, led to their economic woes.

Before benchmarking others, make sure that they have useful objectives as well as compatible goals and objectives to yours. How would you have liked to be in the computer business a few years ago and benchmarked the "leaders," such as IBM and Digital Equipment Corporation? If you did, you would have aligned yourself with failures and disappointments. Both companies are coming back now, one as a refocused corporation and the other as a division of a formerly small and insignificant competitor (who didn't benchmark them before acquiring them).

As Peters[39] and others advise, don't settle for the status quo. If something is working now, it should be continuously improved anyway. And while you are at it, try getting rid of it all together and find something that adds value both internally and externally. If you don't, your competitors are probably doing it.

If anything is worth doing, it is worth doing poorly, at least at first.

The Old Reality was "Anything worth doing is worth doing right." Not anymore, because of increasing pressures for rapid response. And adding value. However, if one waits for perfection to swing into action, the competition will get there first. Define what must be accomplished and get it done. Then use continuous improvement to make what you do and deliver better and better and increasingly useful to all internal and external partners.

As the Nike™ ad notes, "Just do it." Define required and useful results and swing into action and deliver quickly. Then revise as required.

The new professional: a towering competence at something; . . . they have value in the marketplace.[40]

This is simple. Everyone has to be excellent, competent, and relied on to perform and contribute when and where required. And everyone must continue to develop this competence and marketability both within and outside one's organization. After all, if you are not marketable outside your organization, you are not marketable inside it either.

Don't trust any solution that will fit on a bumper sticker.

Interesting, isn't it? Many people want the simple checklist, the "5 magic steps to instant success." Why not simplify, simplify, simplify?

People are complex, and that complexity increases dramatically as they work together in an organization. Simplicity is appealing. But don't oversimplify to get acceptance.

There might be a trend in some professional circles to simplify, shorten, streamline, or short-circuit. I even suggested that we are often "dumbing down" professional roles and responsibilities in order to get acceptance.[41]

Resist the temptation to simplify only to get acceptance. You will have some happy people initially, but it is you who will likely be held responsible when the oversimplifications fail. Focus instead on what useful results must be delivered to benefit all internal and external partners.

▓ Organizational and Personal Success Depends on Using New Realities for Shifting Your Paradigms and Changing How You Think and Do

It is time to shift from old and current realities to new and useful ones. It will be uncomfortable for most. You will often be seen as "out of the mainstream" or not "real world." When you shift your realities, it will be you who will be ahead of the pack, not following it.

Use new and wider boundaries for thinking, planning, doing, evaluating, and continuously improving. Move out of today's comfort zones. This basic New Reality will help you define and achieve personal and organizational success. As you work with the concepts and tools in this book, think of how many of these new realities are addressed; they all are.

EXERCISES

Mind-sets, Paradigms, and Organizational Culture

1. *Calibrating your current mind-sets and actions against what will allow you and your organization to be successful.* Following are a series of questions for you to use in considering your current orientation and actions and what you see as being most helpful to you and your organization to define and then achieve success.

Each **What Is** and **What Should Be** column—on either side of the questions—has the following dimensions in terms of the relative frequency that something does or does not happen:

Consistently (96%-100%)
Quite frequently (85%-95%)
Sometimes (51%-84%)
Not usually (18%-50%)
Almost never (6%-17%)
Rarely, if ever (0%-5%)

Review your current corporate culture—how things are done around your organization—in terms of the following questions. Answer, for each question, both **What Is** (your current practice) and **What Should Be** (your desired practice; that which will best serve your organization):

My organization

WHAT IS — Rarely, if ever (0-4%) · Almost Never (5%-15%) · Not Usually (16-49%) · Sometimes (50-83%) · Quite Frequently (84-94%) · Consistently (95-100%)

WHAT SHOULD BE — Rarely, if ever (0-4%) · Almost Never (5%-15%) · Not Usually (16-49%) · Sometimes (50-83%) · Quite Frequently (84-94%) · Consistently (95-100%)

Please indicate the frequency (in terms of percentage of times) with which the following statements are happening within your organization. Please provide two responses to each question:

⇐ **WHAT IS** | **WHAT SHOULD BE** ⇒

describe how you see your organization *currently* operating. | describe how you think your organization *should be* operating.

WHAT IS			Statement	WHAT SHOULD BE		
① ② ③ ④ ⑤ ⑥			1. Always demands more data before making a decision based on a changed paradigm or frame of reference	① ② ③ ④ ⑤ ⑥		
① ② ③ ④ ⑤ ⑥			2. Bases decisions on current as well as past realities/paradigms and frames of reference	① ② ③ ④ ⑤ ⑥		
① ② ③ ④ ⑤ ⑥			3. Is open to new ideas and frames of reference but usually decides to do conventional things	① ② ③ ④ ⑤ ⑥		
① ② ③ ④ ⑤ ⑥			4. Is open to new ideas and frames of reference and sometimes decides to take a risk on a new paradigm	① ② ③ ④ ⑤ ⑥		
① ② ③ ④ ⑤ ⑥			5. Is open to new ideas and frames of reference and decides to take a risk on a new paradigm	① ② ③ ④ ⑤ ⑥		
① ② ③ ④ ⑤ ⑥			6. Seeks new ideas and frames of reference and adopt and adapts new ones with ease and conviction	① ② ③ ④ ⑤ ⑥		
① ② ③ ④ ⑤ ⑥			7. Makes decisions without hard data when it makes sense in terms of "pushing the envelope" to move into new directions and results.	① ② ③ ④ ⑤ ⑥		

Suggested pattern:

Items 1 through 4: Both What Is, ideally, and What Should Be responses are low.

Items 5 and 6: What Is, ideally, as well as What Should Be responses are high.

Item 7: What Is and What Should Be responses should both be high.

2. To reinforce the potential impact and consequences of shifting your paradigms—using the new realities and "forgetting" about using some old ones—here are some activities for you. You may choose to do these independently or as a team.

1. Identify the Old Realities that you might be using in your
   (A) life and
   (B) organization.
   Identify the risks and gains for continuing to use them.

2. Which of the New Realities would provide the bases to add value to your
   (A) life and
   (B) organization?
   Identify the risks and gains for using them.

3. What organizations in your area of business (or government) are currently using one or more of the old paradigms? What do you think will happen to them in the next 1, 5, and 10 years?

4. What opportunities exist for you and your organization based on others using old paradigms?

Notes

1. Joel Barker's two videos (1989, 1993), as well as his 1992 book, are worth your attention. He has adapted Thomas Kuhn's concepts of paradigms to the social and behavioral sciences.

2. Barker (1989, 1992).

3. Again, in Barker's work, he notes that many opportunities were missed, such as the copying machine, quartz watches, quality management/continuous improvement (to name a few) because the people in the organization didn't see a new paradigm when it was offered them. Barker (1989, 1992, 1993) suggests that there are three roles in change: the paradigm creator, the paradigm pioneer who buys in early and stays with the new paradigm even when there are no hard data on its usefulness, and the "settler" who wants all the data to be in before adopting the new paradigm, by which time it is usually too late.

4. Harold Greenwald, noted psychotherapist, points out the critical role of choice. He reveals in his 1973 book, *Decision Therapy,* that one can select the payoffs they want to get, identify what kinds of behaviors will deliver those payoffs, and decide to change and then support that decision. Just as it is appropriate for decision making in personal life, this advice is also true for organizational life. We are what we do. If we want different payoffs and consequences, then we have to change what we use and do. We can decide to use old paradigms or shift to new ones and realize new payoffs. Every person has choices.

5. We have the anonymous Net to thank for these. Unfortunately, no authorship is usually identified for this and other materials that flow on the Internet, but I extend my thanks to the still unknown creator(s).

6. Futurist Alvin Toffler in an interview in the November 1993 issue of *Wired* attributes this to a lack of imagination and an unwillingness to step outside one's self and organization.

7. I was once asked to testify on educational vouchers for the Florida Senate's Education Committee. When one senator objected to my offering that there is a better way of funding education than on the basis of attendance, he thought that I must be an "egg-headed academic." When I offered that "funding education on the basis of FTE (full time equivalence for attending classes) was like paying a cow for the time she spent standing over the bucket instead of on the basis of the quality and quantity of milk she gave," the good senator leaped to his feet and almost shouted "I understand that! I understand that!" After this experience, he looked first at ends before means as long as he served in the legislature.

8. At the turn of the 20th century, a country's strength was linked to its steel production. As we begin the 21st century, a nation's strength is, and will be, related to its "mindware"—the resources for helping to be creative and productive by working smarter, not harder.

9. Interestingly, Peter Drucker (1998) also has recently suggested some other "new paradigms—not "new realities"—for management." Included on his list are the following: (1) There is only one right way to organize a business; (2) the principles of management only apply to business organizations; (3) there is a single right way to manage people; (4) technologies, markets, and end uses are fixed and rarely overlap; (5)

management's scope is legally defined as applying only to an organization's assets and employees; (6) management's job is to "run the business" rather than to concentrate on what is happening outside the business; and (7) national boundaries define the ecology of enterprise and management.

As usual, Drucker's insights are valuable. However, these "new management paradigms" apply only to what is called "Macro" in the Organizational Elements Model (OEM)—shown in Figure 1.3—and are less comprehensive than the "new realities" suggested here. But they are useful within the context of the OEM.

10. Marshall and Tucker (1992) were among others to point this out.

11. See Taylor (1998).

12. One New Reality that is a basic core of this book is that Society, now and in the future, is of primary concern. This reality is discussed throughout and is the basis for Mega Planning and useful strategic thinking. Also see Kaufman (1998b) for concepts and tools related to this.

13. Stanley and Danko (1996).

14. Among the first authors to suggest this were Marshall and Tucker (1992).

15. Noted later in the book are important distinctions-yet-relationships among needs assessment, needs analysis, front-end analysis, task analysis, system analysis and systems analysis. Frequently, analysis and assessment are incorrectly equated. Also confused are various types of analysis. Also see Watkins, Leigh, Platt, and Kaufman (1998).

16. Mintzberg (1994) points out the pitfalls of conventional wisdom that describes most current "strategic planning." He is correct for most models being used; they are splintered, overly detailed, and narrowly focused—and thus don't work. To overcome this objective, in this book I suggest that the missing element of most strategic plans is the primary "Mega focus," where everything that any organization uses, does, produces, and delivers must add value to external clients and society. This is a new and wider paradigm than that which is part of the current conventional wisdom.

17. There is an enlightening discussion of this by Martin (1993).

18. Triner, Greenberry, and Watkins (1996) make a convincing case for this.

19. I dealt with this formally in Kaufman (1997b) and elaborated it more in the revised edition of my book *Strategic Thinking* (Kaufman, 1998b). Futurist Faith Popcorn (1990) noted that "doing societal good is no longer a corporate option, it is a must."

I no longer feel lonely in this concern for societal value added. As early as 1969 (Kaufman, Corrigan, & Johnson, 1969; see also Kaufman & Carron, 1980), I brought up the concept of making society the primary client and beneficiary of everything every organization used, did, produced, and delivered as the primary focus for any organization. I can only tell you that my position was not popular by the conventional-wisdom crowd at that time. It is getting better now that others have joined me.

Also, other formulations of this appear, including one by the ice cream marketers Ben & Jerry's. In addition, a popular retailer of bath and body items talks in its advertising to a "societal focus." But recently some questions about these organizations actually converting words into reality (as noted in Kaufman, Watkins, Triner, & Stith, 1998) is proposed by controversial writer/researcher Jon Entine. In several publications, including references to his work in *Forbes,* March 12, 1998 ("Numb Nuts") and *Business Ethics,* whose publisher Marjorie Kelly answered critics in a September 13, 1994 letter to its Editorial Advisory Board members, Entine raises the questions of whether so-called "societal bottom line" entrepreneurs really do "walk the talk." It is one thing to talk about societal good and possibly another to actually focus on measurable societal value added.

20. This new reality is based on Drucker (1993b). Drucker is a primary and arguably the best critical thinker in "new paradigm" management. He is even approaching societal value added as a vital element in planning and contribution, but in his articles (Drucker, 1992, 1994, 1995), he seems to back away from my suggestion that every organization must focus on societal value added.

21. In Drucker (1993b).

22. Toffler (1980) also noted this.

23. Interestingly, this reality is not very tough to figure out. Why make a safe car? Dead people hardly ever become repeat clients.

24. Tom Peters (1997) talks on this situation and reality.

25. Of course, there were some on staff who were disturbed by this; it was new paradigm thinking. And they didn't want to deviate from what they already believed and knew how to do. They were caught out of their comfort zones.

26. He also followed Joel Barker's (1989) advice to get outside your own specialty area to find new paradigms. Cognetta did this shift when he saw a possible relationship between being able to smell under the surface of water and being able to smell under the surface of the skin.

27. This is an important insight provided by Peters (1997).

28. In a personal conversation with change expert Daryl Conner, he expressed that he thinks this to be, unfortunately, basically correct.

29. See Critchlow (1996).

30. The work of Barker, especially in his videos *The Business of Paradigms* and *Paradigm Pioneers,* is very useful in getting people to move out of their comfort zones.

31. As noted in Drucker (1993b).

32. Popcorn (1991) emphasizes this point when she notes that doing societal good is no longer a corporate option, it is a must.

33. See Harari (1992, pp. 28-29). Oren Harari is a professor at the University of San Francisco and a consultant with the Tom Peters Group.

34. Instead of worrying about "change management," they could better first work toward "change creation."

35. See Conner (1992, 1998) for an extensive guide to nontinkering and effective change. Also, in commenting on providing a culture for useful change, management expert Gary Rummler (1986) observes that if you pit a good worker against a bad organization, the organization wins every time. All parts of the organization must support useful change.

36. I prefer the term "advance" to keep a proactive stance.

37. This has been suggested by Tom Peters in several of his recent writings and lectures.

38. Kaufman (1998a) and Kaufman and Swart (1995).

39. Peters (1997).

40. Noted by Peters (1997).

41. Kaufman (1997a).

CHAPTER 2

Ends and Means

This chapter focuses on the following three critical success factors (CSFs):

Critical Success Factor 2: **Differentiate between ends and means—focus on "what" (Mega outcomes, Macro outputs, Micro products) before "how."**

Critical Success Factor 3: **Use all three levels of planning and results.**

Critical Success Factor 4: **Prepare objectives—including those for the ideal vision and mission objectives—that have indicators of how you will know when you have arrived.**

Let's start with CSF 2.

Ends and means, what and how. Achieving success depends on correctly defining what success is and how to measure it. In this chapter, I examine three important aspects of this all-important ends and means relationship:

1. Ends are defined in terms of measurable performance objectives.
2. Ends, or results, are related to three levels of concern for every organization: Societal (or Mega level), Organizational (or Macro level), and Individual and Small Group (or Micro level).
3. Ends must be identified and linked at all three levels of planning:
    Mega, Macro, and Micro.

Figure 2.1 shows the relationship between ends and means.

First, let's examine the basics of defining and specifying ends: preparing measurable specifications for objectives that define "where we are headed and how to tell when we have arrived."

E
N
D
MEANS
N
D
S
MEANS

What's the Difference?

ENDS are the results, impacts, or accomplishments we get from applying the means. They are what is achieved.

MEANS are the way in which we do something. They are processes, activities, resources, methods, or techniques we use to deliver a result.

Figure 2.1. The relationship between ends and means.

Ends and results stated in performance terms are vital for success. But shifting to a results orientation—a consequences and payoffs mind-set—won't be easy for everyone. Old habits and past successes for many among us tend to get them to think and act in terms of means and resources while assuming that useful ends will happen. Hope springs eternal. Figure 2.2 shows an algorithm useful for choosing between ends and means.

Is it possible for people to change their ways? Can people give up paradigms and modes of action that have served them well in the past but will get them into trouble now? Many authors agree—what made you successful in the past may get you into trouble now and in the future. Getting out of one's comfort zones in order to be successful in the future is vital to Mega Planning.

We have a tendency to jump right into means before knowing and justifying the ends we are to accomplish. That is why CSF 2 is so basic: focus on ends—what to accomplish—before even thinking about selecting means.

Ends are the results, products, consequences, payoffs, and goals to be accomplished. Ends are the Whats and not the Hows, or resources.

Means are the ways, resources, activities, actions, programs, projects, how-to's that bring about ends. Means are the Hows.

Solutions in search of problems. Because much of our culture is preoccupied with action—getting going—we have a tendency to swing right into activities using solutions, methods,

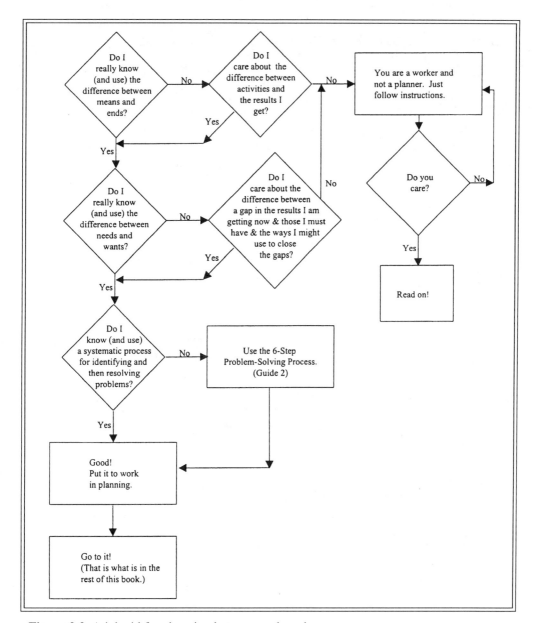

Figure 2.2. A job aid for choosing between ends and means.

and interventions we know and with which we are familiar. We thus often select solutions that don't go with our problems.

Culturally, we think in terms of means or solutions and not results and consequences. Read the papers. Listen to television. Tune in on political speeches. The conversations are almost about processes, or "how." In Table 2.1 are some popular topics. Scan these and sort them mentally as to whether each is a means or an end.

TABLE 2.1 Some Popular Initiatives to Be Sorted Into Means and Ends

FUNCTION	MEANS	ENDS
Reengineering		
360° feedback		
Decrease class size		
Reduce welfare funding		
Increase prison funding		
Develop a quality management program		
Training		
Downsizing		
Privatization		
Outsourcing		
Benchmarking		

Although these topics are the heart and soul of many organizational or political actions, they are all means to unspecified or hoped-for ends. Politicians talk of reducing class size in schools as if they assume that reduced class size will automatically increase learner performance. Politicians have lots of solutions to offer voters that many unquestioningly assume will lead to useful results: budget cutting, vouchers for schools, raising standards, and performance-based budgeting, to name a few. All of the topics in Table 2.1 are means in search of useful ends. They offer solutions—means—before defining the results and consequences to be achieved. A triumph of means over ends.

Concentrating first on means and activities is old paradigm thinking. We have a lot of it. We pay workers by the hours on the job and not on the quality and quantity of the work they produce. We increase funding to programs that have failed, assuming that the only thing missing is money. We talk of the importance of "experience" without asking the value added of that experience. Ends are what we must accomplish and deliver. Let's take a closer look.

▧ Objectives: What They Are

Ends—performance and accomplishments—must be defined before selecting means and resources. Engineers do it. So do physicians. Architects as well. In fact, any group that has to deliver results sets objectives. Objectives contain nothing about the means or resources to get there—just the results. Nothing, ever, about who will do the job!

An objective states "Where are we headed and how will we be able to tell when we have arrived?" Any time you want to get results and be able to prove that the results have been delivered, you prepare measurable objectives.

> ✔ What result will be accomplished?
> ✔ Who or what will demonstrate the accomplishment?
> ✔ Under what conditions will the accomplishment be observed?
> ✔ What criteria—ideally in interval or ratio scale terms—will be used?

Figure 2.3. The elements of a useful measurable objective.[1]

There are a number of formulations for preparing objectives. In training courses, Bob Mager is considered by most to have the clearest exposition of what an objective should look like and provide. Figure 2.3 shows the elements of a useful objective.

Let's look at each element of this formulation, keeping in mind that when defining and using an objective all of the elements must be present in a useful objective.

What result will be accomplished? Results are ends, products, outputs, outcomes, or accomplishments. The statement of results never include means or resources that can or will be used to deliver the accomplishment. Ends, and not means.

Who or what will demonstrate the accomplishment? This element of a measurable objective specifies who or what will display or demonstrate the result. It might be the contributions of a manager, a profit-and-loss statement, a building, a piece of equipment, or the performance of an associate. When a result is to be displayed, this part of an objective specifies the object.

Under what conditions will the accomplishment be observed? This part of an objective states precisely where and in what environment the results are to be observed. The conditions might include such things as "on the job," "at the end of the fiscal year," "during a crisis incident," and "at the time of first implementation."

What criteria—ideally in interval or ratio scale terms—will be used? Criteria are those precise specifications that allow one to prove what has been accomplished. These criteria often carry many names:

Performance Specifications	Products
Performance Criteria	Outputs
Requirements	Outcomes

Measurability is a vital characteristic of an objective. The more precise and rigorous the criteria the better. There are, as shown in Table 2.2, four scales of measurement.

Whenever possible, objectives should have the criteria for results stated in Interval or Ratio scale terms. The greater the precision and rigor, the more clearly purposes and destinations may

TABLE 2.2 Four Scales of Measurement, the Definition of Each, and an Example

Scale of Measurement	Definition	Example
Nominal	Naming, numbering	Jan, Inez, Quality, football player #15
Ordinal	Rank order	Blue ribbon award, world-class livestock judging, more than last year
Interval	Equal scale distances with arbitrary zero point	Average production, temperature in Celsius
Ratio	Equal scale distances with known zero point	Temperature in Kelvin, zero defects

be set and progress and completion determined. (Some examples of useful objectives are in the appendix to this chapter.)

Everything is measurable.[2] An interesting aspect of using this definition of a useful objective and these measurement scales is that everything is measurable. Everything. An item of conventional wisdom is that there are such things as "intangibles," or "unmeasurables." This just isn't true. Everything is measurable: As soon as it is declared that "there are some things that just are not measurable" a measurement has been made: there are two "piles" that can be made, one labeled "measurable" and another "not measurable." How does one decide what pile to sort it into?

In addition, as soon as you name something, you have differentiated it from other things, and that constitutes a nominal scale calibration. If you can name it, you are measuring it-so no more excuses about not being able to set rigorous objectives.

The most useful objectives are written in Interval or Ratio scale terms.

Other Formulations for Objectives

The ABCD model. Another guideline for preparing a measurable objective is the "ABCD" approach.[3] Using the first four letters of the alphabet as a mnemonic guide, Figure 2.4 defines the basic dimensions, or parts, of an objective.

Let's look at each element of the ABCD format:

A: Who or what is the **A**udience, recipient, or target? In terms of the Mager-type objective, this is akin to "Who or what will demonstrate the accomplishment?"

B: What **B**ehavior, performance,[4] accomplishment, end, consequence, or result is to be demonstrated? In the Mager-type objective, this is equivalent to "What result will be accomplished?"

C: Under what **C**onditions will the behavior, performance, or accomplishment be observed? Comparing this to the Mager-type objective, this is exactly equivalent to "Under what conditions will the accomplishment be observed?"

```
                    ┌─────────────────────┐
                    │  A Format for Preparing │
                    │  Measurable Objectives  │
                    │      As Easy As         │
                    │       ABCD              │
                    └─────────────────────┘
```

A: Who or What is the **A**udience, target, or recipient?

B: What **B**ehavior, performance, accomplishment, end, consequence, or result is to be demonstrated?

C: Under what **C**onditions will the behavior or accomplishment be observed?

D: What **D**ata-criteria, ideally measured on an interval or ratio scale, will be used to calibrate success?

Figure 2.4. The "ABCD" guide for defining useful objectives.

D: What **Data**—-criteria, ideally measured on an Interval or Ratio scale—will be used to calibrate success? This is almost the same as the Mager-type objective "What criteria—ideally in interval or ratio scale terms—will be used?"

The "Hey Mommy" Test

An easy guide to the usefulness of a statement of an objective is to ask the question "Hey Mommy, let me show you how I can . . ." and fill in the result. If it makes sense—if it defines a useful result that is clear—it is probably a good objective. For example, how would you rate the statement "Hey Mommy, let me show you how I can develop a deep respect for my associates"? Silly, isn't it? There is no result, even though it might have good intentions. Compare that statement with "Hey Mommy, let me show you how I can prove that there have been no harassment complaints against us this year."

Results must be the primary focus of any objective—precise and rigorous criteria so you can state "where we are headed and how we can tell when we have arrived."

The Importance of Rigor in Mega Planning and Setting All Objectives

There is consistent data, across cultures, that lack of clarity about purposes and criteria lies at the core of organizational ineffectiveness and efficiency.[5] If we don't clearly identify where we are headed and how we will measure if we have arrived, associates don't know what they are to deliver. And if we don't know where we are headed, how can we define how to get there?

Lack of precision and rigor is dehumanizing[6] to our internal and external partners; we don't care enough about them to be clear about what it is we will deliver. It is sensible to know where we are headed. Again, if we don't have rigorous specifications, how can we plan, design, develop, implement, and continuously improve? Simply put, we cannot.

Preparing Objectives (and Performance Indicators)[7, 8]

Objectives (which include performance indicators) provide the intentions and the evidence and proof required to show that an effort, activity, or initiative has achieved a defined result.

Objectives have two uses, one proactive and the other reactive: These are, respectively, to identify what is to be accomplished and to provide criteria for judging success or failure.

Objectives may be used in several ways, ranging from providing staff performance appraisal standards, to supplying criteria for the evaluation of training, for defining the consequences of human resources development, to defining new organizational destinations and purposes. Use them whenever you want to define measurable purpose:

- A clear, unambiguous statement of required results
- Precise criteria to measure actual results
- Specification of who or what will demonstrate the intended results
- Statement of under what conditions the results, or performance, will be observed

Target Ends

But sometimes people want to also take a look at the means to achieve the ends. No matter what we do, or how we do it, organizations are only successful to the extent to which they get results. Useful performance indicators only relate to valid *ends* (results, consequences, performance, payoffs). Indicators that target *means* (how something gets done, processes, methods, techniques) or resources (people, time, money, facilities) provide feedback on procedure *compliance,* fidelity of implementation, or how faithfully or to what degree a specific job is being done: They deal with *how,* not *what.*

"How" is only sensible to look at in terms of what they (methods, means, activities) deliver, so beware of writing objectives for means: Without relating them to ends and consequences, you just might end up with solutions in search of problems. As noted earlier, however, old habits die hard. Until they get the confidence to change to a results orientation, people have a tendency to jump right into defining means. They will even sometimes get angry and argue "I know that is the way to do it" or even perceptually distort a means and think it is an end.[9]

There are two types of indicators in common use, one of which relates to results and the other is concerned with activities and compliance:

Type R: Results-oriented indicators that identify measurable performance, consequences, payoffs, or ends. Results targeted may include individual contributions as well as organizational results and consequences, and external client and societal value added. This type is what I urge you to use exclusively.

Type I: Implementation-oriented indicators that identify fidelity of activity and compliance in the application of methods, means, resources, and/or approaches.

Although both types are widely used today, Type R is strongly urged: if we are not intending to deliver useful results and their consequences, our efforts (means, activities, initiatives, approaches) might be wasted. Therefore, this chapter and this book deals only with Type R performance-results-oriented indicators because the use of ends-based objectives provides the best assurance that selected means will deliver desired consequences.

During operations and implementation, however, a performance improvement professional might want to use a means- or process-oriented (Type I) set of criteria in order to provide an employee with feedback on how well that employee is doing in a particular activity. This can be helpful *if* there is assurance that the activity, when done correctly and to specifications, will deliver important results. Continuous improvement of processes and resources must focus only on the results to be achieved. (By only examining means, however, the user risks begging the question of the *usefulness* of any results that flow from the means, or activities. One may be performing a task as specified, but the task may not be useful to the organization or to external clients.)

Some Important Features of Objectives

Not all results are created equal. Individual accomplishments within an organization must combine with all others to provide useful organizational contributions: Some results are "building blocks" for larger, overall ones. These enroute results are in turn only useful when they "add up," or combine, within the entire organization to properly serve external clients and society.

As I noted earlier in this chapter (and on which I devote more time to in Chapter 3), this "contributing relationship" of all of the ends and means of an organization makes up a "results chain,"[10] This chain, shown in Figure 2.5, spans from organizational resources and efforts to organizational results and finally to client and societal value-added Outcomes.

A results focus is a critical success factor. Now let's expand this critical success factor to demonstrate the three levels of results that must be both identified and linked.

This big-picture perspective encourages—even demands—the formal consideration of the implications of what one's organization does, accomplishes, and delivers to the outside world. Objectives are prepared for all three levels of results. And for all three levels of planning.

Three Levels of Results:[11]
The Organizational Elements Model

Now that I have defined the importance of defining results in measurable—ideally Interval or Ratio scale terms—in order to define and demonstrate success, let's look more closely at one of the basic guides for Mega planning, the Organizational Elements Model (OEM). The OEM iden-

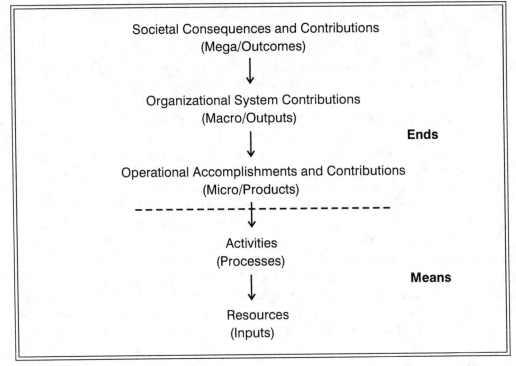

Figure 2.5. Results chain shows the relationships among the Organizational Elements.

tifies and links everything any organization, public or private, uses, does, produces, delivers, and the resulting payoffs for external clients and society. It is the societal level of results that uniquely defines Mega Planning and that is unique to this formulation.

With the introduction of the OEM, I now bring into consideration CSFs 3 and 4, defined at the beginning of this chapter.

The Organizational Elements Model

One of the three basic guides for Mega Planning is the OEM. Now let's see what it is and why it is so important. The OEM defines three levels of results and two types of processes, resources, and means. The organizational elements are as follows:

Outcomes: Results at the external client and societal level. Outcomes are results that add value to society, community, and clients outside of the organization. Planning at the Outcomes level is called Mega Planning. Outcomes could include survival; self-sufficiency; not being under the care, custody, or control of others; and no continuing disabilities that prevent self-sufficiency. Because every organization has external clients and because each must demonstrate adding value for society, Outcomes/Mega Planning constitute the most central and key focus for planning and organizational success. After all, every organization is in the position of having to improve society.

Several of the "new realities" provided in Chapter 1 focus on the demand to be societally responsive and responsible: (a) that useful change has to add value for all internal and external partners, (b) that there are two bottom lines for any organization—conventional and societal, and (c), to paraphrase Faith Popcorn,[12] that doing societal good is now a corporate must, not an option.

Mega planning starts with Outcomes and ends with Outcomes. It defines a societal value-added system. It defines societal value added as the primary focus for planning. management, design, development, implementation, evaluation, and continuous improvement. Mega. Outcomes.

Outputs: The results that an organization can or does deliver outside itself to external clients and society—not the achievement of external results (Mega) but the delivery of results outside the organization that can and should deliver Mega consequences. Planning that stops at the organizational contributions level is termed Macro planning. Macro planning, interestingly, is most often the type of planning that is called (unfortunately) "strategic planning."[13] Interestingly, this is the results level of most conventional "strategic planning" and thus leaves societal and external value added in question.

Products: The building-block results that form the basis of what an organization produces, delivers inside as well as outside itself, and the payoffs for external clients and society. It is the primary focus of most organizational activities and resources application.

Processes: The means, processes, activities, interventions, programs, and initiatives an organization can or does use. Anything that is intended to use resources and deliver results is a "process." Processes are only useful to the extent to which they effectively and efficiently deliver useful results.

Inputs: The ingredients, raw materials, physical and human resources that an organization can use in its processes in order to deliver useful ends.

Figure 2.6 shows an organizational example with some items for each element.

The OEM also can be useful in one's own life and daily affairs. Figure 2.7 shows a personal example with some items for each element.

Each Organizational Element Equally Important

No one Organizational Element is more important than any other. All must not only be used, they also must be linked and integrated. Although Mega Planning has Outcomes as its unique starting focus, it is not any more or less important than any of the others.

The Organizational Elements and the Three Levels of Planning

As I noted in the Introduction, the Organizational Elements, listed in Table 2.3, are related to the three levels of planning:

The literature blurs levels of results. For some reason, the popular literature on planning and performance system improvement tend to use the three levels of results described here—

ORGANIZATION

Mega/ Outcomes	Macro/ Outputs	Micro/ Products	Processes	Inputs
Self-sufficient and people who contribute	Assembled automobiles	Tire	Organization development	Money
Reduced or eliminated illness due to air pollution	Yearly auto production	Fender	Management techniques	Personality
Reduced or eliminated fatalities	Automobiles sold	Production quota met	Manufacturing techniques	Mental and physical characteristics
Positive quality of life	System delivered	Completed training	Operating production line	Resources
No welfare recipients	Patient discharged	Trained workers	Training	Needs (current)
Continued profit		Worker agreement	Reengineering	Goals (current)
Stockholder vote of confidence		Course completed	Curriculum	Desires
Money for continuation		Operation completed	Quality improvement programs	Problems (current)
Zero crime			Doing	Values
Zero homelessness			Learning	Laws
Client's success			Developing	Memories
			Examining patient	
			Strategic planning	
			Strategic thinking	

Figure 2.6. An organizational example of indicators for each of the Organizational Elements.

Outcomes, Outputs, Products—interchangeably. Calling every result an "outcome" blurs the important role of linking results at all three levels of planning.

Results, results, results: Three levels. There are three levels of planning: Mega, Macro, and Micro. When planning targets society as the primary client and beneficiary of what gets delivered, this is a *Mega-level* concern. When the primary client and beneficiary is the organizations itself, this is termed *Macro-level.* When the primary client and beneficiary is an individual or small group, then the focus is *Micro-level* planning.

There are three *ends* (or results) to which the means contribute. Objectives can and should be written for each. The "foundation" and core level of result is **Outcomes** that indicate the Megalevel contributions of everything and organization uses (Inputs), does (Processes), pro-

INDIVIDUAL

Mega/ Outcomes	Macro/ Outputs	Micro/ Products	Processes	Inputs
Expenses less than income	Obtained first career position	Monthly paycheck	Critical thinking	Money
Positive future	Marriage to loved one	Mastery of word processing	Intuition	Personality
Freedom from fear	Good physical health	Purchased car	Guilt	Mental and physical characteristics
Financial	Graduation from college	Clean house	Depression	Resources
Independence	Discharged from hospital	Dinner party held	Task orientation	Needs (current)
Continued health and well-being	Maintenance of desired weight	Achieve desired weight	Valuing	Goals (current)
		No disabling illness	Problem-solving	Desires
			Defense mechanism	Problems (current)
			Going through psychotherapy	Values
			Working	Laws
			Planning	Memories
			Investing	
			Dreaming	

Figure 2.7. A personal example of applying the OEM to one's own life and activities.

duces (Products), and delivers (Outputs). The internal results, processes and resources that are delivered and have consequences to external clients and society.[14] All internal resources, activities, results, and deliverables must render value added to society and external clients (Outcomes). The other two types of *ends* are internal (within-the-organization) results: **Products** are the building blocks of organizational contributions at the Micro level, and **Outputs** are the Macro-level results that can be or are delivered to clients.

Table 2.4 shows the relationships among planning levels, results types, and primary clients.

Objectives, while relating to the three types of ends (Products, Outputs, Outcomes), should have identifiable linkages among all of the five organizational elements. Means and ends should be related. Starting with Mega, the three levels of planning and the three levels of results should be linked in an outside-in fashion, as shown in Figure 2.8.

TABLE 2.3 The Organizational Elements, the Related Results, and Definitions

Name of the Organizational Element	Name of the Level of Planning and Focus	Brief Description
Outcomes	Mega	Results and their consequences for external clients and society
Outputs	Macro	The results an organization can or does deliver outside of itself
Products	Micro	The building-block results that are produced within the organization
Processes	Process	The ways, means, activities, procedures, and methods used internally
Inputs	Input	The human, physical, and financial resources an organization can or does use

TABLE 2.4 Levels of Planning, Levels of Results, and the Primary Clients and Beneficiaries of Each

Level of Planning	Level of Results	Primary Clients
Mega	Outcomes	External clients and society
Macro	Outputs	Internal clients and organization
Micro	Products	Individuals and/or small groups

Several Possible "Templates" for Improving Objectives

Three major considerations for developing useful objectives are the following:

1. Differentiation among means and ends
2. Reliability[15] of the measurability of the results
3. Array and range of organizational elements covered: Mega/Outcomes, Macro/Outputs, and Micro/Products

Means and ends have a dynamic relationship with the organization and what it uses, does, produces, delivers, and the consequences they have. Often, means and ends have dynamic relationships within an organization. Instead of seeing objectives as only important at one level of results, note that they have a contributing, or building-block, relationship with ends and consequences at all levels, as shown in Figure 2.9.

Some considerations when preparing objectives. When preparing (or reviewing) objectives, one, two, or, three "templates" may be used to compare each with these three realms.

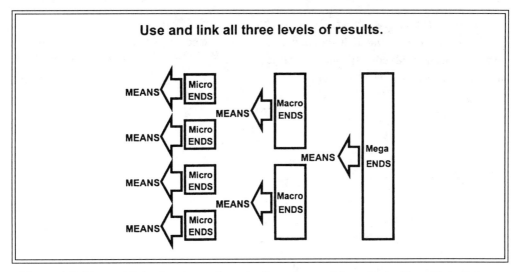

Figure 2.8. Use and link planning and results from the outside to the inside to link all three levels.

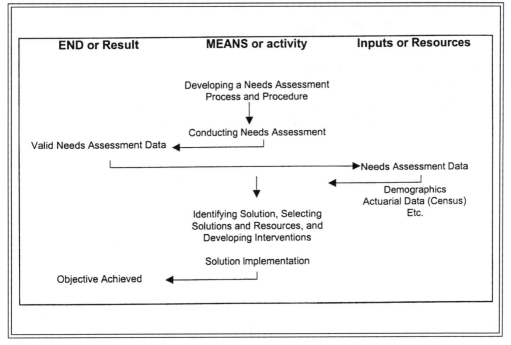

Figure 2.9. The nonlinear (or lock-step) nature of linking means and ends.

Template 1: Means and Ends

The most important factor in deriving a useful performance indicator is whether it deals with results or means, with consequences, or resources (CSF 2). For any would-be objective, determine if it relates to a means or to an end:

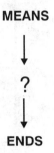

MEANS

↓

?

↓

ENDS

Ends are *results* to be accomplished, *Means* are the possible techniques, procedures, methods, and resources that may be used to obtain ends. Means are best selected only on the basis of the results they are to accomplish. One clue to discriminating a means is if the indicator includes a word with an "ing" suffix (e.g., train*ing,* develop*ing,* learn*ing,* plann*ing,* us*ing,* show*ing,* and demonstrat*ing*). Such "ing" words usually identify a means, not an end.

If a would-be performance indicator only identifies a means to an end, then change it to target only the intended result. To derive an ends-related indicator from means-related ones, ask "What would be the result if this means (or resource) were successfully implemented?" For example, an intent to "improve learn*ing* of basic performance indicator concepts" is better stated "Correctly list four characteristics of a valid objective, including its performance indicators and write one which will identify intended measurable results."[16] Ends-oriented objectives are encouraged here because, sooner or later, performance and results will be the basic test of whether or not any process, resource, or method is worthy.

Template 2: Measurability

Classify each of the objectives as to its level of measurement. There are four scales of measurement:

Nominal	Naming
Ordinal	Rank Ordering
Interval	Equal Scale Distances, Arbitrary Zero-point
Ratio	Equal Scale Distances, Known Zero-point

Objectives are measurable on an interval or ratio scale, whereas goals, aims, and purposes use nominal and ordinal scales. Objectives should be measurable on an interval or ratio scale in order to better assure their accuracy and reliability.

Template 3: Organizational Focus

In order to better assure that the accomplishment of an objective will yield both individual performance improvement as well as organizational accomplishments and useful contributions, sort the performance indicator into one of the five Organizational Elements:

MEGA/	MACRO/	MICRO/	PROCESSES	INPUTS
OUTCOMES	OUTPUTS	PRODUCTS		

Make certain that a possible indicator falls in one of the results elements (Mega/Outcomes, Macro/Outputs, Micro/Products) unless compliance is the only intended consequence. In addition, any performance indicator should have linkages to the other Organizational Elements. This can be accomplished by identifying the interactions between the performance indicator and the total array of elements. So doing will confirm that there will be a results chain that links internal organizational results with external, outside-the-organization consequences.

If there are no linkages for a performance indicator with all five of the organizational elements, this serves as a warning signal that the performance under consideration might not be useful within and/or outside the organization. Without such ties/linkages among the elements, there is little rationale for moving on with a planned effort.

Using the templates. All, some, or one of the three templates may be useful. The use of all three better assures the usefulness of the derived objectives.

The flow of the use of all the three templates are shown in Figure 2.10.[17]

Summary

Mega Planning depends on a results focus. Although it is tempting for people to focus on the comfortable realms of methods and resources, success depends on a results orientation. This ends-first paradigm is vital. It is so important that each of the six critical success factors identified in the Introduction either include or depend on a results orientation.

All objectives (CSF 4: Prepare all objectives . . .) must be precise and rigorous. No fuzzy intentions in Mega Planning.

Two types of objectives are in use today. Type R deals with results; Type I focuses on implementation and compliance. This chapter deals with the recommended results-oriented objectives (Type R).

Objectives should

- relate to ends, not means, processes, or resources in isolation from the results they should deliver;

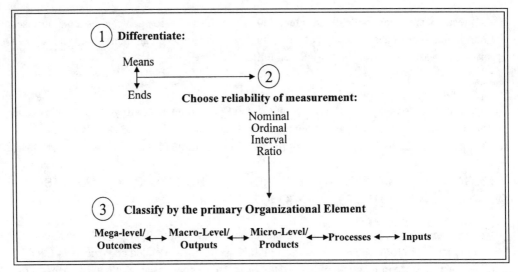

Figure 2.10. Three integrated templates for assuring the relationship among means/ends, reliability of measurement, and the appropriate Organizational Element.

- be precise and measurable on an Interval or Ratio scale; and
- be related and incorporated into a results chain that links all organizational efforts, organizational results, and client and societal payoffs and consequences.

If any objective does not have all of the above characteristics, it is possible that the performances for which one is devising indicators may not be useful and productive.

Critical Success Factor 2 is vital for Mega Planning. Results, ideally on an Interval or Ratio scale, are imperative as you define where your organization should be headed, justify why it should get there, and know how to tell when it has arrived. With precise and rigorous indicators for destinations and accomplishments, you have vital data concerning intentions, objectives, design and development criteria, and continuous improvement criteria,

A results focus is a component in all of Mega Planning. Without it, you risk being fuzzy and missing the point for defining and achieving success.

Expanding the results orientation, the Organizational Elements Model (OEM) identifies what every organization, public and private, must use, do, produce, and deliver along with the external consequences of their outputs. The Organizational Elements must not only be considered, they must also be linked (CSF 3: Use all three levels of planning and results). And, finally, everything any organization uses (Inputs), does (Processes), produces (Products), and delivers outside itself (Outputs) must add value for external clients and society (Outcomes). There are two levels of means (Inputs and Processes) and three levels of results (Products, Outputs, Outcomes).

To ensure that the Organizational Elements are linked, Mega Planning identifies three levels of planning: Mega that focuses on Outcomes, Macro that focuses on Outputs, and Micro that focuses on Products.

Results, results, results. It is all about results. Useful results.

EXERCISES

1. Purposes, Objectives, and Rigor

Review your purposes, objectives, and the precision and rigor of these intention statements—how these are conceived and done at your organization—in terms of the following questions. Answer, for each question, both **What Is** (your current practice) and **What Should Be** (your desired practice; what will best serve your organization).

Each **What Is** and **What Should Be** column—on either side of the questions—has the following dimensions in terms of the relative frequency that something does or does not happen:

Consistently (96%-100%)
Quite frequently (85%-95%)
Sometimes (51%-84%)
Not usually (18%-50%)
Almost never (6%-17%)
Rarely, if ever (0%-5%)

Part A: The Nature of Your Results Focus

My organization prepares purpose statements that define:

WHAT IS							WHAT SHOULD BE					
Rarely, if ever (0-4%)	Almost Never (5%-15%)	Not Usually (16-49%)	Sometimes (50-83%)	Quite Frequently (84-94%)	Consistently(95-100%)	Please indicate the frequency (in terms of percentage of times) with which the following statements are happening within your organization. Please provide <u>two responses</u> to each question: **WHAT IS** describes how you see your organization currently operating. **WHAT SHOULD BE** describes how you think your organization should be operating.	Rarely, if ever (0-4%)	Almost Never (5%-15%)	Not Usually (16-49%)	Sometimes (50-83%)	Quite Frequently (84-94%)	Consistently(95-100%)
① ② ③ ④ ⑤ ⑥						1. Resources and activities to be accomplished	① ② ③ ④ ⑤ ⑥					
① ② ③ ④ ⑤ ⑥						2. General (Nominal or Ordinal scale measurements) results to be achieved	① ② ③ ④ ⑤ ⑥					
① ② ③ ④ ⑤ ⑥						3. Specific and rigorous (Interval or Ratio scale measurements) results to be achieved	① ② ③ ④ ⑤ ⑥					
① ② ③ ④ ⑤ ⑥						4. Results for individual and small groups to be achieved	① ② ③ ④ ⑤ ⑥					
① ② ③ ④ ⑤ ⑥						5. Results for the organization to achieve and deliver	① ② ③ ④ ⑤ ⑥					
① ② ③ ④ ⑤ ⑥						6. Results to add value for external clients and society	① ② ③ ④ ⑤ ⑥					

Suggested patterns:

Item 1 should be rated low on both What Is and What Should Be.

Item 2 should be rated higher on both What Is and What Should Be than ratings for Item 1.

Items 3 to 5 should be rated increasingly higher than Items 1 and 2 on both What Is and What Should Be.

Item 6 is the best choice and should be rated high on both What Is and What Should Be.

Part B: Justifying the Purposes and Objectives

My organization prepares purpose statements that define results and have the following justification:

WHAT IS						Please indicate the frequency (in terms of percentage of times) with which the following statements are happening within your organization. Please provide two responses to each question:	WHAT SHOULD BE					
Rarely, if ever (0-4%)	Almost Never (5%-15%)	Not Usually (16-49%)	Sometimes (50-83%)	Quite Frequently (84-94%)	Consistently(95-100%)		Rarely, if ever (0-4%)	Almost Never (5%-15%)	Not Usually (16-49%)	Sometimes (50-83%)	Quite Frequently (84-94%)	Consistently(95-100%)

WHAT IS describes how you see your organization currently operating.

WHAT SHOULD BE describes how you think your organization should be operating.

① ② ③ ④ ⑤ ⑥	7. Results based on data from defined gaps between current and desired results and the consequences of the results—needs-- for individuals and/or small groups (Micro level).	① ② ③ ④ ⑤ ⑥
① ② ③ ④ ⑤ ⑥	8. Results based on data from defined gaps between current and desired results and their consequences—needs-- for the organization itself (Macro level).	① ② ③ ④ ⑤ ⑥
① ② ③ ④ ⑤ ⑥	9. Results based on data from defined gaps between current and desired results and their consequences—needs-- for external clients and society (Mega level).	① ② ③ ④ ⑤ ⑥

Suggested patterns:

Items 7 and 8 should be rated increasingly higher (Item 8 higher than ratings for Item 7) on both What Is and What Should Be because they are data based.

Item 9 should be rated higher than Items 7 and 8 on both What Is and What Should Be because of including the Mega level of results and consequences.

Part C: Linking Levels of Organizational Results and Their Consequences

My organization prepares purpose statements in terms of:

WHAT IS							WHAT SHOULD BE					
Rarely, if ever (0-4%)	Almost Never (5%-15%)	Not Usually (16-49%)	Sometimes (50-83%)	Quite Frequently (84-94%)	Consistently(95-100%)	Please indicate the frequency (in terms of percentage of times) with which the following statements are happening within your organization. Please provide two responses to each question: **WHAT IS** describes how you see your organization currently operating. **WHAT SHOULD BE** describes how you think your organization should be operating.	Rarely, if ever (0-4%)	Almost Never (5%-15%)	Not Usually (16-49%)	Sometimes (50-83%)	Quite Frequently (84-94%)	Consistently(95-100%)
① ② ③ ④ ⑤ ⑥						10. There is no linking among levels of planning and results.	① ② ③ ④ ⑤ ⑥					
① ② ③ ④ ⑤ ⑥						11. Results linking Micro and Macro levels.	① ② ③ ④ ⑤ ⑥					
① ② ③ ④ ⑤ ⑥						12. Results linking Macro and Mega levels.	① ② ③ ④ ⑤ ⑥					
① ② ③ ④ ⑤ ⑥						13. Results linking Macro, Micro, and Mega levels.	① ② ③ ④ ⑤ ⑥					

Suggested patterns:

Item 10 should be rated low on both What Is and What Should Be.

Item 11 should be rated high on both What Is and What Should Be (but note that they do not directly focus on external clients payoffs).

Item 12 should be rated high on both What Is and What Should Be and is the best choice (because it links all three levels of planning and results).

Part D: The Rigor and Reliability of Measurements

WHAT IS							WHAT SHOULD BE					
Rarely, if ever (0-4%)	Almost Never (5%-15%)	Not Usually (16-49%)	Sometimes (50-83%)	Quite Frequently (84-94%)	Consistently(95-100%)	Please indicate the frequency (in terms of percentage of times) with which the following statements are happening within your organization. Please provide two responses to each question: **WHAT IS** describes how you see your organization currently operating. **WHAT SHOULD BE** describes how you think your organization should be operating.	Rarely, if ever (0-4%)	Almost Never (5%-15%)	Not Usually (16-49%)	Sometimes (50-83%)	Quite Frequently (84-94%)	Consistently(95-100%)
① ② ③ ④ ⑤ ⑥						14. Results and needs are measurable on a nominal and ordinal scale.	① ② ③ ④ ⑤ ⑥					
① ② ③ ④ ⑤ ⑥						15. Results and needs are measurable on an interval and ratio scale.	① ② ③ ④ ⑤ ⑥					

Suggested patterns:

> Item 14 should be rated low on both What Is and What Should Be (but note that at least it is focusing on results, but with less rigor than Item 15).
>
> Item 15 should be rated high on both What Is as well as What Should be. There should be an increasingly higher rating of both What Is and What Should Be as you move from Item 14 to 15.

2. Means vs. Ends

For each item on the list, put a mark in the appropriate column depending on whether it is primarily an END (results, consequence, or payoff) or a MEANS (resources, methods, how-to-do-its, interventions, processes, approaches, methods):

	END	**MEANS**
Learning problem solving		
Looking for a job		
Demonstrate positive self-esteem		
Joining a class action lawsuit		
Downsizing		
Moving to Seattle		
Graduated college		
Survival		
Banning tree cutting		
Reengineering		
Assessing needs		
Training		
Continuous improvement		
Team building		
Loving		

Answer Key

Let's compare answers:

	END	MEANS
Learning problem solving		✔
Looking for a job		✔
Demonstrate positive self-esteem	✔	
Joining a class action lawsuit		✔
Downsizing		✔
Moving to Seattle		✔
Graduated college		
Survival	✔	
Banning tree cutting		✔
Reengineering		✔
Assessing needs		✔
Training		✔
Continuous improvement		✔
Team building		✔
Loving		✔

It is usual for processes, activities, and initiatives that we admire, know how to do, and have used in the past to show up on a list like this as an "end." Calling something an "end" doesn't make it one. Don't confuse ends and means, and do not prepare objectives or any other performance criteria by including in its statement and means, resources, or how-to-do-its. Even if we "love" them.

Appendix: Hypothetical Objectives/Performance Indicators for the Three Types of Results: Mega/Outcome, Macro/Output, and Micro/Product

Following are simplified examples of objectives and performance indicators for each of the three types of results, based on Macro-level planned contributions based on Mega consequences.

Mega/Outcome Linked: All clients, direct and indirect, will suffer no death or disability from accidents or manufacturing. All of the sold and delivered watercraft vehicles turned out by the plant after June 4 will be safe, effective, and efficient as indicated by (1) having no court-ordered changes or mandated modifications based on violations of health and safety laws and regulations resulting in death or disabilities and (2) no upheld successful lawsuits attributed to manufacturing defects or pollution that caused loss of life and/or livelihood of anyone associated with what the organization delivers: There will be no loss of life attributed to defective design, development, or fabrication as certified by the Department of Water Safety for each state where the vehicles are sold.

Macro/Outputs: At least 99% of all parts manufactured by the MB&A Plant after next month will meet all quality acceptance standards without remanufacturing, and be shipped to distribution points and/or to customers on or before the times contracted as indicated by no client complaints about timeliness or quality and no returns for defects or dissatisfaction.

Micro/Products: At least 99.8% of all cellular telephones and each of its components delivered to final assembly and shipping will meet all quality acceptance standards and criteria, as indicated by sign-off by the quality inspector on each shift and no rejects from the quality assurance test laboratory.

Notes

1. Based in part on R. F. Mager (1997).

2. Stevens (1951).

3. Unfortunately, I don't know the origin of this formulation, although I offer my thanks to the person(s) who first thought of it.

4. In his landmark works, Tom Gilbert has emphasized the critical differences between behavior—what a person does—and performance—what a person accomplishes. This important distinction is nicely made in Gilbert and Gilbert (1989).

5. Joe Harless of the Harless Performance Guild notes that, based on data from over 200 front-end analyses, the top reasons for poor performance are (1) lack of clearly defined accountability, (2) no incentive/reward, (3) lack of managerial coaching and reinforcement, and (4) lack of employee skill or knowledge.

6. University of North Florida distinguished Professor Leon Lessinger (some call him the father of educational accountability) long ago stated that we should be "accountable for humanism." To this I add that practical humanism includes forming partnerships with others we can or will be affected by what we use, do, produce, and deliver. As part of this humanism we must be clear about where we are headed and why we want to get there and share that with all partners. Without that clarity, we cannot build the commitment to common purposes.

7. Objectives state where you are headed and how to demonstrate when you have arrived. Performance indicators supply the criteria that any objective must include.

8. This material is based, in part, on my Chapter 5 in Kaufman, Thiagarajan, and MacGillis (1997).

9. In Chapter 3, Needs and Needs Assessment, I again visit this tendency to focus on means and assume that useful ends will surely follow. Using "need" as a verb (or in a verb sense) jumps right over gaps in ends (needs) and selects means prematurely.

10. Kaufman (1992b, 1998b; Kaufman, Thiagarjan, & MacGillis, 1997) emphasizes these points.

11. As a reminder, for each level of results there is an associated level, or focus, of planning: Outcomes/Mega, Outputs/Macro, and Products/Micro.

12. Popcorn (1991).

13. Interestingly, Mintzberg (1994) accurately points out that most conventional "strategic planning" is really limited, narrow, and restrictive and doesn't really focus on important strategic issues. I agree. Most of conventional strategic planning is really tactical (Outputs/Macro) or operational (Micro/Products) and thus is doomed to limited success. Also see Kaufman (1992b, 1998b) for the alternative that I term "Mega Planning."

14. This is the core of what I call Mega Planning and can be reviewed in Kaufman (1992d, 1998b). As noted earlier, it is this Mega/Outcomes focus that is missing from conventional formulations of "strategic planning." I use the label "Strategic Planning Plus" to emphasize the added Mega level.

15. Statistically, validity is the extent to which something measures what it is supposed to measure, and reliability is the consistency with which it is measured.

16. Note that "learn*ing*" is a process; mastery is an end. Thus, a "learning organization" is really an incomplete concept; it is this constant "learning" that results in a constantly improving and consistently responsive organization.

17. In Chapter 3, another element to this template is added to derive useful objectives that intend to identify future requirements for organizational success.

3

Needs and Needs Assessment

This chapter focuses on the following fifth critical success factor:

Critical Success Factor 5: **Define "need" as a gap between current and desired results (not as insufficient levels of resources, means, or methods).**

Defining Need and Needs Assessment

Absolutely vital to a useful needs assessment is the definition of what is a *need.*[1] For the purposes of planning, it is vital to use the following definition:

A **need** is the gap between current results and desired or required results.

A need is not a gap in resources, processes, methods, or how-to-do-its (such as training, HRD, supervising, benchmarking, continuous improvement, reengineering, etc.).

A **needs assessment** identifies gaps between current results and desired (or required) ones and places them in priority order for resolution based on the cost to meet the need as compared to the cost of ignoring it.

Interestingly, most "needs assessments" that are used and provided in the literature focus not on gaps in ends and results but on gaps in processes or resources. This violates CSF 2 that requires a focus on ends before selecting means. An assessment of gaps in means or methods is a "quasi-needs assessment" because there is a concern for gaps, but not gaps in results.

A **quasi-need** is a gap in a method, resource, or process.

These definitions and terms are more than hair-splitting or attention-getting ones. Much more.

"Need" defined as a gap in results? This is more than semantic quibbling.

How can the definition of "need" be so important? Simple. By defining "need" as a gap in results—between current and desired ones—it builds on CSFs 2, 3, and 4. A major emphasis in Mega Planning is a focus on results, not on means, methods, or resources.

It is vital to define need as a gap in results, for it will allow you to justify where you are headed, where your objectives come from, and why they are important. This definition also allows you to tell when you have arrived. As we shall see shortly, a "needs assessment" is based on this definition of need because a needs assessment identifies gaps in results and places the needs in priority order.

With any other (and usually conventional and comfortable) definition of need, this justification is very "iffy." "Need is not a verb" is vital, although my encouraging you to get out of your current comfort zone (remember, CSF 1?) might seem trivial at first. It isn't. Let's see why.

"Need" is a gap in results.

By defining need as a noun (only identifying gaps in results) the firm foundation for planning may be built (see Figure 3.1).

Note that when you define need as a gap in results, it doesn't discount means and resources, it simply places them in their proper perspective: as ways to close the gaps in results. Means and ends are thus related in a sensible way.

Needs assessments that really are not needs assessments.

Most conventional definitions of need, needs assessment, and needs analysis really focus on means. Such familiar phrases (or orders) as "We need training," "We need to hire more engineers," "We need to get on the Web" really jump us right over defining the gaps in results that training, more engineers, or getting on the Web might be responsive to. In other words, when we define need as a verb, we are assuming that we know the needs. And that doesn't happen very often.

A popular (and comfortable) technique is called "training needs assessment." Again, according to research,[2] if one starts at the Micro or Process level—realizing that training is a means and not an end[3]—you will be wrong 80% to 90% of the time. Eighty to 90% wrong! So, a "training needs assessment" usually comes from a premature selection of training as the solution before defining gaps in performance and the contributions of the resulting performance.

Why is starting with a means, such as training, likely to get you into trouble? Again, according to quality gurus Deming and Juran,[4] most (80% or 90%, depending on the author's report) performance problems are not usually individual problems but system breakdowns. Thus, if you start with "training" (or other means, activities, or interventions) as the solution, you attack individual performance problems and ignore the overarching system problems that are causing the problem in the first place. You will likely be treating the symptoms and not the causes. Starting at

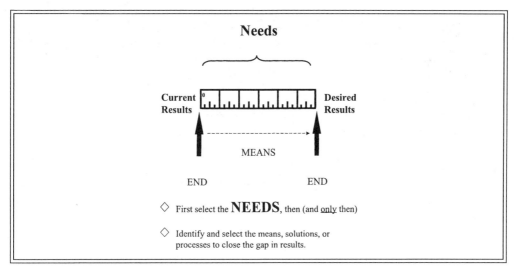

Figure 3.1. Needs are gaps in results, not gaps in processes or resources.

"training needs" and the Micro level present breathtakingly bad odds. Why would anyone continue to use a "training needs assessment"? With this kind of track record, it is comfortable, conventional, straightforward, and wrong.

But bosses often demand solutions, assuming they already really know the problem and, indeed, the correct solution.[5] They jump right into means before defining the ends to be accomplished. Open conversation can be useful in overcoming a boss's tendency to be solution/process oriented. Simply, without sarcasm or hostility but in a spirit of "let's reason this out together," ask "If the training were successful, what performance would you want to observe? And what contribution will that change in performance have on our internal and external success?" Work together to define the gaps in results that are to be closed or reduced, and then consider other alternatives as well.

If you simply accept the assignment and design, develop, and implement the request, if and when it fails (and recall, it will fail 80% to 90% of the time) it will be you that is blamed. By defining "need" as a noun, you can justify any intervention.

Three bonuses for defining "need" as a gap in results.
When you use this suggested definition of need, you get three bonuses:

1. The "What Should Be" dimension of an identified need serves as the measurable objectives. It states where you are headed and how to tell when you have arrived.
2. The "What Should Be" dimension serves as the evaluation and continuous improvement criteria. You don't have to go out and develop a separate evaluation plan, it is already there.
3. You have the justification for never having a proposal turned down again. With the data from a defined need and the gaps in results, you may now compute the costs-consequences[6] for

not meeting the needs. Conventionally, we only submit proposals for doing something on the basis of our objectives (What Should Be) and the costs for getting from "What Is" to there. With data about both dimensions of "What Is" and "What Should Be," we can price out (a) the cost to meet the need and (b) the cost to ignore the need.

We most often get our ideas and proposals rejected because "this just costs too much." We usually only submit our objectives and our costs to meet them, but we don't usually also state the consequences of not meeting the needs. If you do submit both the costs to meet and the costs to ignore the need, then if your proposal is rejected, the person rejecting it now has to take the responsibility for not meeting the needs. Most bosses have never thought of needs in these terms, and your providing costs-consequences data—what it costs to meet the needs as compared to the costs to ignore them—is usually seen as refreshing and useful. Try it.

Needs are identified at three levels of results: Mega, Macro, and Micro.[7]
There are three levels of results—Outcomes, Outputs, and Products—and needs may (and should be) identified at each level. The linking of needs at the Mega, Macro, and Micro levels of planning is vital. It is from this linking that we get strategic alignment and can better assure that what our organizations, use (Inputs), do (Processes), produce (Products), and deliver (Outputs) will add value to external clients and society (Outcomes). Doing so is a hallmark of Mega Planning.

Conducting a needs assessment at each of the planning and results levels (Mega, Macro, and Micro) allows the linkages among external payoffs and internal results and activities. Figure 3.2 shows this relationship.

In Chapter 4, the Mega level of results and consequences is completely defined. But for now, note that there is a cascading down based on needs assessment data that links the Organizational Elements. This assures strategic alignment with tactical and operational results.

After identifying the needs—gaps in results—for the elements in the Ideal Vision, those that you and your organization commits to deliver and move ever closer toward become the basis for the Mission Objective—the results at the Macro level—which identifies the Ideal Vision elements that

- you and your organization commit to close the gaps in results;
- those parts of closing the gaps in results that you and your organization commit to deliver and move ever closer toward *in partnership with other agencies, agents, and partners*; and
- those parts that you and your organization will not be directly responsible for but which are important for your success and for which you must have the data in order to do your planning and evaluation/continuous improvement.

This process of rolling down from the Ideal Vision (see Chapter 4) to define (a) your Mission Objective and the associated Macro-level needs and then (b) your functions (building-block results) and their associated needs assures strategic linkage. Strategic linkage assures the align-

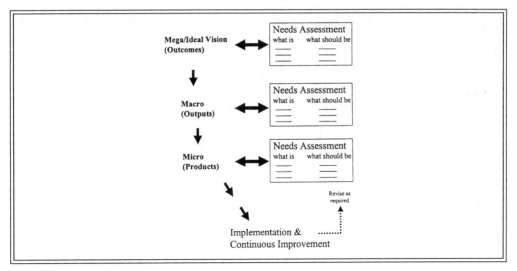

Figure 3.2. The organizational roll-down defines needs at each level, starting with Mega, to provide needs assessment data.

ment among what you use (Inputs), do (Processes), produce (Products), deliver outside your organization (Outputs) with external client and societal value added (Outcomes).

All of the concepts and tools of Mega Planning relate.

The relationship of needs assessment and the levels of planning and results are interactive. Chapter 4 provides more detail (see Figure 4.4) on how to do a needs assessment for each organizational level. It will make more sense after the definition of an Ideal Vision—the Mega level of planning—is provided.

If you don't use needs assessment at the three levels of planning and results, you cannot assure yourself or others that what you use, do, produce, and deliver will be appropriate or useful: strategic alignment. This process allows you to align strategies (Mega-level results and consequences) with tactics (Macro-level results and consequences) with operations (Micro-level results and consequences). This rolling-down relationship linking Mega, Macro, and Micro is seen in Figure 3.2.

What Is a Needs Assessment?

Wants and needs. Means and ends. Activities and competence. Methods and consequences. Training and competence. Human resource development and performance. Benchmarking and performance improvement. While these pairs might be related, they are different. What they do have in common is that the first in each pair is a *means* and the second is an *end*. If you want to select a useful destination (an end), you best proceed by defining the gap in results, a *need*, between where you are now and where you want to be, between "What Is" and "What Should Be" for results. The process of defining those gaps in results and selecting the most important ones for reduction or closure is called *needs assessment.*

Needs assessment is part of holistic Mega-level strategic planning. Whether it is selecting the organizational destination or defining and relating what contributions must be delivered from within the organization to be successful, needs assessment provides the performance data for those decisions: rigorous and justifiable data on needs.

Chapter 2 identified how to prepare useful performance objectives and how to use those objectives in the identification of needs. It is also important to realize that the data from a results-referenced needs assessment provides basic information for evaluation and continuous improvement. Measurability and rigor are an essential part of needs assessment and of Mega Planning.

Choosing a Proactive Approach

Performing a needs assessment to identify and document problems seems, at first, more time-consuming than jumping right into a solution. The urge to "look active and get moving" is deceptively attractive, but it often turns out that initial hunches don't resolve the real problems. We often act in haste and repent in leisure. This tendency to want to "get right into solving our problems" is what leads to premature use of identifying training (before justifying performance problems and value added to the organization and external clients) or analyzing needs before identifying and justifying them first.

A proactive needs assessment identifies and justifies the problems in the beginning of performance improvement initiatives, not jumping directly to training or other solutions-in-search-of-problems. If you decide you don't have the time to do a needs assessment, you likely will later be forced to go back and repair the damage from not having resolved the basic problem in the first place.

An additional focus on the future. Another consideration is the future. The past is prologue to the future, and planning is an attempt to make change and create a positive and attractive future. But the future is murky, unpredictable, and fickle. It is also where we will spend the rest of our lives. Some people view it with respect and trepidation and seem to want to leave it unaddressed. Others see the future, as does Peter Drucker, as something we can create if we so choose.

A needs assessment should look at "futures" in order to identify where the organization is going, where it could be going, and where it should be headed. Planning that attempts only to improve on favored or in-vogue solutions that have worked in the past ignores the possibility that these solutions might be the seeds of future failure. The world changes, often in dramatic and systemic ways. We can and must choose between being the victims of change or the masters of it.

Selecting where to head. Most performance planners, including performance improvement specialists, start with a problem to resolve[8] or a deficiency to fix. Planning, thus, is done reactively by responding to some situation to be changed. Identification of the problem to be resolved is usually, unfortunately, left up to a client, or an "expert" who defines both the problem as well as the purposes. These specialists are primarily concerned with *resolving* problems.[9]

As significant as such "repair" efforts are, it is usually much more important to first identify and justify the actual problem and also to search for and identify opportunities—that is, to be proactive.

Although setting measurable objectives is the usual starting place for applying planning, it is almost always vital to first make certain that the objectives are the right ones and that their accomplishment will lead to organizational success and usefulness of what the organization delivers to external clients. Here enters the key role and contribution of needs assessment.

Needs assessments provide the direction for planning and then useful problem resolution through identifying, documenting, and selecting appropriate problems.[10] By selecting important problems and deriving useful objectives before rushing off to resolve them, planners and performance system professionals may improve the effectiveness and efficiency of any organization and its individual operations.

Needs assessment is best used as an integral part of Mega Planning. It may also provide the database for other important initiatives, including human resources development (HRD) and all organizational improvement projects.

There are many models and processes that get called "needs assessment." But most do not (a) define "need" as a gap in results and (b) identify needs at the three planning levels (Mega, Macro, Micro) or the three related results levels (Outcomes, Outputs, Products). The various approaches to needs assessment vary substantially in terms of which of the Organizational Elements they cover.[11] Most are not really needs assessments, as suggested here, but are usually better termed "wants assessments" or "solutions assessments" because they don't focus on gaps in results but, rather, on gaps in processes, interventions, and/or activities.

▨ The Nine Steps of Needs Assessment

Following are nine steps for doing a needs assessment. Each step uses different results-focused tools and techniques. The specific choice of tools and when to use each depends on the type of needs assessment you choose.

Step 1: Decide to plan using data from a needs (not a "wants") assessment.

A plan is a blueprint that delivers useful results. It identifies the functions—deliverable Products—an organization must produce in order to get from current results and consequences to required and desired ones. It also focuses on adding value for internal and external clients. A *management plan*—a flow of building-block functions required to get from What Is to What Should Be for results—derives from determining where you want to go and justifying why you want to get there.

Planning is only a substitute for good luck. If you can count on good luck, don't go to the trouble of doing a needs assessment.[12] A properly completed needs assessment replaces good luck in determining and justifying where you should be headed and why you want to get there.

Using a needs assessment to define current and desired results affords you the data and tools for gaining control over events and/or keeping things working appropriately before problems appear. All the partners in planning (see Step 3 below) must agree to all commitments. Planning partners include those who will be affected by the results and those who will have to implement any resulting plan.

Step 2: Identify the three needs assessment (and planning) levels to be included—Mega, Macro, and Micro—and commit to needs assessment (and planning) that starts at the Mega level.

How much of your operational world (and realities) should you consider and tackle? The following three levels or units of analysis are possible:

- *Mega.*[13] This level is the result of everything an organization uses, does, produces, and delivers—Products and Outputs—to its external clients and to the external world. It links all the Organizational Elements.[14]
- *Macro.* This level combines the Micro-level contributions (Products) together in order to deliver useful results outside the organization to external clients. The Macro level's unit of analysis is the total to form what an organization can or does deliver (Outputs) to its external clients, including society. This level is made up of what an organization uses, does, and delivers to itself as well as to its external clients.[15] It does not include external results and consequences.
- *Micro.* This level of needs assessment and planning includes a concern for the cumulative contributions of (a) organizational resources (Inputs) plus (b) the procedures and methods (Processes) to be employed in organizational activities that deliver (c) immediate results (Products).[16]

You may, and should, assess needs at all of these three levels. Choosing the Micro or Macro level assumes that the contributions of those results will be responsive to client and societal requirements and realities—a rather large assumption.

The Organizational Elements Model (OEM), shown in Table I.1 and discussed extensively in Chapter 2, provides a holistic framework for identifying needs, analyzing them, defining useful objectives, and then selecting effective and efficient interventions. Using this model will help you identify, define, and relate what organizations use, do, and deliver. The OEM links internal and external resources and Processes with three kinds of results (as shown in Table 3.1): Products, Outputs, and Outcomes. Notice the relationship among the Organizational Elements and the three levels of planning and needs assessment:

Assuring the linkages among levels of results and value added. Linking Mega/Outcomes, Macro/Outputs, and Micro/Products is vital to assure strategic alignment. If you don't link the

TABLE 3.1 Relationship Between Three Levels of Planning and Their Associated Three Types of Results

Level of Planning	*Type of Result (based on the OEM)*
Mega	Outcome
Macro	Output
Micro	Product

three levels of planning and results, your effectiveness might be compromised. Figure 3.3 is a job aid[17] for asking the appropriate needs assessment questions and better assuring the linking of the three levels of results.

Step 3: Identify the needs assessment and planning partners.

Successful needs assessment and any resulting plans, procedures, projects, activities, and resulting payoffs that are derived from the needs assessment data, depend on choosing the correct planning partners to guide the process and to "own" it when it is completed. An otherwise good plan might fail simply because uninvolved or unrepresented people may not see that an imposed change, no matter how rational, might benefit them. You can usually aid in any plan's adoption and resulting changes by having affected people participate as partners in the planning or have them represented in the needs assessment and resulting plan's creation.

Who are the Mega Planning partners? It isn't enough to identify just the partners. They must be active participants and contributors. The partners should be representative of (a) implementers, (b) recipients, and (c) community and society. These partners represent those who might implement any interventions, those who might be directly affected by them, and the external clients and society who might also be impacted by whatever you and your organization selects to do and deliver. Resist the temptation to put friends or powerful people on the planning partners group. For useful data and for credibility, the planning partners must be both representative and seen by all as truly representative.

After identifying the planning partners, you ask them to collect data on "What Is" and "What Should Be" for results. In addition, there are the "hard" data concerning self-sufficiency and self-reliance and the gaps between what is and what should be for this set of indicators (Figure 3.4).

There are three human needs assessment and planning partner groups and one performance databased one. The human partners are (a) those who will be affected by the results of the plan, (b) those who will implement the plan, and (c) clients or society that will receive (and/or be affected by) the results.

The planning (and needs assessment) partners selected depend on the type of organization and who are its clients. Usually, the planners and their operational unit (such as personnel, engi-

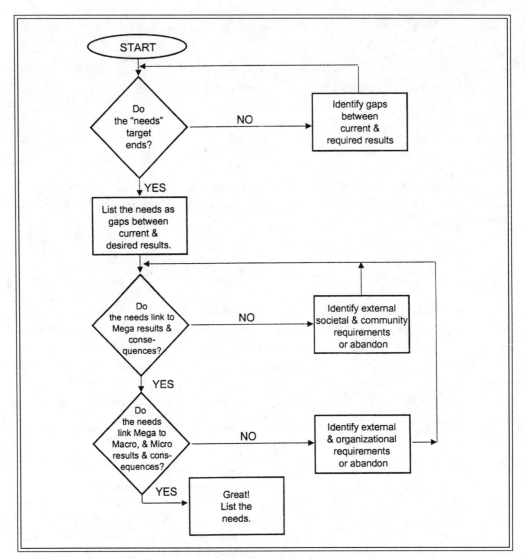

Figure 3.3. An algorithm, or job aid, notes the questions and sequences of questions and answers for doing a Mega-level needs assessment.

neering, quality) are the implementers and the planners' immediate clients, such as trainees, supervisors, or patients, are the recipients.

"Society" is an inclusive term for those who will be affected by what an organization and its external clients deliver as well as the entire community in which they live. For example, a community service for the handicapped might include those who are paraplegic, blind, hearing impaired, physically impaired, mentally diminished, ailing and infirm elderly, as well as their neighbors. For a computer software developer, "society" might include wholesale and retail

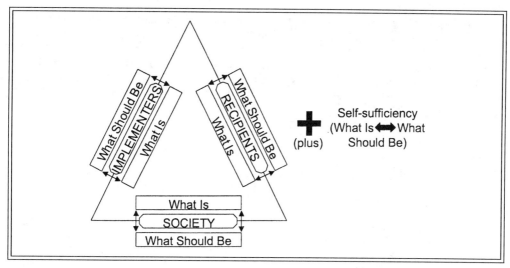

Figure 3.4. The three partners for needs assessment (Society, Recipients, and Implementers) and the "hard data" partner that adds information on self-sufficiency and survival.

sales organizations and the end users as well as those people who are directly or indirectly affected by the use of the software (for example, a bank's software might affect the bank accounts of those who make payments to their clients if there are "glitches").

When selecting the planning partners, make sure that they are typical representatives of their constituencies. If, for example, ethnic or age composition is important, secure a representative sample that includes these variables. If particular skills are critical, make sure that these are represented among the partners.

Usually, a stratified random sample[18] of each partner group will provide representativeness. But don't create huge groups, only representative ones. The number of planning partners depends on what you are planning and who the planned changes are supposed to serve. Because the partner group should represent the actual operational world, it should not include "tokens" nor be packed with friends.

Again, the word *need* has, unfortunately for human and organizational performance purposes, several conventional and thus commonly accepted meanings. Make sure that all the partner groups are working with the same (and recommended, as defined earlier) definition. The importance of using *need* (as a noun, not a verb) to describe a gap in results cannot be overemphasized.

The human partners will supply data concerning perceived needs. Because these needs are based on personal experiences, observations, and feelings, they are termed "needs sensing" or, more commonly, "soft" data.[19] Sensed needs often provide perceived reality and sensitivity to issues of values and preferences about current problems and consequences. They also may reveal observations concerning the processes, conditions, and procedures that led to the currently undesired results.

TABLE 3.2 The Organizational Elements Model and Associated Scopes, Clusters, and Their Relationship to Mega, Macro, and Micro Planning and Needs Assessments[20]

Organizational Level	OUTCOMES (the value added of Outputs in and for society and external clients)	OUTPUTS (the collective Products of the system that are delivered or deliverable to society)	PRODUCTS (enroute—building-block—results)	PROCESSES (how-to's, means, activities, methods, procedures)	INPUTS (human, capital, and physical resources, ingredients)
Examples	Self-sufficient, self-reliant, productive individual; continued funding of organization, continued projects over time, positive corporate image, etc.	Delivered automobile, graduates, client accepted consultant report, etc.	Completed fender, training course completed, competency test passed, 14,000 hrs. certification, etc.	Benchmarking, reengineering, total quality management, continuous improvement, teaching, learning, training, managing, self-managed teams, accountability, etc.	Existing personnel; identified needs, goals, objectives, policies, regulations, and laws; money, values, principles, and societal and community characteristics; current quality of life; instructor competencies; buildings; equipment, etc.
Cluster	SOCIETAL RESULTS/ IMPACT	ORGANIZATIONAL RESULTS/ ENDS		ORGANIZATIONAL EFFORTS/ MEANS	
Scope	EXTERNAL (Societal)	INTERNAL (Organizational)			
Planning Level	MEGA	MACRO	MICRO		
Primary Client or Beneficiary	SOCIETY/ COMMUNITY	ORGANIZA-TION	INDIVIDUALS OR SMALL GROUPS		
Strategic-Planning Question	Do you commit to add value for society and all partners?	Do you commit to deliver outputs that meet client requirements and desires?	Do you commit to deliver products that meet all performance requirements?		

Involving significant others, or partners, in the proactive needs assessment and planning decision. People who are important in defining and making required change, as well as supporting the results of a plan for change, should be included in any decisions. List those people who will (1) participate in the planning, (2) approve or support what flows from a needs assessment, and (3) be affected by any plans that flow from a needs assessment. These potential "gatekeepers" include the following:

- Members of the planning team
- Supervisors, managers, associates, and executives who will use the plan
- Important and representative community members
- External clients or customers
- Those who could influence the success of the effort

Including significant other partners in the total planning process makes sense from a number of perspectives:

- They will supply useful information that might be otherwise overlooked.
- Their participation reduces the possibility of selecting an approach that is a quick fix or simply politically acceptable or popular.
- They will come to "own"[21] both the planning process and its results. And, rather than being indifferent or obstructive to it, they will tend to become its "champion" or sponsor.

To ensure that those being asked to make the needs assessment and planning decision share an understanding of the alternative payoffs and consequences, it is useful to present to them the rationale we have just gone through. The importance of a primary Mega focus is very important to keep them from the usual tendency to leap directly to considerations and selection of Inputs and Processes-favored solutions.

Step 4: Obtain the participation of your needs assessment (and planning) partners.

When the partners are identified, contact the selected partners and reveal to each your expectations, required time commitments, desired Products, and level of contributions. Disclose how much in the way of funds, travel, data, materials, support services, and the like that you will provide them. Be clear concerning how you will use and consider their Inputs. Assure them, and follow through on, that they are not rubber stamps, that the plan is not already in place and their meeting is only façade, and that you will not bias them or attempt to manipulate them. Tell them that they should only deal with facts and focus on ends and consequences, not means or resources.

After getting commitments from the partners, design and schedule the first meeting. Meetings can be simple face-to-face affairs or can include written surveys, Delphi techniques, teleconferencing, or computer interface. Replace partners who don't come to meetings or who don't contribute.

Step 5: Obtain acceptance of the needs assessment (and planning) frame of reference as Mega.

Share with the partners the three needs assessment and planning levels—Mega/Outcomes, Macro/Outputs, and Micro/Products (see Step 2). Get their commitment to Mega. By familiariz-

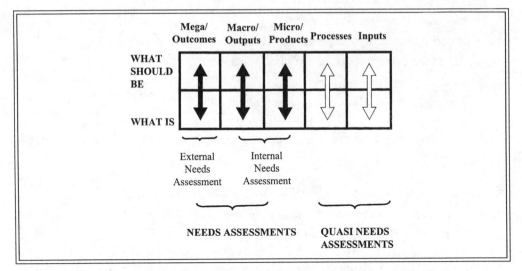

Figure 3.5. The two-tiered Organizational Elements Model. Needs, as gaps in results, are shown as solid arrows for the elements of Outcomes, Outputs, and Products. Quasi-needs are shown as clear, outlined arrows for Process and Inputs. Needs analysis becomes possible after needs are identified.[24]

ing them with the optional levels of needs assessment and planning, and the advantages and disadvantages of each, you afford the partners an informed choice. It is important that all partners know the scope of the needs assessment and have a common set of understandings and expectations. If they select a level below Mega, be sure they know *and* will assume the risks of doing so in terms of their accountability for not delivering societal- and external client-useful results.[22]

Explain to the partners the basic concepts of needs assessment. Tell them that needs assessment is the process for identifying, documenting, justifying, and prioritizing the gaps between "what is" and "what should be" concerning the three types of results identified in Table I.1: Outcomes, Outputs, and Products. Figure 3.5 illustrates that there may, and should, be three kinds of needs assessments; one relating to each of the three types of results. The Mega level (Outcomes) of needs assessment is strongly recommended as the safest, most pragmatic, and most practical starting place.[23]

Using the OEM for organizational analysis. This two-level format for the Organizational Elements may be used for organizational diagnosis. By filling in each of the 10 cells, you may identify "what is" and "what should be" for your organization and note where there are empty cells and also where appropriate linkages among and between the cells are missing.

A taxonomy of needs and quasi-needs assessments.[25] Based on the OEM, there are three varieties, or types, of needs assessments and two types of quasi-needs assessments. Table 3.3 identifies the alternatives and provides a descriptive label that also relates to each of the steps in the

TABLE 3.3 A Taxonomy of Needs and Quasi-Needs Assessments and Their Relationships With the Organizational Elements Model and the Six-Step Problem-Solving Process

Primary Organizational Element (and Type of Result) Focus	*Type of Needs or Quasi-Needs Assessment*	*The Step of the Six-Step Problem-Solving Model With Which Related*
Mega/Outcomes	Alpha	1.0
Macro/Outputs	Beta	2.0
Micro/Products	Gamma	3.0
Processes	Delta (Quasi-need)	4.0
Inputs	Epsilon (Quasi-need)	5.0
(Evaluation and Continuous Improvement)	Zeta	6.0

six-step problem-solving model (shown in Table I.1—one of the basic useful guides for Mega Planning and strategic thinking).

Using this taxonomy, the most powerful starting place for a needs assessment is Alpha, or a primary focus on Mega. Starting below the Alpha type of needs assessment risks not relating what your organization uses, does, produces, and delivers to external client and societal value added. When conducting a needs assessment, a quick determination of its usefulness (and perhaps unexamined assumptions) may be accomplished by asking what type of process it is in terms of this taxonomy.[26]

Needs analysis[27] consists of taking the determined gaps between adjacent elements and finding the causes of the inability to deliver required results at one level (e.g., Products, when aggregated, to deliver required results, or Outputs), and/or why Outputs did not deliver positive results for external clients and society (Mega/Outcomes). A needs analysis also identifies possible ways and means to close the gaps in results—needs—but does not select them.[28]

Some confuse needs assessment and needs analysis, perhaps not realizing the basic functions required: To analyze anything, including needs, one has to identify *what* to analyze in the first place. Thus, needs analysis rationally only comes after identifying the need—gaps in results—to be analyzed.

A few practitioners even fail to distinguish among needs assessment, needs analysis, problem solving, trouble shooting, problem isolation, and problem diagnosis.[29] Regardless of what a needs analysis is called, it rationally follows needs assessment and needs selection and is a part of identifying and solving problems. While it is tempting to start with needs analysis, one rationally should identify the need-gap in results to be analyzed.

Step 6: Collect both internal and external needs data.

Internal needs data concern performance discrepancies within an organization,[30] and external needs data concern performance discrepancies of your clients and our shared world.[31]

When collecting data on internal performance, look at two information sources: the perceptions of the planning partners ("soft" or qualitative data, defined as personalized views of reality that are not independently verifiable) and the actual performance discrepancies collected from objective observations ("hard" or quantitative data, defined as objective findings that are independently verifiable).

Perceptions: Not enough, alone, for useful planning. Useful planning is not based on soft data alone, even though it is currently popular to base organizational change (such as training, human resource development, and reorganization) only on people's perceptions, that is, on qualitative data. Several realities have to be merged:

- The actual results being delivered (current results)
- The results that should be delivered in the future (desired results)
- The perceptions of the people involved about both current and desired results

Both hard and soft data are used to answer questions for Mega-, Macro-, and Micro-related questions.

What objective hard-performance data measures. In addition to the "human" planning partners (and their qualitative perceptions), useful planning also requires a "non-human" partner in the form of "hard," performance-based independently verifiable indicators. Such quantitative indicators of actual (and later, required and desired) results could include measurements of the following:

- Positive client and social impact (such as customer satisfaction, continuing profits,[32] and the environmental impact and safety of what is delivered)
- Self-sufficiency[33]
- Self-reliance
- Products that meet internal and external quality standards
- Quality of life
- Social spin-offs
- On-the-job safety

You may view the performance-based data as a "non-human" partner because it supplies additional facts you should consider in identifying, documenting, and selecting needs apart from any subjective and personal impressions. Together, the sensed needs (soft data) from the implementers and recipients, and external society/clients plus the performance-based measures (hard data) provide the integrated and complete needs assessment data. The hard and soft data are provided by the planning partners either directly by them or under their supervision and guidance.

Some *personal* criteria that can be used as indicators for self-sufficiency and self-reliance are these:

- No adult will be under the care, custody, or control of another person, agency, or substance.
- Each individual will achieve a condition of functional, physical, and mental well-being that allows them to be continually self-sufficient and self-reliant.
- An individual's consumption will be equal to or less than his or her production.

Some other indicators of social impact are the following:

- Satisfactory (or better) credit rating
- Independence from government transfer payments (such as food stamps and unemployment benefits)
- Health, both physical and mental, resulting in self-sufficiency
- Positive participation in and contribution to society (votes in elections, public service, etc.)
- Not being in a jail or mental institution or on parole
- Good quality of life (happily married, employment satisfaction, socially contributing, contributing to the arts, etc.)
- No deaths or disabilities from pollution
- No suicides
- No murders

It is important to project these social indicators into the future, so that when they are used they will represent that reality. To develop a program of planned change on "yesterday's news" would be disappointing for everyone concerned.

You also require data concerning gaps in performance as well as impact on and for external clients.[34] These independently verifiable needs may be both in human and organizational performance. Such data are termed "hard" because they derive from actual observed performance. Hard data focus only on results and performance. Hard data may be obtained for all three levels of planning and results. Let's see.

External results (Outcomes) might include such indicators of consequences as continued profits over time (as an indicator that what is delivered is safe and useful on an ongoing basis), positive organizational image, death rates, numbers of people with positive credit ratings, return of people to a healthy life and their maintenance of that full functioning, quality of community life, and the like.

Hard data also can (and should as we link internal and external results and consequences) include internal organizational performance indicators (Outputs and Products). Hard data for Outputs could be delivered services to customers, client returning goods or complaints, welfare case discharges, and on-time delivery of a computer or automobile. Hard data for the Products level could include indicators such as productivity, production rejection rates, absenteeism, morale, and corporate climate.

In measuring organizational accomplishment and contributions, the following indicators of performance could apply:

- Profit (especially continuing)
- Social acceptance (e.g., sales of public stock)
- Disabling accidents
- Adjudicated grievances
- Convictions
- Repeat business
- Rejection/return rates
- Accepted deliveries of goods and services
- Employment levels

Remember that performance indicators for results can, and should be, chosen at each of the three results levels: Products, Outputs, and Outcomes.

Quality of Life: An Important Planning Dimension

Some performance criteria, especially those dealing with Outcomes, seem firmly based on such values as individual and social self-sufficiency, self-reliance, and survival.[35] These basic criteria are essentials—if we don't meet these criteria, little else would matter. (Consider being without nourishing food or safe water for a week and then being asked to choose between a Vivaldi concerto, a Wagner opera, and a showing of Lautrec posters. Wouldn't you be more concerned about ingesting some food and drink first? Don't you think it more important for workers to be paid on time than it is to have employee lounges and company picnics?)

However, when (as is usually true in the developed nations) the survival of citizens is generally ensured, then the quality of life becomes quite important. Being self-sufficient and independent of the care, custody, or control of another person, agency, or substance lets us know that we will survive. Quality-of-life indicators respond to the question "Now that we are surviving, how do we make life worth living?"

It is essential that we consider organizational, social, and individual survival; once these are taken care of, it is then—and only then—appropriate to plan to contribute to the quality of life as well. Table 3.4 illustrates the OEM in relation to quality of life.

Both hard and soft data must be used. Figure 3.6 shows how both types are compared, and only when there is agreement between the two types of data do you move ahead.

TABLE 3.4 The Organizational Element Model as Applied to Both Self-Sufficiency and Quality of Life[36]

	INPUTS	PROCESSES	PRODUCTS	OUTPUTS	OUTCOMES
WHAT IS					
WHAT SHOULD BE					
SELF-SUFFICIENCY LEVEL					
QUALITY OF LIFE LEVEL					

In application, both hard and soft data are collected and compared. When comparing the data from the two sources, one might use a matrix similar to the one in Figure 3.6. Agreements and disagreements are identified and where there is not agreement, additional data should be collected. Going ahead without agreement among hard and soft data can be very risky.[37]

You may collect partners' perceptions concerning performance discrepancies—referred to earlier as needs sensing, or soft data—by using a variety of tools and methods ranging from face-to-face meetings to remote data collection methods including rating scales, questionnaires, Delphi technique, nominal group technique, structured interviews, or some paper-and-pencil assessments.[38]

The sensed needs of the partners will supply data concerning performance discrepancies they feel are important. People's perceptions are their realities. Be sure to collect both hard and soft data, for needs assessments are more than just questionnaires (which only harvest soft perception data).

Social spin-offs. As well as individual payoffs and consequences, social spin-offs are important. Social spin-offs are organizational contributions made over and above individual payoffs. For example, reducing the pollution in a river running through a city may have immediate positive health consequences for the people living directly in the flow, but additional spin-offs would be increased in area watershed purity—thus a healthier environment for people in the region.[39]

Collecting Needs Assessment Data

In designing or selecting needs sensing data collection instruments, be sure they pose the correct questions without bias. Make certain the instrument and its questions focus responses on results, not on resources (Inputs) or methods and techniques (Processes). Also, be sure the questions are comprehensive—collect needs data at the Outcomes, Outputs, and Products levels—in

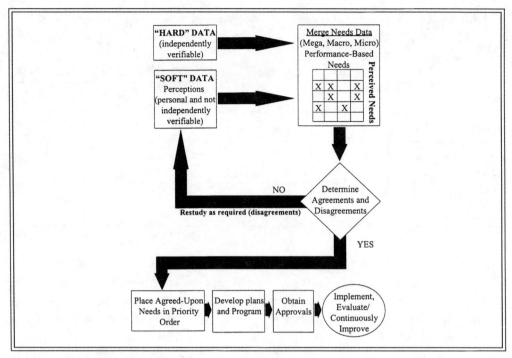

Figure 3.6. Using both hard and soft data to conduct a useful needs assessment.[40]

order to cover the possible array of needs without imposing on respondents with overly complex issues and time-consuming responses. The data collection instruments must be both valid (measuring that which they are really supposed to measure) and reliable (measuring the same thing consistently).

Collecting internal organizational performance data is usually simpler than it first appears. Most organizations have much hard data; you only have to identify what you want and then locate it. Useful data areas might include absenteeism, production rates, cases closed, audit exceptions, ethics violations, disabling or polluting accidents, on-site fatalities, grievances, courses completed, certified competencies, sick leave taken, work samples, and rejection rates. Assure the validity and reliability of these data, and use them only when they will supply useful information concerning performance and consequences. Don't collect data that do not answer the questions you are posing, and don't allow important questions to go unanswered simply because the data are not conveniently available. Sometimes, you will have to create the appropriate data sources.

For the Mega assessment level, collect external performance and consequences data. When doing so, you frequently find useful information both within and external to the organization. Some examples are data concerning clients' satisfaction, repeat business, return rates, recidivism, complaints, profits each year, arrests and convictions, successful lawsuits, return on investment, and income over time.

TABLE 3.5 A Needs Assessment Summary Format

| | | | | Need Level | | |
Current Results	*Possible Means*	*Required Results*	*Related Ideal Vision Element*	*Mega*	*Macro*	*Micro*

Even though you'll use hard and soft data, both must focus on results, not on methods, means, processes, techniques, procedures, resources, or personnel (such as time in training, computers, budget level). Targeting results in needs assessment is essential in relating means and ends.

What to do with the needs data. What do you do with these reliable and valid data when you get them? Following is a needs assessment summary format (Table 3.5) that allows the needs to (a) be openly listed and assure that all levels of needs (Mega, Macro, and Micro) are represented (and also linked)[41] and (b) relate it to assure linkages with the Mega, Macro, and Micro levels of planning:

Getting agreement. Before setting priorities, deriving objectives, and selecting interventions, the partners must agree on needs. When there are disagreements, you might have to help the partners come to agreement. Tools for getting agreement are (1) technical, and (2) group-process oriented.

Technical resolution possibilities include these:

- Reconcile the sensed needs with those based on the hard data.
- Derive a common set of needs supported by both the hard and soft data and obtain additional data if there are formidable differences.
- Translate the disputed perceived needs into results and ask the partners if the revision represents their concern. If it doesn't, ask them to revise it into a results-oriented statement that will address the concern. Most arguments over needs concern an incorrect (and usually stubborn) adherence to talking about gaps in methods and resources, best called "quasi-needs," rather than actual gaps in results.
- Ask the disagreeing partners to define the result that will be obtained if a certain "need" were to be met. Keep asking the question "If we were successful with this or achieved this, what would the result be?" Keep up this inquiry until (a) results are identified, and (b) there are links among all of the organizational elements. This questioning methods

encourages the partners to track the linkages from Inputs and Processes to results and then to a defined gap in results. Then they can sensibly rank the needs, now gaps in results, for resolution on the basis of the costs to meet the need as compared to the costs to ignore it. Don't forget to link all needs with Micro/Products, Macro/Outputs, and Mega/Outcomes.

Group-process oriented resolution possibilities include these:

- Discourage special interest/single issue groups from pushing a pet solution (e.g., Web-based instruction, more funding, reengineering, or training), a method (e.g., self-paced or multimedia instruction), or a resource (e.g., money or people) without first identifying and selecting the need that their favorite solution is intended to address.
- Encourage (and model the behavior yourself) all partners to define needs as gaps in results.
- Be certain that everyone knows that needs assessments are not public relations vehicles to favor one intervention over another.
- Be patient and open. Listen. Be ready, willing, and able to revise as required.

When things come to a halt. Sometimes, there are differences that seem to stall everything. Don't go ahead without substantial agreement, and don't cave in and equivocate just to keep peace. Most planning partners are honorable, concerned, and want to identify and meet the right needs. Often, what is missing are additional data focused on gaps in results, not gaps in resources or programs.

Sometimes, the hard and soft data may disagree. When that happens, get additional and more responsive data by using a revision of the techniques you selected in Step 6. By merging both opinion and empirical results, performance, data, you will usually find areas of common agreement on needs.

It is important that there be basic agreement between data obtained from different sources. Otherwise, the partners, and the interests they represent, won't perceive the needs assessment database as useful and they won't accept the results. Where there isn't accord, do further fact finding or reeducate the needs assessment and planning partners so they can agree. Figure 3.6 showed a flow process for merging the two types of data (hard and soft) and deciding the areas for collecting additional information.

After collecting the data, put it into a form that helps you make sure that it is complete. Enter it into the needs assessment matrix suggested in Table 3.5.

Keep refining the entries in the matrix until there is agreement about the data entered and the entries deal only with results. This might take several cycles. Also, remain consistent with your choice of planning, starting at the Mega level.

Agreement among the partners should be obtained concerning the needs to be addressed. Such judgments should also be consistent with the hard data. People's perceptions and external performance data should agree. By listing and then comparing needs based on both hard and soft data, planners can compare the matches and mismatches (agreements and disagreements).

Do not move on in your planning to select and meet any need unless there is substantial agreement. When there is disagreement between the hard and soft data or among partners (or both), dig deeper. Some causes for disagreements are these:

- Incomplete hard data
- Incomplete experience base of partner(s)
- Unavailable hard data
- Vested interests and territoriality

Now is the time to encourage objective, unbiased consideration of all data. When appropriate, collect more hard data and work with the disagreeing partners to take into account the perceptions of others along with the hard data. People who usually "trust their instincts" can be encouraged to look at performance data, and those who desire hard numbers may be helped to realize that sometimes we don't have all of the hard data required. Deliberate, talk, and reason. Provide data and review what is known and what is yet to be obtained.

It might be frustrating at first to watch some of the partners "lock in" to pet solutions and "tried and true" methods, even though it is apparent that the overall results clearly do not meet the needs. Be patient while you notice that some people will become resistant to change. Such people will confuse means with ends and argue that the system cannot be changed, that the bosses will never accept "deep change" and—well, just about every excuse imaginable. Be calm, listen, and quietly insert cool reality at each opportunity. Fear of change is almost universal, and planning does mean change. It will take some time for the partners to get comfortable with a results-oriented approach (in spite of what they say). Review the Ideal Vision (Chapter 4) of a better tomorrow, and encourage proactive planning.

Sooner or later, rationality will win out. When disagreement remains, you often will have to revisit the historical context and the futures data to provide a frame of reference concerning "what was," "what is," "what will be," and "what could be" and finally selecting "what should be." Again, most disagreements stem from (a) confusing ends and means, (b) insisting on a favored means and not being open to first defining and justifying gaps in results (needs) before finding a means, and/or (c) people involved in power games and territoriality. Bring these possibilities up with the planning partners, and list the existing "needs." Develop a simple chart with the "needs" in a first column, and two other columns marked "ends" and "means." Have the group fill out the chart; they will usually notice that some premature "means" have slipped in.[42]

Step 7: List identified, documented, and agreed-on needs.

Using a needs assessment summary format (Table 3.5), list the agreed-on needs. These listed needs will become basic information for both the needs assessment findings that will be used to identify and select programs, projects, activities, and interventions. These same data will also provide basic data for strategic planning.

The past and the future are important to consider in a needs assessment. Two variables, often assumed or ignored, are worth considering in a needs assessment: (a) past history and (b) the future. Time to perform, are most important for shaping the future, for it provides the potential to manage forthcoming events. Responding to here-and-now problems and criteria requires us to react and provides us with the opportunity to design and deliver a more useful future. After needs have been identified, selected, and used for planning and implementation, patience (defined as time to have things happen) must be allocated. Of course, the speed of change in our individual and collective worlds is accelerating, but at the same time, we cannot expect to implement a program and have it work right away. Because of this rapid change while taking time for any intervention to "take hold," we can (and should) use "formative evaluation" to check our progress.

> **Formative evaluation**: the checking of progress toward an objective to assure that means and methods are contributing to move ever closer toward the objective. It is the process of comparing your progress toward and objective in terms of getting closer to and finally achieving the intended purposes.[43]

We cannot be in such a hurry for a change to take place that we destroy the process by always questioning its effectiveness before impact can occur. (Do we take medication and really expect, not just want, results within 3 seconds?)

History (past accomplishments and influences) helps us evaluate the past and make predictions about the future. Needs assessment and planning are useful in helping us define the extent to which we will move toward a more productive and satisfying future.

Step 8: Place needs in priority order (based on the costs to meet and not meet the needs), place in priority order and reconcile differences.

Provide each of the planning partner groups with the list of needs they must prioritize (based on the results of the previous seven steps). This prioritization must include both soft data and the hard data from actual performance. From the listed needs in Step 7, ask each partner and then partner group to set priorities among the needs.

Costs-Consequences Analysis[44]

To set priorities among the needs, select criteria for weighting them. One useful priority-setting method is asking the partners to assign a value, often in monetary terms, for each need in terms of what it will cost to reduce or eliminate the need and what it will cost to ignore the need. You can view "cost" in financial terms as well as in quality-of-life terms. This process of estimating a detailed return-on-investment analysis is termed a *costs-consequences* analysis.[45] Costs-consequences analysis asks two basic questions simultaneously: What do you give, and what do you get? Based on these estimated costs-consequences, each group may meet with one of the others and derive a common set of rankings.

Step 9: List problems (selected needs) to be resolved and obtain agreement of the partners.

Compare the needs selected for resolution to a projected budget and use the priorities to assign funds until you exhaust the anticipated total sum. Sometimes, you can justify additions to the budget by asking decision makers to reconsider the previous budget allocation based on the solid needs assessment data and the partnership-derived priorities.

Using "need as a noun," you can justify your recommendations on the basis of (a) the cost to meet the need (close the gaps in results) and (b) the cost to ignore the need (what it will cost to allow the need to continue or even get more serious).

Problems are needs selected for reduction or elimination. After the partners have selected the problems to be resolved and you have obtained the budget, but before work proceeds, make certain the partners agree with the final results. If they do, fine. If they don't, have them recommend modifications and justify revisions to the decision makers.

The relationship between needs and problems comes into clear focus here. A need is a gap between current and desired results. Problems are needs to be reduced or eliminated. No needs, no problems (but also assure that no needs and problems later emerge: i.e., maintenance). As Mega Planning moves from planning to implementation, the selection of problems is the critical juncture. When the problems are identified and selected in the manner described here, they are justifiable in terms of costs-consequences—what do you give, and what do you get for meeting the identified needs?

Some important-but-subtle payoffs for using this approach to needs assessment. The data provided from the multi-level needs assessment will allow you to make justifiable decisions regarding organizational and human performance improvement interventions. By identifying the gaps in results and associated consequences, you can justify what you propose to use, do, and deliver on the basis of what it costs to meet the need as compared to what it costs to ignore the need.

Such justification is impossible to derive if one does not use the definition of "need" as a gap in results. Reviewed earlier in this chapter, when using "need" as a noun—a gap in results—there are two more "bonus" consequences:

- The "what should be" criteria provide the design and performance improvement criteria.
- The "what should be" criteria provide the bases for evaluation and continuous improvement. There is no requirement to develop a separate evaluation and continuous improvement plan or initiative.

Needs assessments provide cost-effective alternatives to designing interventions which, while meeting Product-level objectives, often fail to contribute to the organization's value to its clients, communities, and employees. It seems less expensive to find out where your organization should be headed, why it should go there, and tailor interventions to accomplish this than it is to fail and have to determine what went wrong and try again.

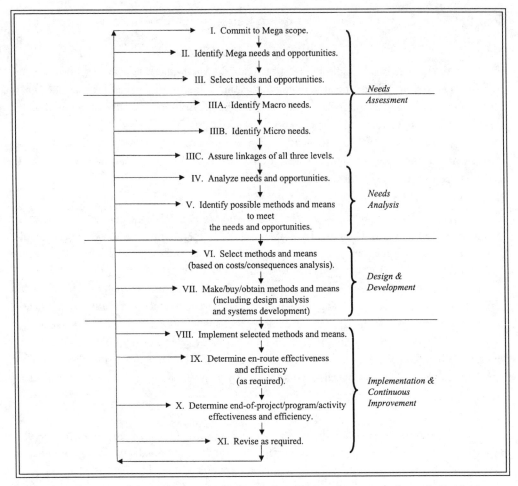

Figure 3.7. An overview and downward flow of needs assessment, needs analysis, design and development, and evaluation and continuous improvement.

Now, let's shift gears. Let's turn now to applying needs assessment—identifying needs and putting them in priority order on the basis of the costs to meet the needs as compared to the costs to ignore them—to your organization.

Figure 3.7 provides an overview of the sequence involved in doing a needs assessment. Note that there are four phases identified: needs assessment, needs analysis, design and development, and implementation and continuous improvement.[46]

Applying Needs Assessment to Your Organization[47]

Following are some tools and concepts that should be useful to applying the concepts of needs assessment to your organization.

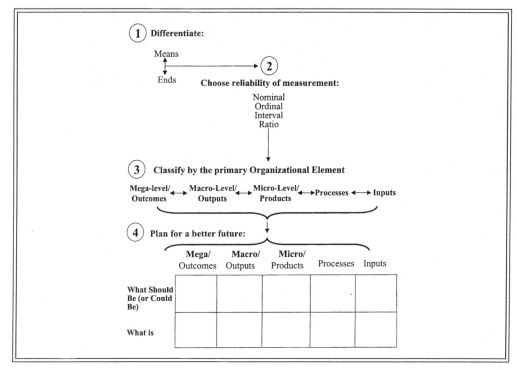

Figure 3.8. Four possible "templates" for developing useful objectives. Any or all may be used. The numbers 1 through 4 show a recommended sequence.

Ensuring That the Objectives Are Comprehensive

In Chapter 2, the topic of concentrating on ends before selecting means was presented and a set of templates provided to help you confirm that ends do indeed relate to all Organizational Elements (also covered). Now that the concept of needs and needs assessment has been presented, a fourth template (Figure 3.8) links those earlier described templates to the OEM and the two levels of What Is and What Should Be:

A Needs Assessment Audit Checklist

Using these definitions, here is a brief needs assessment checklist you may use to "audit" any needs assessment you are using or are considering:

_____1. Needs are identified as gaps between current results and desired results (or stated another way, the gap in results between "what is" and "what should be").

_____2. There is a clear distinction made between *ends* (results, consequences, payoffs) and *means* (resources, methods, how-to-do-its).

_____3. There are three levels of results identified *and* linked and related: one for societal and client contributions (*Mega* level), one for organizational contributions (*Macro* level), and another for individual performance (*Micro* level).

_____4. Any statement of need is free from any indication of how the need will be met (training, computers, technology, etc.).

_____5. Any statement of need is free from any indication of what resources will be used to meet the need (personnel, time, money, equipment, etc.).

_____6. Needs are prioritized, and listed, on the basis of what it costs to meet the need versus what it will cost to ignore it.

_____7. Interventions are selected on the basis of a costs-consequences analysis for each need or cluster of related needs.

_____8. Evaluation/continuous improvement criteria are taken directly from the "what should be" dimension of the selected needs.

_____9. Evaluation/continuous improvement results report the extent to which needs or families of related needs have been reduced or eliminated.

Rating Your Needs
Assessment Process

In a needs assessment's most powerful—and practical—application, you will have a "yes" for each of the nine items. Such a high rating is rare, however, because much of the conventional wisdom in the field steers people toward the more comfortable "training needs assessment," which might be better seen as a "training requirements analysis," or, unfortunately, a "solutions wish list" approach.

Some simple advice: You should not go ahead without at least a "yes" for guidelines 1, 2, 4, 5, 6, and 7. Although this approach will not link what your organization delivers outside itself and the payoffs for external clients, it does form the basic and lowest level of a needs assessment.

If you also can answer "yes" to guidelines 3, 8, and 9, you and your organization will most likely excel as compared to your competition. The inclusion of all nine suggested needs assessment characteristics is the safest approach you can take, for it will allow you and your organization to (a) meet societal responsibilities, (b) provide for external client satisfaction, (c) provide internal client satisfaction and assistance, and (d) provide the data for continuous improvement.

Tools for Conducting
Needs Assessments

Here is a series of possible management tools to help keep the assessment on target and results oriented in Mega-, Macro-, and Micro-level needs assessments and also in a quasi-needs assessment.

MEGA-LEVEL NEEDS ASSESSMENT	DATE ASSIGNED	DATE COMPLETED
Determine your organization's Ideal Vision,[48] including indicators of its impact on the survival and quality of life of its external clients and society (Mega level).		
Assure that the indicators are in measurable performance terms (interval or ratio scale).		
Determine your organization's current status with regard to its impact on clients' and society's survival and quality of life.		
Place Mega-level gaps (i.e., needs) between your Ideal Vision and the current status in a priority order, based on the cost to ignore vs. the cost to successfully address the need.		
Write a responsive Ideal Vision-linked mission objective that includes a specific subobjective for each gap you decide to address (e.g., what you will have accomplished 5 or more years from now).		
Break down your mission objective into building-block objectives, that is, into functions.		
Present your Mega-level needs to your clients and obtain concurrence.		
List (but don't select) alternative methods and means for addressing your Mega-level need(s) and identify the advantages and disadvantages of each.		

MACRO-LEVEL NEEDS ASSESSMENT	DATE ASSIGNED	DATE COMPLETED
Specify the desired quality of what your organization delivers to external clients. (Remember, starting here assumes that you have linked to the Mega/Ideal Vision level.)		
Determine the quality of what your organization now delivers to external clients.		
List the identified, agreed-on Macro-level need(s).		
Align the needs identified at the Macro level with the vision and mission of your organization.		
Place Macro-level needs in a priority order, based on the cost to ignore versus the cost to address each identified need.		
Present your Macro-level needs to your clients and obtain concurrence.		
List alternative methods and means for addressing your Macro-level need(s) and identify the advantages and disadvantages of each.		

MICRO-LEVEL NEEDS ASSESSMENT	DATE ASSIGNED	DATE COMPLETED
Determine individuals' and/or groups' required performance in terms of measurable accomplishments. (Remember that starting at this level assumes linkages to the Macro and Mega levels.)		
Determine individuals' and/or groups' current performance status vis-à-vis the required standards established in Step 1.		
List the identified, agreed-on Micro-level need(s).		
Align the needs identified at the Micro level with the vision and mission of your organization.		
Place Micro-level needs in a priority order, based on the cost to ignore versus the cost to address each identified need.		
Present your Micro-level needs to your clients and obtain concurrence.		
List alternative methods and means for addressing your Micro-level need(s) and identify the advantages and disadvantages of each.		

"QUASI-NEEDS" ASSESSMENT	DATE ASSIGNED	DATE COMPLETED
Specify the desired availability and/or quality of the organizational resources and methods. (Remember that starting here assumes the established links with the Micro, Macro, and Mega levels of results.)		
Determine the current quality and/or availability of the organizational efforts: activities, methods, procedures and/or approaches.		
Determine quasi-needs—the gaps between the desired and the current organizational efforts.		
Align the quasi-needs identified with the needs at the Mega, Macro, and Micro levels.		
Place quasi-needs in order of importance, based on the cost to ignore versus the cost to address each identified quasi-need(s).		
(or Step 1 if you have already identified needs at the Mega, Macro, and Micro levels.) Identify alternative methods and means for addressing the identified quasi-need(s) and/or need(s).		
(or Step 2 if you have already identified needs at the Mega, Macro, and Micro levels.) Identify advantages and disadvantages of each possible method and means available to get the job done.		
(or Step 3 if you have already identified needs at the Mega, Macro, and Micro levels.) Identify constraints and eliminate them if possible.		
Present alternative methods and means for addressing all agreed-on needs and quasi-needs to your clients for agreement on the methods and means to be selected for action and obtain agreement.		

Some Guidelines for Developing Needs Assessment Questionnaires

Although a questionnaire is only one way of harvesting (soft) needs data, if you decide to collect perceptions to help identify needs, here are some guidelines for developing one.

Things to Consider in Developing a Needs Assessment Questionnaire[49]

_____ 1. Make certain that the questions are about results, not about processes or inputs.

_____ 2. Ask about perceptions of gaps in results for both dimensions—what is and what should be.

_____ 3. Ask about the three levels of needs:

- External

- Organizational contributions

- Building-block results (Products)

_____ 4. Assure validity (assesses what it is supposed to assess) and reliability (consistency of measuring).

_____ 5. Make the questionnaire balanced: long enough to get reliable responses but short enough so people will actually respond.

_____ 6. Use an approach that makes it clear to respondents exactly what is wanted. People usually don't like to write long answers, so a checklist will reduce their burden while making the questionnaire easier to score.

_____ 7. Don't ask questions that reveal, directly or indirectly, a bias. Don't use the data-collection vehicle to set up the responses you really want.

_____ 8. Ask several questions about each dimension or issue. Ask about each concern in different ways, to assure reliability in the responses. Basing any decision on answers to one question is risky.

_____ 9. Try out the data-collection instrument on a sample group to identify problems in meaning, coverage, and scoreability. Revise it as required. (This step is the same as Step 6 in the problem-solving model: formative evaluation.)

When collecting performance (or "hard" data),

_____10. Make certain the data collected relate to important questions for which you want answers.

_____11. Assure yourself that the data are collected correctly and that the methods used for both gathering and reporting it are free of bias.

_____12. Assure yourself that the data are based on enough observations to make them reliable, not a one-shot happening.

_____13. Make certain that the data can be independently verified and cross-checked.

One questionnaire format that can be very helpful provides results-oriented questions, for all three levels of results included, and for each requests a response for both What Is and What Should Be. A sample is shown in Table 3.6.

▨ Why Bother?

Our culture is action oriented. We like to get moving, get results, get the action going. But such an orientation is not necessarily productive. Act in haste and repent in leisure, the old adage tells us. And so it is with doing needs assessments. If you are in too much of a hurry to get going, it will be tempting to fall into some convenient (and conventional) traps.

Here is a list of potential hazardous shortcuts, and some reasons why you might want to avoid them:

1. *Starting with a "training needs assessment."* Many organizations start with the assumption that performance problems, at every level of organizational concern, can be resolved by training. As noted earlier, this is dangerous. By starting at the Micro/Product level—the focus of "training"—you will be wrong 80% to 90% of the time![50]

According to Juran and Deming (depending on which one you read), 80% or 90% of all performance problems are not individual performance problems but are system breakdowns. Thus, if you start at the individual performance level—Micro/Products or Processes—as training does, you may well treat symptoms of a system problem. Although it is tempting to view training as the solution-of-the-month, it might not solve basic performance problems.

Rather than spending time and money working at this lower level, regardless of how conventional and comfortable it is you might find a solution to the wrong problem. Again, if you fail to link all of the Organizational Elements, you are stacking the deck against yourself. Although it is tempting to apply training right away, if you already know that training is the solution, why go to the trouble of doing a needs assessment?

The term "training needs assessment" is, perhaps, better termed "training requirements analysis" and is applied *after* a needs assessment has identified gaps in results, problems selected, and training selected in detailed planning. People who are very well trained may not be competent in areas important to organizational success.

2. *Starting with a problem analysis and just identifying current performance discrepancies.* Although you will identify performance deficits (usually at the Processes and/or Products level), their resolution might not have any impact at the upper organizational levels, at the Macro and Mega levels. Be careful not to just treat the symptoms instead of the causes.

3. *Sending out questionnaires and asking people what they "need."* Getting the involvement of others is important, but simply asking them such questions will end up in a "dump" of favored and comfortable methods and solutions. Using "need" as a verb encourages people to provide solutions to problems that they probably have not calibrated in terms of results and payoffs. Solutions are best considered after you have identified the needs—gaps in results to be closed—and

TABLE 3.6 A Questionnaire Format for Harvesting "What Is" and "What Should Be" Needs Data

WHAT IS						WHAT SHOULD BE				
SA	A	N	D	SD	*Question (results related*[a]*)*	SA	A	N	D	SD
					1. This organization is client centered.					
					2. Our performance objectives are written in measurable performance terms.					
					3. We plan for the Mega level.					
					4. Results, not politics, are rewarded here.					
					5. Evaluation is conducted at the three levels results: Mega, Macro, and Micro.					
					6. Minority employment policies are attracting and keeping competent people.					
					7. The accident rate here is as low as possible.					
					8. Personnel policies encourage individual productivity.					
					9. Resources are timely and of the proper quality.					
					10. All deliveries are on time.					
					11. All deliveries meet customer requirements.					
					12. There are zero customer complaints.					
					13. Associates are 100% competent in all skills, knowledge, attitudes, and abilities.					
					14. There are no deaths or disabilities from what we deliver.					
					15. Our workplace is completely safe.					
					16. There are no negative environmental impacts from our work and activities.					
					17. There are no negative impacts from our Outputs.					
					18. All trained associates make a contribution to their work assignment, the organization's Outputs, external client success, and societal well-being.					
					19. Etc . . .					

a. Mixed Outcomes, Outputs, and Products.
Scoring key: SA = strongly agree; A = agree; N = neutral; D = disagree; SD = strongly disagree.

selected the high-priority problems to resolve. Such a conventional "ask them what they need" approach, even though quick and yet sounding concerned, can raise unreasonable expectations because of the assumption that if you are asking them about their "needs," then their dreams will obviously be answered. This quick fix to assessing needs only serves to confuse means (solutions, methods, procedures, and resources) with ends (results, consequences, and payoffs).

4. *Using soft data only.* Opinions are perceived reality. They can and should be tempered by performance, accomplishments, and consequences.

5. *Using hard data only.* We often collect performance data on the easy-to-measure variables. Sometimes, people's observations, feelings, and perceptions can provide additional clues to performance problems and opportunities. Combine both hard and soft data sources in your needs assessment. Make certain that there is agreement among the hard and soft data.

6. *Restricting your needs assessment to the Micro/Product level.* When you do this, you assume that the individual splinters of positive performance will integrate and add up to organizational efficiency and client/societal payoffs.

7. *Confusing needs and wants, ends and means.* Use the term "need" as a verb. Ends are not means. Means are most sensibly selected on the basis of ends to be accomplished. It is common to use the vernacular of common discourse and confuse "need" with want.

8. *Seeing yourself as a powerless "victim" who cannot make changes or provide suggestions to upper management and/or external clients or partners.* If you see yourself as powerless, you will achieve that self-fulfilling prophecy. Contemporary leadership principles[51] tell us that without each member of the organization working to define and achieve positive results, the organization will falter. Empower yourself and others to contribute. Be proactive, not just reactive. Give yourself permission to forget the past[52] that is no longer functional, define the future, and work together toward the perfection of adding value to external clients and society.

It is interesting to notice how often people disempower themselves: "My boss doesn't want to hear anything about this—she wants training, and training I will deliver," "My organization doesn't want anyone to question anything," "They will fire me if I bring up Mega or even this approach to needs assessment." Before they even probe the possibilities or think about how it might be approached, they let the fear and conventional wisdom take over and disempower themselves. They become self-exiling victims. Most organizational supervisors, managers, and executives are more open than their associates are willing to recognize. Give all people a chance to do the right thing.

9. *Continuing to work with others who confuse "public relations" with needs assessment.* Some organizations, especially those who want to prove a point (or justify a mission), naively turn to "needs assessment" to show that what they do is important. Be clear that a needs assessment is an impartial process for defining and prioritizing gaps in results, not gaps in services, demands, or desires.

Conducting a results-oriented needs assessment doesn't have to be expensive or time consuming. Outcome data are readily available, as are many sources for Output and Product data. You can collect needs-sensing information by using or modifying a number of instruments on the market or in the literature, or you can construct your own needs assessment data collection vehicle.

Deriving and using needs assessment and planning partner groups may, at first, seem a bit bothersome, but modern management thinking increasingly promotes such quality-type activities, and such partnership groups represent the growing trend toward involving significant others—your associates and partners—in organizational decisions and activities. Useful empowerment flows from working together, finding a common set of purposes, and trusting each other to make appropriate contributions.

EXERCISES

1. Needs and Needs Assessment

Each **What Is** and **What Should Be** column—on either side of the questions—have the following dimensions in terms of the relative frequency that something does or does not happen:

> Consistently (96%-100%)
> Quite frequently (85%-95%)
> Sometimes (51%-84%)
> Not usually (18%-50%)
> Almost never (6%-17%)
> Rarely, if ever (0%-5%)

Review your needs assessment processes and methods—how needs assessments are conceived and done at your organization—in terms of the following questions. Answer, for each question, both **What Is** (your current practice) and **What Should Be** (your desired practice; what will best serve your organization).

My organization

WHAT IS						Please indicate the frequency (in terms of percentage of times) with which the following statements are happening within your organization. Please provide <u>two responses</u> to each question:	WHAT SHOULD BE					
Rarely, if ever (0-4%)	Almost Never (5%-15%)	Not Usually (16-49%)	Sometimes (50-83%)	Quite Frequently (84-94%)	Consistently (95-100%)		Rarely, if ever (0-4%)	Almost Never (5%-15%)	Not Usually (16-49%)	Sometimes (50-83%)	Quite Frequently (84-94%)	Consistently (95-100%)
						WHAT IS / **WHAT SHOULD BE** — describes how you see your organization currently operating. / describes how you think your organization should be operating.						
①	②	③	④	⑤	⑥	1. Needs are defined as gaps in desired resources (Inputs)	①	②	③	④	⑤	⑥
①	②	③	④	⑤	⑥	2. Needs are defined as gaps in desired solutions or activities (Processes)	①	②	③	④	⑤	⑥
①	②	③	④	⑤	⑥	3. Needs are defined as gaps in desired or required individual and/or small group performance (Products)	①	②	③	④	⑤	⑥
①	②	③	④	⑤	⑥	4. Needs are defined as gaps in desired or required customer or client deliverables (Outputs)	①	②	③	④	⑤	⑥
①	②	③	④	⑤	⑥	5. Needs are defined as gaps in desired or required external client and societal value added (Outcomes)	①	②	③	④	⑤	⑥

Suggested patterns:

Items 1 and 2 are best rated low on both What Is and What Should Be.
Items 3 and 4 are best rated low on both What Is and What Should Be, but
    better high on these than high on items 1 and 2)
Item 5 is best rated high on both What Is as well What Should Be.

2. Fuzzy World-Wide Industries: A Hypothetical Case Study

Here is a hypothetical example of the results of a "needs assessment"[53]
done by Fuzzy World-Wide Industries:

Fuzzy World-Wide Industries
"Needs Assessment" Summary

1. We have to have supervisors managing with vision.
2. We have to be world-class.
3. We have to be competitive.
4. We need to have more executive training.
5. We need to cut down on training time.
6. We need to make quality "Job 1."
7. We must all work together.
8. We must increase our production by 18%.
9. There must be no injuries or deaths from what we deliver.
10. We must make a profit each year.
11. We must not pollute the environment bringing harm to living things.
12. We need to use performance technology.

Examine the "needs assessment" and identify which elements of it:
   a. Identify a **need** as a gap in results
   b. Identify a **quasi-need**: a "need" as a gap in methods or a gap
       in resources
For each need identified, classify it as:
   Mega/Outcomes-related
   Macro/Outputs-related
   Micro/Products-related (Note the needs listed for each results
       level. Anything missing?)
For each quasi-need, ask "If I did or delivered this, what result would I get?"
Keep asking that question until you have identified needs at the three levels of
results. List them.

Using the Needs Assessment Self-Assessment (previous), review an existing "needs assessment" and identify if it is likely to be useful and appropriate. If
the reviewed "needs assessment" does not meet the basic criteria, what
changes to it should be made?

Let's compare asnswers.

1. *We have to have supervisors managing with vision.*

    This is a means (Process). It states nothing about what results and payoffs there will be from "managing with vision" nor does it state what the vision will be.

2. *We have to be world-class.*

    This aspiration never defines what "world class" is or how we would measure it. It also does not state what the results and payoffs will be from being "world class." This does not relate to a need but is an intention, and a Fuzzy one at that.

3. *We have to be competitive.*

    This aspiration never defines what "competitive" is or how we would measure it. It also does not state what the results and payoffs will be from being "competitive." This does not relate to a need but is an intention, and—like #2—another Fuzzy one.

4. *We need to have more executive training.*

    This is a means. Your first clue that it is the use of "need" as a verb and that dumps one into means without defining the ends to be accomplished. In this case, what gap in results would be closed by "more executive training"? What gap in results would this deliver at the Micro, Macro, and Mega levels?

5. *We need to cut down on training time.*

    This is also a means. Your first clue again is the use of "need" as a verb and that dumps one into means without defining the ends to be accomplished. In this case, what gap in results would be closed by "cutting down on training time"? What gap in results would this deliver at the Micro, Macro, and Mega levels?

6. *We need to make quality "Job 1."*

    Again, this is a means. Your clue again is the use of "need" as a verb and that dumps one into means without defining the ends to be accomplished. In this case, what gap in results would be closed by "making quality Job 1"? What is "quality," and how do we measure it? What gap in results would this deliver at the Micro, Macro, and Mega levels?

7. *We must all work together.*

    This is also a means. In this case, what gap in results would be closed by "working together"? What gap in results would "working together" deliver at the Micro, Macro, and Mega levels?

8. *We must increase our production by 18%.*

    At last a result—at the Micro-level. If stated as a need—a gap between current results and desired ones—it might read "Current production is at X and we will increase it to at least Y, an increase in production of at least 18%."

9. *There must be no injuries or deaths from what we deliver.*
    This will deliver results at the Mega level. If stated as a need, it might read "Last year there were three disabling injuries and one death from our Outputs. Next year and all following, there will be no disabling injuries and no deaths from our Outputs."

10. *We must make a profit each and every year.*
    This will deliver results at the Mega level, to the extent to which profit is earned without bringing harm to anyone or the environment. Profit over time is an indicator of a Mega-level contribution. If stated as a need, it might read "Last year we had a loss of $2.23 million. Next year and all following, we will show a profit each and every year."

11. *We must not pollute the environment, bringing harm to living things.*
    This will deliver results at the Mega level, to the extent to which what Fuzzy does and delivers does not bring harm to the environment and living things; they are "good neighbors." If stated as a need, it might read "Last year we had two spills cited by the environmental council for being toxic and destructive. Next year and all following, we will have no incidents causing toxic damage or other kinds of destruction each and every year."

12. *We need to use performance technology.*
    "Performance technology" is a means, even though it can be a very powerful means. Ask "If we were successful at using performance technology, what would the results of that be?"

Notice that *none* of **Fuzzy World-Wide Industries** "needs" were stated as gaps in results. This is a common mistake, and one you can avoid. Also, notice how many times "need" was used as a verb (e.g., "We need to use perform-ance technology") and thus moving anything the organization uses, does, and delivers toward a focus on solutions rather than results and value added.

3. Comparing Needs Assessments With the Mega Planning Frame of Reference

1. Compare your needs assessment—one with which you have been involved—and determine if it includes Mega-, Macro-, and/or Micro-level concerns. (It might be that it is none of the above.)
    Note: A way to determine if it is Mega (societal) focused is to deter-mine if the elements of an Ideal Vision (see Chapter 5) are included.

2. What are the implications for your internal (organizational) and ex-ternal clients' success with the plan with which you have worked?

3. If the needs assessment does not include a Mega-level focus or links, what will it take to modify it?

4. What are the penalties and payoffs for you and your internal and external clients for using a Mega-level-linked needs assessment?

5. Why do you think most needs assessment models and frameworks do not include or link to the Mega level?

4. Adding Value: Relating the Results of Strategic Planning, Needs Assessment, Reengineering, Benchmarking, and Quality Management/Continuous Improvement

There is little reason to plan if the plan is not applied and useful results are obtained. It is important to link everything an organization uses, does, produces, and delivers with the external payoffs for clients and society. Here is a simple form to use to better assure the linkages and to add value to your organization, your clients, and society.

1. Use any intervention you are considering or have used. Place its focus in the following *results chain* form:

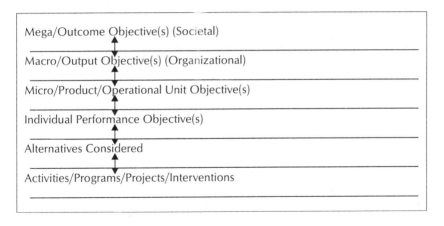

Mega/Outcome Objective(s) (Societal)
_____
Macro/Output Objective(s) (Organizational)
_____
Micro/Product/Operational Unit Objective(s)
_____
Individual Performance Objective(s)
_____
Alternatives Considered
_____
Activities/Programs/Projects/Interventions
_____

2. Checking to assure that an intervention will have positive payoffs at the Micro-, Macro-, and Mega-planning levels:
   a. Trace the intervention's results up the form for each category.
   b. Make sure you don't rationalize any objective. It either contributes and links or it does not.
   c. Change if required. It doesn't make much sense to pursue an intervention if it is not going to make the required contributions.

3. If you have not yet implemented an intervention (the preferred approach), start at the top item and derive downward, including considering alternative methods-means (interventions), to assure the linkages and payoffs.

For each step of the "results chain," identify the needs: gaps in results between current and desired results. Based on these needs for each of the results levels of the results chain, you may ensure that any intervention you select and implement will be responsive to meeting the needs.

5. Analyzing a Needs Assessment

Using a needs assessment you have created, used, or with which you have been asked to participate, do the following:

1. Examine the "needs assessment" and identify which elements of it:
   a. Identify a need as a gap in results
   b. Identify a quasi-need: a "need" as a gap in methods or a gap in resources

2. For each need identified, classify it as Mega/Outcomes-related, Macro/Outputs-related, and/or Micro/Products-related.

Needs Assessment Summary Format

				Need Level Focus		
Current Results	Possible Means	Required Results	Related Ideal Vision Element	Mega	Macro	Micro

Note the needs listed for each results level. Anything missing?

3. For each quasi-need, ask "If I did or delivered this, what result would I get?" Keep asking that question until you have identified needs at the three levels of results. List them.

4. Using the Needs Assessment Audit Checklist (provided earlier in this chapter), review an existing "needs assessment" and identify if it is likely to be useful and appropriate. If the reviewed "needs assessment" does not meet the basic criteria, what changes to it should be made?

Note: Most existing "needs assessments" are really oriented to identifying means and resources desired—more of a "wish list"—and assume that obtaining the means and resources will deliver useful results. The above self-assessment is designed to help you identify what is useful and what might be missing from any "needs assessment."

▓ Notes

1. There are differing views of what is a "need" (cf. Kaufman, 1992d, 1998b; Sleezer & Gradous, 1998); Witkin, 1984). It is strongly urged that problems of definition, statements of purpose, justifications for selection of methods and means, and evaluation are significantly clarified and simplified by defining "need" as a gap in results.

2. Triner, Greenberry, and Watkins (1996).

3. Ask yourself "If training is successful as a means, what would the worthwhile results be?" Training, as are most English words that end in "ing," are means. Isn't it interesting how often people want to jump right into a means, or solution, before defining and justifying the associated needs as gaps in results?

4. Deming (1982, 1986) and Juran (1988).

5. Kaufman (1991a).

6. Muir, Watkins, Kaufman, and Leigh (1998).

7. Recall that Outcomes are results at the Mega level of planning, Outputs are results at the Macro level of planning, and Products are results at the Micro level of planning.

8. However, it is more likely that they start only with a symptom of a problem.

9. Based on my research and observations, "subject matter experts," while perhaps well-meaning, often supply recommendations that (1) may not be current in terms of operational requirements, (2) might reflect only what they feel the client wants to hear, and/or (3) leave the recommendations based on "what is" and not on "what should be," or "what could be"—reactive and not proactive. It is for this reason that I have taken to calling them "subjective matter experts" due to the frequent lack of validity and usefulness. It is tempting, however, to use such sources, for it is convenient and has "face validity"—that is it *seems* to be valid.

10. Although this refers to identifying and resolving *problems,* they should be thought of as "problems and opportunities." Needs assessment can be used to identify both gaps between current and required results as well as the gaps between current and desired (but currently not included) results.

11. Kaufman (1998b), Kaufman, Thiagarajan, and MacGillis (1997), and Watkins, Leigh, Platt, and Kaufman (1998).

12. I would much prefer good luck, but I can't always count on it.

13. Sometimes referred to as the holistic level of needs assessment and planning because Macro and Micro are included, or nested, within the Mega level.

14. A manufacturing example: combining the contributions of quality-assured resources and materials (Inputs) used by trained and competent welders (Processes) who turn out products that are used by competent manufacturing workers, managers, executives, with continuous improvement to certify that every product meets or exceeds quality standards (Products). The deliverables of this organization (Outputs) will have sufficient quality and value to increase the number of new clients, retain the existing ones, and measurable help clients become successful as well as economically and personally self-sufficient: They will not only be satisfied, but the Outputs will be safe, effective, and efficient. In addition, they must not pollute or bring harm to any living thing, as indicated by zero returns for defects and no successful lawsuits or government actions for harming anyone or anything (Outcomes).

15. The manufacturing example continued: a welder's competence combined with the fabricated Products of other workers, the contributions of a continuous improvement/quality management initiative that will increase the price and attractiveness of the company's Outputs to existing an potential buyers.

16. This level of needs assessment, for example, might be directed toward improving the competence of welders or addiction counseling specialists. Improving employee proficiency may require you to find resources (Inputs and/or Processes) such as money, trainees, and/or unique training methods that will deliver the measurable performance objectives.

17. Some people don't care for job aids, or algorithms. To them, I apologize. These are provided to simply help readers see what functions might be performed and in what order.

18. Just using a "random sample" is the second worst sampling method possible—second only to no sampling. With a random sample, gross distortions can define your data simply from a table of random

numbers. By stratifying and then random sampling within each stratum, you better assure the representativeness of your data.

19. This type of data is often termed "soft" because of its attitudinal/perceptual origins and because it is not independently verifiable.

20. Based on Kaufman (1992d, 1998b) and Kaufman, Thiagarajan, and MacGillis (1997).

21. Peter Drucker (1972) speaks to the vital ability to "transfer ownership" from any planners to those who will effect any plans and resulting programs and interventions.

22. Usually, the reason for not wanting to deal with Mega is fear. Most people don't know how to think or measure at that level (remember that most of what they learned in school, get from the media, and hear from politicians is about Inputs, Processes, and occasionally Products). If they are questioning whether or not one can measure at the Mega level, think of an example they would identify with, such as aircraft safety being the result of all of the Inputs, Processes, Products, and Outputs. If Mega is not the focus, how can they be sure that any of the lower-order resources, activities, and results will be useful?

23. Drucker (1993, 1994, 1995), Kaufman (1992d, 1998b), and Popcorn (1991) agree on this.

24. Based on Kaufman (1992d, 1998b) and Kaufman, Herman, and Watters (1996).

25. I originally suggested this kind of taxonomy in the book I wrote with Fenwick English (Kaufman & English, 1979).

26. Most so-called needs assessments are Gamma at best, and many are really quasi-needs assessments. As Mega Planning continues to gain more acceptance, there should be a shift toward Alpha needs assessments.

27. Watkins and Kaufman (1996).

28. Selecting the methods-means to meet needs are based on a costs-consequences analysis (cf. Kaufman, 1998b).

29. Lewis and Bjorkquist (1992), for example. I find this kind of reasoning incomplete as noted in Kaufman and Gavora (1993).

30. At the Outputs and Products levels.

31. At the Outcomes level.

32. Profits that continue over time provide an indicator that what is being delivered to external clients and society are useful. Unlike only considering quarterly profits, or other short-term indicators, continued profits over time tend to show that there is both perceived and actual utility of organizational Outputs.

33. One *indicator* for individual self-sufficiency expressed as ($C \leq P$: Consumption is less than or equal to Production) is money (or any other medium of exchange). People generally put money where their values lie—they spend on what they value. Thus, one proxy—the integration of a number of variables—for self-sufficiency and self-reliance is the consumption/production relationship: Consumption is anything that causes an outflow of money, and Production is anything that brings an inflow of money.

34. Again, the difference between performance (accomplishment) and behavior (some actions that may results in some end but not necessarily required ends) is vital.

35. Criteria for these are provided in Chapter 4 on Ideal Vision.

36. Based on Kaufman (1992d).

37. It is tempting to move forward without agreement, but often discrepancies indicate that proper data have not been uncovered. Perceptions—soft data—are realities for most people and without the agreement with hard data they will feel that their concerns are not addressed. Often, hard data may only be collected on "easy to measure" variables leaving more important indicators unmeasured. Collect the required data, not just the easily available type.

38. There are many books and other guides on instrumentation and data collection vehicles. Kaufman (1992) has some of these provided as well as many references. Another good source of data collection procedures and instruments is provided by Rossett (1987).

39. Sobel and Kaufman (1989).

40. Based on Kaufman (1992d).

41. Based on Kaufman (1992d, 1998b).

42. In the Needs Assessment form suggested here, note that the second column is for listing possible means. This is done to allow planning partners to note when means and resources might be prematurely considered.

43. Formative evaluation is a "standard" element of Scriven's "holy trinity" of evaluation: formative, summative, and goal free (Scriven, 1967, 1973).

44. Much more on this in Chapter 7.

45. Kaufman and Watkins (1996) and Muir, Watkins, Kaufman, amd Leigh (1998).

46. Based, in part, on Kaufman, Rojas, and Mayer (1993).

47. My thanks to Ryan Watkins, Nova Southeastern University, and Doug Leigh of Florida State University and the Office for Needs Assessment & Planning for helping with the development of many of these. Also, see Kaufman, Rojas, and Mayer (1993) for more details on doing a needs assessment.

48. To be extensively defined and explained in Chapter 4.

49. Based on my "Needs Assessment Basics" in Kaufman, Thiagarajan, and MacGillis (1997).

50. Kaufman (1998b), Triner, Greenberry, and Watkins (1996), and/or Watkins, Leigh, and Kaufman (1998).

51. Argyris (1991), Barker (1989, 1993), Block (1993), Conner (1992, 1998), Drucker (1973, 1985, 1988, 1992, 1993a, 1993b, 1994), Forbes (1998), Garratt (1987, 1994), Handy (1995-1996), Hanford (1995), Hammer and Stanton (1995), Kaufman (1998b), Kaufman and Swart (1995), Kaufman et al. (1997), Kaufman, Watkins, et al. (1998), Peters (1987, 1997), Roberts (1987, 1993, 1997), Rummler and Brache (1990) and Senge (1990).

52. As also suggested by Peters (1997).

53. Although I have gleaned these from actual so-called needs assessment.

4

An Ideal Vision

The Underlying Basis for All Planning and Doing

Visions and visioning have grown from being seen as "flaky" and "soft" to being increasingly accepted and expected as a central element in defining organizational directions and purpose.[1] This chapter provides the basis for identifying and accepting an Ideal Vision that defines the kind of world we want to help create for tomorrow's child—as the basis for all public and private planning, as the driver for everything any organization uses, does, produces, and delivers.

An Ideal Vision is the "Mega" of Mega Planning and strategic thinking. It is the cornerstone of future-oriented successful planning and using it constitutes the sixth critical success factor:

> *Critical Success Factor 6:* **Use an Ideal Vision as the underlying basis for all planning and doing (don't be limited to your own organization).**

As was noted in the earlier chapters, there are three levels of planning—Mega, Macro, and Micro—and three levels of results—Outcomes, Outputs, and Products. The Mega level is an Ideal Vision.

Visions and Visioning

A lot has been written about visions and visioning.[2] Much of it is old-paradigm thinking because it starts and stops with the organization itself. A useful Ideal Vision is not for an organization or any part of it but for external clients and society: Mega level.[3]

The literature is not always helpful in terms of application to Mega Planning, for it usually suggests that the CEO defines a "vision for the organization" and "shares" it with associates. This approach has several potential flaws:

1. It focus on one's organization as the primary client and beneficiary of what is planned, done, and delivered.
2. It is authoritarian and paternalistic. It fails to involve internal or external partners in defining the future contributions of the organization.
3. It ignores or assumes the organization's role and responsibilities relative to external clients, including society.

When the CEO prepares a conventional vision statement, it usually ends up

- being general and without specifics about results to be delivered;
- including the means and methods to be used and thus skipping right into solutions before defining and justifying required results and value added; and
- focusing only on the organization and so is self-absorbed and self-serving. It assumes or ignores adding value to society and external clients.

There is, however, a shift from a Macro (organizationally focused) to a Mega focus.[4] The trend is experiencing a relatively slow shift, and whether or not stated intentions for a societal focus is followed up with a real Mega orientation and action is one that must be tracked closely. I suggest that this shift from an internal focus to an external one is both vital and is occurring.

Enough about what is not useful. Let's look at applying CSF 6.

What Is an Ideal Vision?

An Ideal Vision states, in measurable terms, the kind of world we want to create together for tomorrow's child. An Ideal Vision has no Inputs, Processes, Products, or Outputs. It only contains Outcomes.[5]

There are two varieties of Ideal Visions: "Positive" and "Basic Measurable." We have a choice: either make the statement of an Ideal Vision comfortable or make it basic, measurable, and useful.

Some planners, especially those new to Mega Planning and thinking, want to frame an Ideal Vision in positive terms. Keeping within that comfort zone, here is a "positive" Ideal Vision:

A Positive Ideal Vision: All people will live in a healthy, positive, safe, and satisfying environment where all things both survive and thrive. People may create any type of world they desire as long as they don't violate the Basic Ideal Vision.

There is a practical problem, however, with this positive vision statement: There is little that can be used to measure progress or success. How might you quantify "healthy," "positive," "safe," or "satisfying"? It is important for Mega Planning to be able to both define the future to be delivered and "keep score" on our progress toward that future. Measurability is important (see Chapter 2), and the positive Ideal Vision identifies intent[6] but not the required rigor and precision for planning, design, development, implementation, and evaluation/continuous improvement.

The positive Ideal Vision is useful to help people understand about defining the preferred future but doesn't provide the rigorous and precise metrics required for detailed planning. The Ideal Vision, based on the positive one, can be defined in measurable performance terms. To get a really practical and useful Ideal Vision, using an existing basic Ideal Vision, based on research, is suggested.

Getting from positive to useful. In my work, I have collected, from virtually around our world, the measurable definition of a Basic Ideal Vision.[7] This has been done by asking a valid and representative sample of people "What kind of world, in measurable terms, do you want to help create for tomorrow's child?" From these responses, Inputs, Processes, Products, and Outputs are deleted (sometimes by asking the participants "If we were to accomplish this, what would the result be?" until Mega-level results are identified).

Determining your own Ideal Vision. A format that can be used, if you opt to create your own Ideal Vision, is to ask representative people to describe the world they want to help create for tomorrow's child and then add measurable performance indicators for each (see Figure 4.1).

IDEAL

Describe the world in which you want tomorrow's child to live:

_____

_____

_____

_____

_____

_____

ENDS/Results Criteria

(e.g., 0 deaths or disabilities from drugs; 0 murders; 0 disabilities from rapes; 0 species that become extinct from unintended human intervention; 0 deaths from pollution)

_____

_____

_____

_____

Figure 4.1. Useful questions when developing your own Ideal Vision.

It is usually faster, easier, and more accurate, however, to use the Basic Ideal Vision, shown below, to ask planning partners to "add, subtract, multiply, or divide the Basic Ideal Vision in terms of societal results." By using the existing "consensus Ideal Vision" as a starting place, time is saved by not going over Inputs, Processes, and Products that are conventional thinking for inexperienced Mega planners.[8]

It is fascinating, and satisfying, to notice how much agreement there is, even across diverse cultures, about the ideal world and Ideal Vision for all organizations and individuals to move toward. By asking people about their children and grandchildren, and not about themselves, there is a willingness to be idealistic as well as realistic. I call the defining of the kind of world we want to create for tomorrow's child "practical dreaming" because if we are not intending to define and move ever closer to a perfect world, what do we have in mind?[9]

▨ A Basic Ideal Vision

Remember, this Basic Ideal Vision is the *minimum,* or underlying definition of the kind of world we want to help create for tomorrow's child. It is, and should be, idealistic. It is the minimum, not the maximum. It also must provide the measurable criteria for setting objectives and measuring progress.

It is also important to realize that the Ideal Vision elements should be considered as a fabric—interwoven strands—rather than single discrete elements or threads. The individual parts may interact with others and thus should be seen as a related whole rather than just parts.

Further, note that the basic stem of the Ideal Vision is this:

There will be no losses of life nor elimination or reduction of levels of well-being, survival, self-sufficiency, and quality of life from any source . . .

What follows in this Basic Ideal Vision statement are really Macro-level results and consequences that lead to changes in value added at the Mega level. Psychology Professor Dale Brethower also suggests that not only must we think about value added but also "value subtracted" when we are considering the consequences of programs, projects, activities, or organization. This suggests a balance sheet with positive and negative effects.

A basic underlying indicator of self-sufficiency. Although it is not always satisfying to reduce consequences to money,[10] there is an indicator[11] for individual survival and self-sufficiency in terms of costs and consequences.[12] For any individual, a calibration for self-sufficiency is this:

Consumption is less than or equal to Production.

$$C \leq P.$$

BASIC IDEAL VISION:
The world we want to help create for tomorrow's child

There will be no losses of life nor elimination or reduction of levels of well-being, survival, self-sufficiency, and quality of life from any source, including (but not limited to)

➤ war and/or riot
➤ unintended human-caused changes to the environment including permanent destruction of the environment and/or rendering it nonrenewable
➤ murder, rape, or crimes of violence, robbery, or destruction to property
➤ substance abuse
➤ disease
➤ pollution
➤ starvation and/or malnutrition
➤ destructive behavior, including child, partner, spouse, self, elder, and others
➤ accidents, including transportation, home, and business/workplace
➤ discrimination based on irrelevant variable including color, race, age, creed, gender, religion, wealth, national origin, or location

Poverty will not exist, and every woman and man will earn as least as much as it costs them to live unless they are progressing toward being self-sufficient and self-reliant. No adult will be under the care, custody, or control of another person, agency, or substance. All adult citizens will be self-sufficient and self-reliant as minimally indicated by their consumption being equal to or less than their production.

Using this indicator, each person can be calibrated in terms of the extent to which each legally is at the survival level or beyond. It should be noted that this indicator is indifferent to how much one is above the equal point; the only important point is whether they are making enough to be self-sufficient.

Using this minimal indicator, it is the Mega-level objective that "no one will be under the care, custody, or control of another person, agency, or substance." An interesting aspect of this definition of self-sufficiency is that it provides a precise criteria for discrimination: If one can tell the difference among individuals on the basis of irrelevant variables—color, race, creed, sex/gender, national origin, and/or location—then there is discrimination. This definition has the advantage that discrimination can thus be based on consequences rather than on compliance with processes.

Arguments often provided for resisting using a Basic Ideal Vision.[13] Not everyone, at least at first, is comfortable with such an "idealistic" statement of a vision. After all, it is quite different from the Macro-level conventional wisdom of most visions. Here are some arguments against this provided definition of an Ideal Vision and some responses:

1. "This is not 'practical' nor 'real world.' It is 'utopian' and will never be achieved. After all, objectives must be realizable and attainable and these clearly are not."

First, let's deal with the Basic Ideal Vision not being practical or "real world." If persons are not intending to move ever closer toward this Basic Ideal Vision, what do they have in mind? Do they agree to some murders, some rapes, some deaths from infectious disease? If so, then they are responsible for identifying exactly those who may be murdered, raped, or die or become disabled from disease: They must define the triage. It is practical, very practical, to define and move toward a perfect world, measure our progress toward that destination, and use the performance data to continuously improve what we use, do, produce, and deliver in terms of external/societal results and consequences.

Ask most people what the murder rate, or death from infectious disease rate should be in their community, and most will answer "zero." That is "practical dreaming."

Why not ask our own organization to focus on Mega as we do with organizations that serve us? Interestingly, there is usually a difference on what we want an organization to deliver when we speak of our own or of ones that serve us. Frequently, we hear the kind of objections above when speaking of Mega and our own operations. However, when asked if we want organizations we deal with (e.g., airlines, car manufacturers, and food processors) to have a Mega focus, most give a resounding "yes!" All organizations should add value for external clients and society.

Second, let's deal with "utopian." The conventional definition of this is in terms of means, not ends.[14] This statement of a Basic Ideal Vision is about ends, results, and consequences. It should be the intent of every person and every organization to move, individually and together, toward it. It is not utopian. It is practical, and we can move continuously toward it.

Third, don't all objectives have to be achievable? And, if so, this Basic Ideal Vision doesn't seem to be achievable! This is a piece of conventional wisdom that is not only dangerous, it also seems to strain rationality. Just as a person's reach should exceed their grasp, objectives should define "stretch" in terms of intentions. If we only take on objectives that are achievable, we will be forever mired in yesterday. When we don't reach our objectives, we use the performance data to improve and not to place blame.

2. "There are no data for these. And without data, we can't plan or evaluate. And besides many of these Basic Ideal Vision elements are 'not measurable'."

This shows much old-paradigm thinking. As I noted before in Chapter 2, everything is measurable: If you can name it (nominal scale), you are measuring it. If you can't at least name it, what is it? Calling something "intangible" is a cop-out. We can (and should) measure everything.

And about data availability? There is plenty; all we have to do is find it. Most organizations and governments are almost awash in data for these elements.[15] Libraries, governmental agencies, public service organizations, charities, and local governments have valid and reliable data for most of the parts of the Basic Ideal Vision. Ask for them.

3. "It is not the concern of me or my organization to add value to society. The business of business is business. Let someone else worry about society while we worry about keeping people employed and adding to stockholder value."

This response flies in the face of many contemporary thinkers, not to mention the "new realities" for organizational success, about practical organizational planning and success.[16] If any organization, public or private, does not add value to external clients and society, they just don't have a future. After all, society is where we as well as all of our clients live. If we don't add value there, clients, including society, will find other vehicles.[17]

Identifying Your Organization's Current Contribution to Society

Without formally recognizing the fact, all organizations impact external clients and society. For each of the basic elements of an Ideal Vision, check if your organization currently makes a contribution to that element and thus to the total Ideal Vision.

It is interesting to note how much your organization does contribute, either directly or indirectly, to Mega results and consequences. Please recall that the elements of an Ideal Vision are related and should be seen as a group, or woven fabric, rather than as stand-alone elements.

Using the Basic Ideal Vision for Mega Planning. How do you get from the Basic Ideal Vision to practical planning, that is, to Mega Planning? Simply use it to define the elements of your Mission Objective.

Based on the selected Basic Ideal Vision elements (see Chapter 3), the planners next define what parts of it they commit to deliver and move ever closer toward. Thus, Mega provides the elements that the organization commits to deliver and move ever closer toward yielding the Mission Objective, the Macro level of planning. And the Mission Objective is used to identify the building-block Micro-level planning and results that together identify and define the results the organization is to produce. This relationship is shown in Figure 4.2.

Rolling-down/outside-in planning. Using this roll-down-from-Mega process, the elements of the Basic Ideal Vision that the organization commits to deliver and move ever closer toward form the Mission (Macro) Objective. Rolling down is a proactive process. It starts outside the organization, defines needs at the Mega level, and these data are used to derive the Micro-level Mission Objective.

Figure 4.3 shows how outside-in works and how it compares and links with inside-out planning:

By starting from outside the organization, the Mega focus is better assured. Then, the Macro level—the Mission Objective—is derived, followed by Micro/Product-level objectives. This results in strategic alignment among what the organization produces and delivers and the external consequences.

Basic Ideal Vision Elements — There will be no loss of life or elimination of the survival of any species required for human survival. There will be no reductions in levels of self-sufficiency, quality of life livelihood, or loss of property from any source including:	Makes a Contribution		
	Directly	Indirectly	None
War and/or riot			
Shelter			
Unintended human-caused changes to the environment, including permanent destruction of the environment and/or rendering it non-renewable			
Murder, rape, or crimes of violence, robbery, or destruction to property			
Substance abuse			
Disease			
Pollution			
Starvation and/or malnutrition			
Child abuse			
Partner/spouse abuse			
Accidents, including transportation, home, and business/workplace			
Discrimination based on irrelevant variables, including color, race, creed, sex, religion, national origin, age, and location			
Poverty will not exist, and every woman and man will earn as least as much as it costs them to live unless they are progressing toward being self-sufficient and self-reliant.			
No adult will be under the care, custody, or control of another person, agency, or substance: All adult citizens will be self-sufficient and self-reliant as minimally indicated by their consumption being equal to or less than their production.			
Consequences of the Basic Ideal Vision: Any and all organizations—public and private—will contribute to the achievement and maintenance of this Basic Ideal Vision and will be funded and continued to the extent to which they meet its objectives and the Basic Ideal Vision is accomplished and maintained. People will be responsible for what they use, do, and contribute and thus will not contribute to the reduction of any of the results identified in this Basic Ideal Vision.			

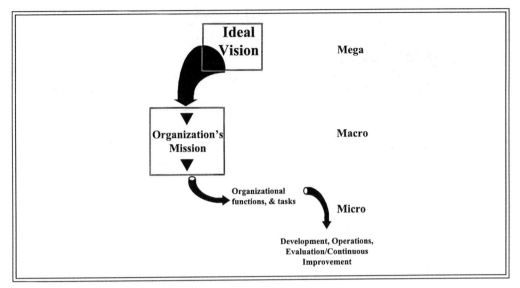

Figure 4.2. Missions derive from the Ideal Vision. An organization selects what portion of the Ideal Vision it commits to deliver and move ever closer toward it.

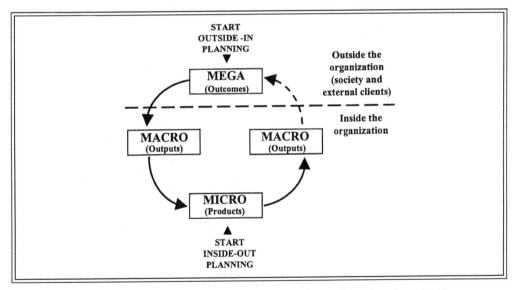

Figure 4.3. Planning can either start from the outside-in (preferred) or from inside-out. Outside-in as a starting place is essential for Mega planning.

If one starts, as is the conventional approach, with inside-out, one usually is assuming (perhaps without recognizing it) that Inputs, Processes, Products, and Outputs will yield useful Mega results. They usually don't.

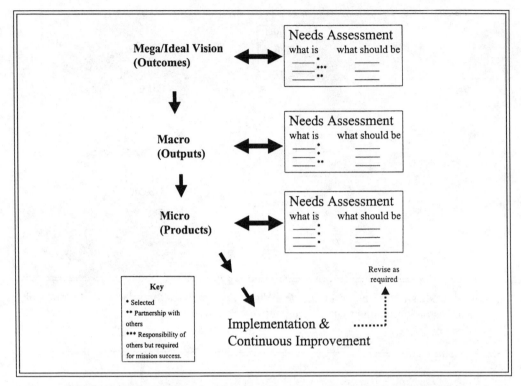

Figure 4.4. The roll-down flow of a Mega-level needs assessment. Note that each planning level does a needs assessment. Also shown is the "key" for selecting Ideal Vision components to form the Mission Objective (Macro). The elements that form the Ideal Vision, based on needs, are selected to form the Mission Objective and the functions.

By using the needs assessment process (Chapter 3), the gaps at the Mega level are defined and then used to identify those that will form the mission for the organization (see Figure 4.4).

Reviewing from Chapter 3 this process, planners identify the elements of the Ideal Vision they have derived (or ratified) and determine those they select on the basis of the costs to meet the need as compared to the costs to ignore it. Then, they identify each in terms of being

- selected as a prime responsibility for closure, noted by "one star" next to the need;
- selected as a responsibility for closure with another agency or agent in cooperation, noted by "two stars" next to the need; and
- selected as the responsibility of others but requiring the data for mission success, noted by "three stars" next to the need.

The intersection between the Ideal Vision and needs assessment is vital. Each level of planning—Mega, Macro, and Micro—requires having its own needs assessment done.

TABLE 4.1 Format for Checking the Ideal Vision Elements to Ensure They Are Mega Focused[18]

Ideal Vision Element	Mega/ Outcomes	Macro/ Outputs	Micro/ Products	Processes	Inputs
1.					
2.					
3.					
N.					

Checking to determine if your Ideal Vision statement is complete. Table 4.1. provides a format for checking the elements of your Ideal Vision to assure that it is societal value-added focused. Sort the elements into this table, by number, and find out if there are any statements included in your draft that are not Mega/Outcomes focused by asking for each "What result would we get if we were successful with this?" Keep asking that same question until you either reach Mega or discard it.

Also, be careful of "logic leaps" from a means or a resource directly to so-called Mega-level results are made. For example, "Because people have positive self-concept, peace will happen as a result." This kind of jumping from unwarranted assumptions to foregone conclusion will show up if you use the table objectively.

Deriving the Mission Objective from the Ideal Vision. The elements in the Ideal Vision are subjected to a needs assessment—what are the gaps between current results and desired ones? Then, each is subjected to the question "What does it cost to meet the need as compared to the cost to ignore it?" The relative costs-consequences estimates provide the priority for each. When operating at the Mega level, these estimates will likely be very broad. As you move down from Mega to Macro to Micro, the needs data become more precise and so also do the costs-consequences data.

This rolling down from outside the organization (Mega) to the inside is a vital aspect of getting strategic alignment. This process provides strategic alignment between external clients and society and what your organization uses, does, produces, and delivers.

The Organizational Elements and the basic questions you and your organization must ask and answer. Table 4.2 shows the relationship for each of the several Mega Planning questions and the associated Organizational Element. This should help keep means and ends and needs and wants in useful perspective.

Mega planning and new business. If you plot the parts of the total Ideal Vision your organization "covers" and then plot the coverage of other organizations (both public and private), you will be able to identify (1) overlaps and redundancies (and thus opportunities for cooperation or reducing wasted duplication) and (2) blank spaces[19] that no organization now is responsive to; these are market niches for possible new business.

TABLE 4.2 Basic Mega Planning Questions and Which of the Organizational Elements to Which Each Relates

| Basic Questions | The Organizational Elements | | | | | Revision |
	Mega	Macro	Micro	Process	Input	Evaluation and Continuous Improvement
1. Do you commit to deliver organizational contributions that add value for society and external clients?	X					
2. Do you commit to deliver organizational contributions that have the quality required by your external partners?		X				
3. Do you commit to produce internal results that have the quality required by your internal partners?			X			
4. Do you commit to have efficient internal programs, projects, and activities?				X		
5. Do you commit to create and ensure the quality and appropriateness of the human, capital, and physical resources available?					X	
6. Do you commit to deliver products, activities, methods, and procedures that have positive value and worth (add value)?						X
7. Do you commit to deliver the results and accomplishments defined by your objectives?						X
Some Additional Questions:						
8. Do you commit to improve on-the-job effectiveness and competence of individual associates?			X			
9. Do you commit to improve the accountability and availability of useful resources?					X	
10. Do you commit to improve the efficiency of work and associates?				X		

Visions and Visioning

1. Review your organization's purpose statements, values, and/or guiding principles. Check What Is and **What Should Be** for each statement.

Each **What Is** and **What Should Be** column—on either side of the questions—has the following dimensions in terms of the relative frequency that something does or does not happen:

Consistently (96%-100%)
Quite frequently (85%-95%)
Sometimes (51%-84%)
Not usually (18%-50%)
Almost never (6%-17%)
Rarely, if ever (0%-5%)

My organization's stated purpose and direction has a primary focus on:

WHAT IS						Please indicate the frequency (in terms of percentage of times) with which the following statements are happening within your organization. Please provide <u>two responses</u> to each question:	WHAT SHOULD BE					
Rarely, if ever (0-4%)	Almost Never (5%-15%)	Not Usually (16-49%)	Sometimes (50-83%)	Quite Frequently (84-94%)	Consistently (95-100%)		Rarely, if ever (0-4%)	Almost Never (5%-15%)	Not Usually (16-49%)	Sometimes (50-83%)	Quite Frequently (84-94%)	Consistently (95-100%)
						WHAT IS ⟵ **WHAT SHOULD BE** ⟶ describes how you see your organization currently operating. / describes how you think your organization should be operating.						
①	②	③	④	⑤	⑥	1. Operational efficiency	①	②	③	④	⑤	⑥
①	②	③	④	⑤	⑥	2. Operational effectiveness	①	②	③	④	⑤	⑥
①	②	③	④	⑤	⑥	3. Organizational efficiency	①	②	③	④	⑤	⑥
①	②	③	④	⑤	⑥	4. Organizational effectiveness	①	②	③	④	⑤	⑥
①	②	③	④	⑤	⑥	5. Quarterly profits	①	②	③	④	⑤	⑥
①	②	③	④	⑤	⑥	6. Shareholder value	①	②	③	④	⑤	⑥
①	②	③	④	⑤	⑥	7. Customer/client satisfaction	①	②	③	④	⑤	⑥
①	②	③	④	⑤	⑥	8. Societal value added	①	②	③	④	⑤	⑥
①	②	③	④	⑤	⑥	9. Societal value added first and then on client satisfaction and then on shareholder value and then profits and then internal effectiveness and efficiency	①	②	③	④	⑤	⑥

Suggested patterns:

Items 1 through 3 should be rated low on both What Is and What Should Be.

Items 4 through 8 should increasingly be rated at higher levels on both What Is and What Should Be (because they move ever more toward external value added).

Item 9 should have the highest ratings on both What Is and What Should Be (because it has a Mega focus and progression of results and consequences not explicit in the previous items).

The focus of the Ideal Vision used in our organization:

WHAT IS / WHAT SHOULD BE

Rating scale (each side): Rarely, if ever (0-4%); Almost Never (5%-15%); Not Usually (16-49%); Sometimes (50-83%); Quite Frequently (84-94%); Consistently (95-100%)

Please indicate the frequency (in terms of percentage of times) with which the following statements are happening within your organization. Please provide two responses to each question:

← WHAT IS | WHAT SHOULD BE →

WHAT IS describes how you see your organization currently operating.

WHAT SHOULD BE describes how you think your organization should be operating.

WHAT IS (① ② ③ ④ ⑤ ⑥)	Statement	WHAT SHOULD BE (① ② ③ ④ ⑤ ⑥)
① ② ③ ④ ⑤ ⑥	10. Focuses on a group, department, or operation.	① ② ③ ④ ⑤ ⑥
① ② ③ ④ ⑤ ⑥	11. Focuses on the organization itself.	① ② ③ ④ ⑤ ⑥
① ② ③ ④ ⑤ ⑥	12. Focuses on the kind of world we want to help create for tomorrow's child.	① ② ③ ④ ⑤ ⑥

Suggested patterns:

Item 10 should be rated low on both What Is and What Should Be (because it restricts itself to a part of an organization and doesn't link to the organization and external clients).

Item 11 should be rated low on both What Is and What Should Be (because it restricts itself to a part of an organization and doesn't link to the external clients). It should be rated higher than Item 10.

Item 12 should be rated high on both What Is and What Should Be (because it links what the organization uses, does, produces, and delivers to adding value to external clients and society).

2. Using the form *Finding Direction: Questions All Organizations Must Ask and Answer* below, check off your commitment by answering each of these questions.

FINDING DIRECTION

Questions All Organizations Must Ask and Answer	*Commitment*	
	Yes	*No*
Do you commit to deliver organizational contributions that adds value for your external clients AND society? (**MEGA**/Outcomes)		
Do you commit to deliver organizational contributions that have the quality required by your external partners? (**MACRO**/Outputs)		
Do you commit to produce internal results that have the quality required by your internal partners? (**MICRO**/Products)		
Do you commit to have efficient internal products, programs, projects, and activities? (**PROCESSES**)		
Do you commit to create and ensure the quality and appropriateness of the human, capital, and physical resources available? (**INPUTS**)		
Do you commit to deliver: a. products, activities, methods, and procedures that have positive value and worth?		
b. the results and accomplishments defined by our objectives? (**EVALUATION/CONTINUOUS IMPROVEMENT**)		

3. Using the same form *Finding Direction,* please respond to the following as a small group.

1. Which of the questions do you think your organization *and* any of your internal and external clients can afford to NOT address formally? (This means without identifying and dealing with each in measurable performance terms.)

Level of Planning and Type of Results	*Can Afford to Not Address Formally and Rigorously*	*Must Address Formally and Rigorously*
MEGA/OUTCOMES		
MACRO/OUTPUTS		
MICRO/PRODUCTS		
PROCESSES		
INPUTS		
CONTINUOUS IMPROVEMENT		

2. Which of the questions do you believe your organization *and* any of its internal and external clients currently do and do not formally and rigorously address in measurable performance terms?

Level of Planning and Type of Results	Do Not Address Formally and Rigorously	Do Address Formally and Rigorously
MEGA/OUTCOMES		
MACRO/OUTPUTS		
MICRO/PRODUCTS		
PROCESSES		
INPUTS		
CONTINUOUS IMPROVEMENT		

3. What are the risks for starting at the Mega level? What are the risks for NOT starting at the Mega level?
   In what ways are you adding value to your organization? To your external clients? To our society community? What could you be doing and contributing?

4. Mega Planning: Choose a societal-, community-, or external client-focused result that you and/or your organization would like to achieve. Beginning with that result (or objective), complete the OEM table below.

MEGA	*Start with a societal result you and your organization would like to achieve*
	①
MACRO	
	②
MICRO	
	③
PROCESS	
	④
INPUT	
	⑤

5. Developing a Mission Objective and function objectives derived from an Ideal Vision: From the elements of the Basic Ideal Vision in the previous exercise (during which you or your organizational group indicated as your organization's "primary responsibilities" and contributions to the attainment of the Ideal Vision) compose a Mission Objective for your organization that focuses only on those results.

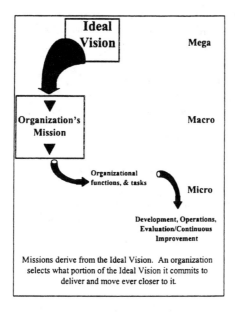

Missions derive from the Ideal Vision. An organization selects what portion of the Ideal Vision it commits to deliver and move ever closer to it.

(Put aside, for the time being, what your organization currently uses as its mission statement.)

_____

_____

_____

▨ Notes

1. There have been some interesting insights into visions and visioning. Once it was all about the chief executive pontificating in vague terms about the organization and the methods and processes to be used to be successful (read "profitable" or "continuingly funded"). These kinds of visions were doomed to failure because, as I note further in the chapter, they are self-centered and self-absorbed. Relatively early in this drama, in my *Strategic Planning Plus* (Kaufman, 1992d), I called for an external focus for visions and visioning, and so did Peter Senge in 1990.

Still, the conventional wisdom has the chief executive talking about a glossy future and in nonmeasurable terms about the destination of the organization. However, my colleagues and I noted a trend to have purposes statements—regardless of what they might be called—from Products and Outputs ever closer to Outcomes and a Mega perspective. In our research (Kaufman, Watkins, Triner, & Stith, 1998), we notice this shift and suggest carefully monitoring organizations to make sure that the intentions for adding societal value is followed by actions that actually do so. I fully expect that the focus on societal value added will become increasingly important and demanded by both clients and society.

2. Here are some of the many useful writings about visions and visioning and useful factors to be considered in preparing and using visions: Barker (1989, 1992, 1993), Block (1993), Forbes (1998), Handy (1995-1996), Kaufman (1991a, 1993a, 1996a, 1997b, 1998b, 1999), Kaufman, Thiagarajan, and MacGillis (1997), Muir, Watkins, Kaufman, and Leigh (1998), Nanus (1992), Peters (1997), Popcorn (1991), Roberts (1993), Sobel and Kaufman (1989), Toffler (1990), and Triner, Greenberry, and Watkins (1996).

3. Kaufman (1998b).

4. Kaufman, Watkins, Triner, and Stith (1998).

5. Again, this is using the Organizational Elements Model and the three levels of planning.

6. Purposes, or "goals," measured in nominal or ordinal scale terms, but not in terms of objectives which are measurable in interval or ratio scale terms. See Stevens (1951) for the mathematical discussion of appropriate scales of measurement. For applications, see Kaufman (1992d, 1998b) and Kaufman, Thiagarajan, and MacGillis (1997).

7. "Basic" because it sets the minimum, not the maximum.

8. Unlike the conventional wisdom that we will never agree on an Ideal Vision, my experience is that once the ground rules are set that (1) only results at the societal level are to be included and (2) no Inputs, Processes, or Products may be included, the progress is excellent and satisfying. The longest time I have taken is half a day to come to agreement on an Ideal Vision. The usual conflict in setting any Ideal Vision comes from arguments over Inputs and Processes, that is, favored programs, projects, and activities.

9. Management expert Wess Roberts (1993) builds on my Mega/Ideal Vision in quoting my definition of this as "practical dreaming." See Kaufman (1995f).

10. Some planners, especially Australians, often rail against "economic rationalism" that seems, superficially, to do what I suggest but doesn't. When usually applied, silly and short-sighted "economic rationalism" only looks at the costs side of any social equation and ignores the societal return on investment. By only looking at costs and not consequences, social and organizational distortions will likely occur.

11. An "indicator" is a metric that people accept as a proxy for a more accurate and complete measure, such as degrees F or C reported on the news that we know is for only one reporting station but feel it is close enough to represent the general area. Indicators are widely used, and useful, in planning because they are "close enough" for further useful work.

12. Kaufman (1992d, 1998b), Kaufman and Carron (1980), Kaufman, Corrigan, and Johnson (1969), Sobel and Kaufman (1989), Wilkinson (1989), and Windham (1975).

13. It is not my intention to set up "straw people" but to accurately reflect some of the concerns that I have heard and attempted to overcome. These are representative of those I have heard in my teaching and consulting, and the responses often work with those who are open to positive change.

14. This statement is also true of Marxism, Communism, and Fascism. These are all Processes, or means, not ends.

15. Recently, when presenting this Basic Ideal Vision to the senior staff of the Australian Bureau of Statistics (ABS), there were some who thought that there were no data available for many items or that some items were not measurable. By reviewing each element with the entire professional staff, it was noted by almost all that the ABS did have data for all. This is also true in most free nations. Data do exist and are available.

16. The following support, in whole or in part, this contention: Block (1993), Forbes (1998), Kaufman (1998b), Kaufman, Thiagarajan, and MacGillis (1997), Peters (1997), Popcorn (1991), and Senge (1990).

17. In my experience, the more senior the organizational executive/manager/professional, the more that person is willing to focus on societal value added. It would seem that junior-level people, including "new hires" believe they must "be practical and real world" instead of focusing on the reality of having to add value to external clients and society.

18. From Kaufman (1998b).

19. This concept is similar to the insight offered by Rummler and Brache (1990). Although they deal very competently with the Macro and Micro levels, this Ideal Vision approach adds Mega to the considerations.

5

A Mega Planning Framework

In most organizations, there has been planning, even what they call "strategic" planning. Therefore, there is likely not an issue of not planning but a problem of incomplete planning.[1] I have identified the rationale and basic concepts and tools for Mega Planning: base all planning and doing on the delivery of external client and societal value added. A hallmark question for Mega Planning and strategic thinking is to ask "If my organization is the solution, what's the problem?" Viewing your organization as a means to client and societal ends puts the external value-added issue in graphic relief. It avoids the egocentric assumption that your organization deserves to exist simply because it has been there in the past.

The focus on Mega has become timely because conventional strategic planning has attracted the attention of serious organizational and performance improvement specialists and executives who want to ensure that their organization is both doing things right and doing the right things.[2]

Valid and useful strategic planning—Mega Planning that includes deciding where to head and justifying why go there in the first place based on societal value added—is essential for anyone in any organization who must decide on what job should be done and what resources should be acquired or developed and/or used. As was noted earlier, most organizations attempt strategic planning, but most of what gets done is actually tactical and/or operational planning.

Relationship between level and type of planning. Not all planning is Mega Planning, nor is all planning strategic. Table 5.1 shows the relationships between level of planning and the type of planning each really is.

In the literature, many things get called "strategic planning," but most of it is not; it is usually tactical or operational. Some planning is really related to efficiency (Process oriented) or even taking account of resources (Input oriented). When you first focus on Mega, the other types of planning will link to that and make a better contribution.

TABLE 5.1 Relationship Between Level and Type of Planning

Level of Planning	Type of Planning
Mega	Strategic
Macro	Tactical
Micro	Operational
Process	Efficiency
Input	Inventory

TABLE 5.2 The Relationships Among Levels of Planning, Types of Results, Sponsorship, and Type of Planning

Level of Planning	Type of Result	Primary Sponsor	Basic Type of Planning
Mega	Outcomes	Executive	Strategic
Macro	Outputs	Manager	Tactical
Micro	Products	Supervisor	Operational

Most of this so-called strategic planning does not focus on the Mega level but, instead, pursues a more comfortable and conventional concern with Macro and/or Micro, such as seeking only to find greater market share or increased funding.[3]

Mega Planning links societal value added with what the organization can and should deliver.

Table 5.2 shows the relationships and sponsors for levels of planning, types of results, and the basic type of planning each represents.

This chapter defines a basic framework for strategic planning[4]—a *Mega*-planning focus—that better assures that society, external clients, and organizational (internal) clients are well-served as well as served well.[5] This process identifies ways to provide the sensible and rational database for defining useful purposes, as well as sensibly identifying and selecting responsive and responsible interventions, including programs, projects, activities, and products.

In providing the Mega Planning framework, there is a review of many of the basic concepts provided in earlier chapters, including the relationships among the six critical success factors and Mega Planning, in order to show how the concepts and tools furnished earlier get put to use. It is an overall guide to Mega Planning.

Effective strategic planning depends on people being able to appropriately get out of their comfort zones and enlarge their paradigms. This is so important that it forms the first strategic planning critical success factor (already noted in Chapter 1 and Introduction):

Critical Success Factor 1: Use new and wider boundaries for thinking, planning, doing, and evaluation/continuous improvement. Move out of today's comfort zones.

When widening your paradigm, think globally as you act locally. Focus on Mega[6] understanding that all of the Organizational Elements must be strategically, tactically, and operationally aligned to deliver useful results—and deliver organizational success.

This future-oriented societal focus provides the unique dimension to Mega Planning so often missing or assumed in other approaches.[7]

Because practical planning, management, and evaluation[8] depend on defining the right destination in the first place, let's turn now to the Mega Planning framework that shows the clusters and associated elements included in defining and achieving organizational success.

The Mega Planning Framework[9]

The strategic planning process for defining useful objectives, and then linking those with tactics and then operations to meet them, is applicable to all organizations—public and private—that intend to define and deliver useful contributions, to be both successful and good neighbors.

This Mega Planning framework has a number of clusters and elements (see Figure 5.1), starting with the decision concerning the primary focus, or frame of reference: Who is to be the primary client and beneficiary of what gets planned and delivered? The framework has three major clusters: (1) Scoping, (2) Planning, and (3) Implementation and Continuous Improvement.[10]

Defining and Using the Three Clusters or Phases of Mega Planning

The following provides the Mega Planning elements, or activities, in terms of the three clusters.

As noted in detail later, the first decision concerns the scope of planning in terms of who is to be the primary client and beneficiary of the strategic plan. There are three possible client groups that planners might select:

1. **Mega:** External clients, including customers/citizens and the community and society that the organization serves
2. **Macro:** The organization itself
3. **Micro:** Individuals or small groups (such as desired and required competencies of associates or supplier competencies)

Practical strategic planning targets the current and future well-being of one's community and society as the primary client; this is Mega-level planning.[11]

A brief review of some of the basics of Mega Planning. To assure that your strategic plan has tangible and useful purpose, the following menu of questions, shown in Table 5.3 (and earlier in Figure I.3), that any organization can (and should) address are suggested for use.

Based on each of these questions, Table 5.4 provides, once again, the identification of the level of planning and the Organizational Element associated with each.

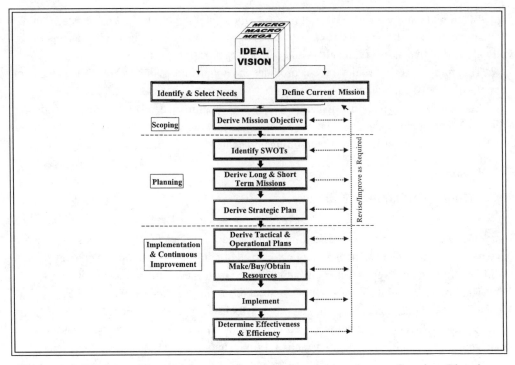

Figure 5.1. The Mega Planning framework and its three major clusters: Scoping, Planning, and Implementation and Continuous Improvement (evaluation).

TABLE 5.3 Finding Direction: The Basic Questions Any Organization Must Ask and Answer

?	Do you commit to deliver organizational contributions that have positive impacts for society? (**MEGA**/Outcomes)
?	Do you commit to deliver organizational contributions that have the quality required by your external partners? (**MACRO**/Outputs)
?	Do you commit to produce internal results that have the quality required by your internal partners? (**MICRO**/Products)
?	Do you commit to have efficient internal products, programs, projects, and activities? (**PROCESSES**)
?	Do you commit to create and ensure the quality and appropriateness of the human, capital, and physical resources available? (**INPUTS**)
?	Do you commit to deliver (a) products, activities, methods, and procedures that have positive value and worth, and (b) the results and accomplishments defined by our objectives? (**EVALUATION/CONTINUOUS IMPROVEMENT**)

When strategic planning starts at the Mega level and thus includes the Macro and Micro levels (as defined in Table 5.2), there will be a linking and synergy—strategic alignment—among all of the elements, actions, and activities of the organization. This approach avoids a linear, lock-step, and narrow approach in favor of a dynamic human-centered process that is built upon synergies among levels.

TABLE 5.4 The Basic Questions Any Organization Should Ask and Answer and Each One's Association With the Level of Planning and the Organizational Element With Which It Is Associated

Organizational Question	Level of Planning	Organizational Element
1. Do you commit to deliver organizational contributions that adds value for society?	Mega	Outcomes
2. Do you commit to deliver organizational contributions that have the quality required by your external partners?	Macro	Outputs
3. Do you commit to produce internal results that have the quality required by your internal partners?	Micro	Products
4. Do you commit to have efficient internal products, programs, projects, and activities?	Operations	Processes
5. Do you commit to create and ensure the quality and appropriateness of the human, capital, and physical resources available?	Resource	Inputs
6. Do you commit to deliver (a) products, activities, methods, and procedures that have positive value and worth? (b) The results and accomplishments defined by our objectives?	Evaluation and Continuous Improvement	Evaluation and Continuous Improvement

The use and linking of the three levels of planning (and their associated results) form the third critical success factor:

Critical Success Factor 3: Use all three levels of planning (Mega, Macro, Micro) and the three related levels of results (Outcomes, Outputs, Products).

Mega-level planning incorporates Micro and Macro planning. When we select it, the three types of planning are aligned and integrated, and we increase the likelihood of achieving organizational success.[12]

A focus on results, consequences, and payoffs. This strategic planning framework is results based and results centered. Confusing means—*how*—and ends—*what*—has profound implications for success. Or lack of it. When resources and methods (collectively called means) are selected before relating them to the results to be accomplished, one risks jumping into solutions before knowing the problems and opportunities. The ends/means distinction is so important that it is the second critical success factor:

Critical Success Factor 2: Differentiate between ends and means—focus on "what" (Mega/Outcomes, Macro/Outputs, Micro/Products) before "how."

Assuring that your identified results link to all three levels of results. Figure 5.2 provides an algorithm to use to make certain that all results use the Mega paradigm. It pays to check during your planning to assure yourself that you are doing Mega Planning.

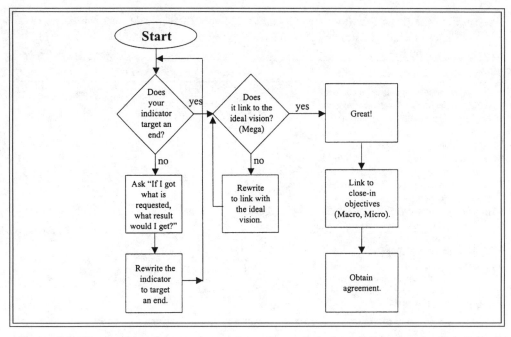

Figure 5.2. An algorithm for assuring your results are linked to all three levels of planning and results.[13]

The Mega Planning Framework and Descriptions of the Basic Elements and Tools

Referring to Figure 5.1, each of the three phases and associated elements are described below.

Scoping (Elements 1-4)

Scoping has four elements, as shown in Figure 5.3: (1) Select the Mega level of planning, (2) identify and select needs, (3) define current mission, and (4) derive the primary mission objective.

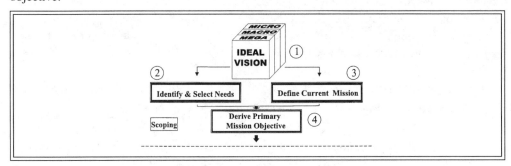

Figure 5.3. The four elements of the Scoping cluster of Mega Planning.

Let's take a detailed look at each element.

1. Select the Mega level of strategic planning from among the three alternatives.[14]

Select the Mega level from among the three types of strategic planning based on who is to be the primary client and beneficiary from what is planned and delivered: Mega, Macro, or Micro. The Mega-level option includes Macro and Micro as embedded within it. When you select Mega, you get the others automatically.

If you don't select the Mega level, you assume that positive societal consequences will surely flow. Failure to formally and directly select and target the Mega level leaves the organization and everyone in it vulnerable to legitimate claims of selecting means and resources that cannot be justified.[15]

Basic to selection of the Mega level is the development of a shared *Ideal Vision,* as discussed in Chapter 4. The building of this shared vision is an integral part of the first phase of Mega planning: the **Scoping** process. The Ideal Vision is what defines the Mega-level choice and commitment. As soon as the Mega choice is made, then the next step is to develop the Ideal Vision. Mega-level strategic planning is long-range planning that defines and continuously moves ever closer toward achievement of this Ideal Vision. At the Scoping step, the planning partners identify and define results for what should be and what could be in terms of the ideal society.

An Ideal Vision is related to contributions, not to procedures, resources, or methods. It defines ends, not means. If we don't stretch toward a better future through strategic planning, how will we ever know where to begin the journey? And in which direction to move? And if and when we have arrived? And how is our progress to be accurately calibrated?

By first identifying an Ideal Vision and selecting its contribution to it, an organization can also identify other agencies and agents and what they will contribute to the total. Thus, synergies among and between societal partners, are identified and delivered. It is an essential ingredient in creating the future, not reacting to it.

An Ideal Vision is stated in measurable performance terms. It is understood that we might not achieve it in our lifetime, but we must set our compass to that destination. The selection of the *primary organizational mission* (based on the Ideal Vision) is a commitment to the future and discourages a drift in the same direction as the organization and/or current operations are now heading.

What About Beliefs and Values?

It is almost conventional dogma that planners formally consider the planning partners' beliefs and values. This Mega Planning omits this determination as a formal element but doesn't fail to consider them.[16] Embedded in the process of deriving a shared Ideal Vision is dealing with the planning partners' beliefs and values. Beliefs, values, and wishes all drive the ways in which partners will address the strategic planning process. Usually, without questioning these personal and usually unchallenged frames of reference, people apply their existing paradigms of how they view and deal with their life, associates, clients, competitors, relationships, families, neighbors, and thus planning. Beliefs and values are usually strongly held and unexamined and commonly focus on means and resources (some people call these their "philosophy," or "core values").[17]

Deriving an Ideal Vision allows the partners *in the context of future societal good* to compare their beliefs and values with the Ideal Vision. The comparison of one's beliefs and values with the measurable and rigorously defined specifications for what kind of world we want to help create together for tomorrow's child provides the planning partners the opportunity to revisit and possibly revise old paradigms based on the Ideal Vision. This is usually effective. The success of the entire Mega Planning process might hinge on the planning partners' ability to consider new outlooks and paradigms and/or basic beliefs about people, prejudice, business, government, health, and what the organization should accomplish and deliver and who is to be the primary client and beneficiary.

When one begins strategic planning with raw and unexamined beliefs and values, processes, interventions, programs, how-to-do-its, means (such as "profits are exploitive," "setting objectives is inhumane," "computers are the solution to our problems," or "money is the primary motivator") are imposed before the useful ends that any means or program should deliver are identified and justified. Thus, with this premature starting point, organizations head off to do their work with solutions that do not fit the problems and opportunities—solutions in search of problems.

An Ideal Vision that is cooperatively derived and shared will allow partners to revise their current beliefs and values paradigms. Reconciling beliefs and values while developing the Ideal Vision might get people outside their comfort zones because it challenges long-held perceptions. Be patient and allow the planning partners to grow, develop, and change. The results will pay great dividends in terms of what the organization will be able to develop and contribute to our external clients, shared communities, and society.

2. Identify needs.

Using the definition of a *need* as a gap in results, and employing both performance (hard) and perceptions (soft) data, the gaps between current results and desired results—a needs assessment—are identified (starting with gaps for the Ideal Vision).[18] This has been extensively presented in Chapter 3, including the necessary concepts, tools, and procedures.

The importance of conducting a needs assessment—the identification and prioritization of needs—(as a gap between current and desired results) is basic and fundamental. To do otherwise will allow means and resources to be selected without justifying them on the basis of getting from current results, payoffs, and consequences to desired ones.[19]

This definition of need is so vital that it is the fifth critical success factor:

Critical Success Factor 5: Define NEED as a gap between current and desired results (not as insufficient levels of Resources, Means, or Methods).

Needs are sensibly prioritized on the basis of "what do you give as compared to what do you get?" A needs assessment allows a decision to be made on the basis of what it costs to meet a need versus what it costs to ignore it.[20] An added "bonus" of using "need" as a gap in results is that it then provides the basic criteria for evaluation. In evaluation—the comparing of intentions with accomplishments—the "what should be" criteria are used for evaluation. Thus, one does not have to develop an independent evaluation process but, rather, simply uses the "what should be" criteria directly from the statement of need.

3. Define the current mission.

At the same time as doing Element 2 (above), the current mission is obtained and (as is usually necessary) rewritten to state it in results terms. These revisions will include developing measurable—Interval or Ratio scale—indicators of "where are we headed?" and "what criteria will allow us to prove when we have arrived?" Objectives should be results related and only target ends, never means.

Writing objectives, all objectives, in results terms is so important that it is the fourth critical success factor:

Critical Success Factor 4: Prepare objectives—including those for the Ideal Vision and mission objectives—which have indicators of how you will know when you have arrived.

4. Identify the primary mission objective.

At this fourth element, the primary[21] mission objective (including detailed performance criteria) is derived. It is based on the part of the Ideal Vision the organization commits to deliver and to continuously move toward. The mission objective will serve as the basic direction in which your organization will head—a "guiding star." It states the Macro-level results (Outputs) to be delivered.

The **primary mission objective** is derived from the Ideal Vision: the needs identified and selected and the measurable definition of the current mission. When the needs have been identified at the Ideal Vision level, the Mega Planning partners estimate the costs versus consequences for meeting the needs and not meeting them. From that, the planners identify those elements of the Ideal Vision they commit to deliver.

The primary mission objective is based on (a) the selection of, and commitment to, the Mega level for strategic planning, (b) the derivation of a results-referenced Ideal Vision (including reconciled beliefs and values), (c) identified needs, (d) costs-consequences estimations based on what it costs to meet the needs as compared to what it costs not to meet them (cost being both financial and social), (e) the elements of the Ideal Vision the organization commits to deliver, and (f) the existing mission (that, as is usually required) has been transformed into measurable performance terms).

If one selects a mission objective that is not derived from the Mega/Ideal Vision, they severely risk the entire enterprise. If one does not intend to contribute to getting continually closer to the Ideal Vision, what are their intentions? Are they willing to risk the conduct of an entire organization that does not contribute to creating a better world?

The primary mission objective is based on a comparison among current intentions (the results-defined current mission) and desired results (based on the Ideal Vision and the meeting of priority needs) in order to define what it will take to get from "what is" to "what should be," or from current results to desired ones.

A primary mission objective identifies the measurable destination on an interval or ratio scale.[22] A mission *statement* identifies destination intentions that are measurable only on a nominal or ordinal scale:

mission statement + interval/ratio scale criteria = mission objective.

The skills of preparing measurable performance indicators and writing mission objectives in terms of results at the appropriate (and selected) level are the key to planning success.

The primary mission objective sets the benchmark for enroute, or building-block, mission objectives. A primary objective is the basic, long-term, future-seeking mission for the organization. It is the one that has the direct link to the parts of the Ideal Vision (Chapter 4) that the organization commits to deliver and move ever closer toward. From this primary mission objective, as will be noted later, build-block missions are derived for intermediate years, such as the year 2020, 2010, next year, this year. Thus, there is defined a chain, or ladder, of missions that identifies organizational objectives that span from the Ideal Vision to this year.

Planning (Elements 5-7)

The planning phase has three elements, as shown in Figure 5.4: (1) identify strengths, weaknesses, opportunities, and threats, (2) derive long- and short-term missions, and (3) derive the strategic plan.

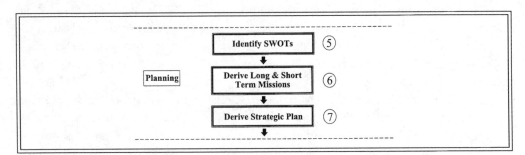

Figure 5.4. The Planning cluster of the Mega Planning framework.

The products from the Scoping elements provide the basis for building the Mega-referenced strategic plan. In the Planning phase, the three elements described next are important.

5. Identify SWOTs: Strengths, Weaknesses, Opportunities and Threats.

The determination of the organization's *s*trengths, *w*eaknesses, *o*pportunities, and *t*hreats (SWOTs) is usually accomplished and analyzed through both internal and external scanning[23] of the inside- and outside-the-organization environments. It is important to ensure that scanning includes objective examination of the SWOTs. Further, it is self-deceptive to lie to your own analysis or even not recognize that old ways and means—frames of reference, paradigms, organizational approaches, and climates—might be antagonistic to current and future realities. Future trends as well as opportunities are identified and documented at this step.[24] Although many may be tempted to only examine weaknesses and threats, this element allows the identification of possibilities that might otherwise remain obscured.

6. Identify long- and short-term missions.

Based on the shared Ideal Vision, identified needs, the primary mission objective, and the SWOTS, select the building-block—long- and short-term destinations—mission objectives. These linked enroute mission objectives—from the year 2020 to 2010, from next year to this year—contain the measurable specifications for the organization in terms of their Outputs. These long- and short-term missions build a results bridge between current results and the achievement of the primary mission objective.

These building-block mission objectives are based on trend data and what is currently known and possible. The SWOTs information from the previous element provides a database for the determination of the long- and short-term missions. They are written in measurable performance terms, as are all objectives. The Ideal Vision and the related "results ladder," which defines intended accomplishments from today toward the ideal, provide the basis for the continuous improvement of the system and its components.

The primary mission objective (derived in Element 4) is based on the Ideal Vision, and the building-block missions identify the results that the organization commits to deliver based on the primary mission objective. Also, the mission objective provides the criteria for enroute, building-block missions that will bridge from this year to that future: year 2020 mission, year 2010 mission, to this year. This relationship is shown in Figure 5.5.

This sixth element identifies measurable objectives that are precise, rigorous, and clear statements of "where we are headed" plus "what criteria we will use to know when we have arrived" for close-in and distant destinations.

Figure 5.5. Derive a "chain" of missions that link this year, through time and performance, to the Ideal Vision.

7. Derive the strategic plan.

Based on the products from the preceding six strategic planning elements, the product of this element is answering the key questions: What? Who? When? Why? Where?

Reconciling differences among the planning partners might have to be done here once again. It is important that the strategic plan be based on the Ideal Vision, identified needs, the primary mission objective, and the associated long- and short-term missions. Every part of the plan must be selected and justified on the basis of the contribution to the missions and the Ideal Vision.[25]

At this element, the planning partners frequently have to go back and collect new and different data that came from the statement of the Ideal Vision and related needs—gaps in results—as compared with the existing mission.[26] A continuing emphasis on the difference-yet-relationship between ends and means is vital.

Operational, or enroute, milestone results, called *functions*—for the implementation of all that has been planned up to this point are set, along with the identification and selection (from alternatives) of the tactics and approaches (methods-means) to be used. The functions—building-block results that when completed will deliver the required results—may be arrayed to form a management plan called the mission profile. The **mission profile** identifies the results, or functions, to be accomplished and the order in which they are to be completed. The mission profile is a graphic representation of the flow and sequence of functions to be completed in the order in which they are to be accomplished so as to get from "what is" to "what should be" as defined in the mission objective.

Strategic plans should not be long nor complex. About 10 pages in length is about right to be used and useful for most organizations.

To keep plans in proper perspective, tactics—the ways and means to get required results—and operational plans that should be based on the strategic plans are best provided in a separate document. The tactical and operational plans are based on the strategic plan and also usually contain budgets, personnel requirements, and resource requirements. To have a strategic plan that is longer than 10 pages cries out for the rightfully dreaded micromanagement that will get in the way of freeing competent organizational associates to make the required contributions.

Another contribution of this plan development element can be the derivation of decision rules: results-referenced policies. Decision rules, or policies based on results to be accomplished, are necessary so that all organizational partners have the same "marching orders" as they move toward their shared destination. These decision rules provide strategic objectives, complete with measurable criteria for each rule. They differ from any so-called policies that are really compliance guidelines. Any compliance guidance should be based on validated results to be achieved.

Implementation and Continuous Improvement (Evaluation) (Elements 8-12)

Elements 8 through 12, shown in Figure 5.6, move from Mega Planning to operations and improvement.

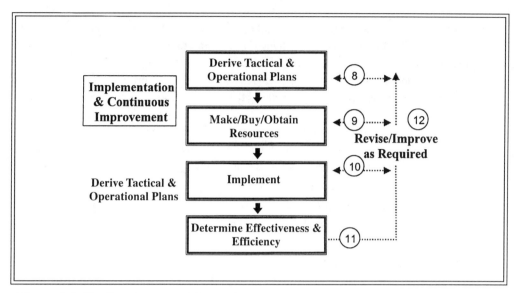

Figure 5.6. The five elements of the Implemention/Continuous Improvement cluster of Mega Planning.

8-10. Put the strategic plan to work.

The activities and results of these elements and activities include the following:

- **Element 8:** *Developing a tactical plan*—the identification, definition, and selection of the best ways and means (how-to-do-its) to deliver the results required in the strategic plan. The tactical plan includes the specifications that will be used for the designing of methods, means, and resources, justifying what is to be accomplished and how it will be done on a costs-consequences basis. During this element, you may identify both what should be delivered through your organization and what you might outsource, privatize,[27] or subcontract.

  Developing an operational plan—a plan based on the tactical plan that has identified the elements for the how-to-do-its (methods-means), including the development of timelines for accomplishing each product and delivering it to where it has to be and when it has to be there. The operational plan (1) defines the details of getting all of the tactics (methods-means) delivered, including the developing (or acquiring) of the resources, (2) implementing what has been planned, (3) conducting formative evaluation, and (4) revising as, and whenever, required while implementation is being carried out.

Now that you know where you are headed, why you want to get there, and what are the detailed requirements for the building-block results, you may sensibly and justifiably obtain the next element.

- **Element 9:** *Obtaining the factors of production*—the methods and means for meeting the objectives. The literature is rich with methods, means, tactics, and tools for making, buying, and/or obtaining the methods-means for getting from "what is" to "what should be" based on the strategic and tactical plan. The entire field of performance improvement, pioneered and provided by the journal published by the International Society for Peformance Improvement (ISPI) and its professional members and more recently by the publications of the American Society for Training and Development (ASTD), is worth your attention. In addition, there are many books written about the elements of making/buying/obtaining the methods-means, including many listed in this book's Bibliography section.

- **Element 10:** *Implementing the plan*—an activity that involves putting the plan to work and tracking progress in order to change what is not working and continuing what is.

11-12. Quality management and continuous improvement.[28]

These elements provide the process for continuous improvement in delivering useful results. When used consistently and properly, excellent results occur.[29]

Continuous improvement is similar, in some ways, to needs assessment: It compares results with intentions and provides the criteria for deciding what to change and what to continue. It involves a discrepancy analysis. It is, like the other elements, vital. It tells you what is working and what is not as you move ever closer to the primary mission objective and the Ideal Vision.

Although it might be time consuming to get these Implementation and Continuous Improvement steps accomplished—completing all of the previous elements in this Mega-level strategic planning framework—but now all of the requirements are stated and justified on the basis of

1. an Ideal Vision that defines the world we commit to deliver and move ever closer toward for tomorrow's child;
2. gaps in results (needs);
3. priority needs to be reduced or eliminated, based on the costs to meet the needs as compared to the costs to ignore them;
4. mission objectives that identify the results to be accomplished to get from current results to the achievement of the Ideal Vision; and
5. measurable performance specifications for functions (building-block results) that provide the basis for identifying and then selecting the alternative methods-means based on a costs-consequences analysis.[30]

This final Mega Planning phase includes a summative evaluation[31] where purposes (goals and objectives) are compared with results. Based on the evaluation—comparing results with intentions—decisions are made about what to continue and what to revise/continuously improve. In addition, the evaluation/continuous improvement criteria are directly taken from the "what should be" portion of the needs assessment.

Mega Planning is a continuing process. It is a way of thinking—strategic thinking—as well as a tool for deriving a formal plan. By taking a Mega perspective, the linkages will be

**CURRENT AND FUTURE SOCIETAL AND EXTERNAL CLIENT SURVIVAL,
WELL-BEING, AND SELF-SUFFICIENCY (Mega)**
↓
STRATEGIC PLAN OBJECTIVES
↓
DELIVERY UNIT (e.g., marketing, health services) OBJECTIVES
↓
**PROGRAMS, PROJECTS, ACTIVITIES, METHODS,
PROCESSES, AND PROCEDURES**
↓
RESOURCES
↓
IMPLEMENTATION   Revise as required
↓
EVALUATION AND CONTINUOUS IMPROVEMENT   ↗

Implementing Mega Planning

Following are steps for a proactive and holistic Mega Planning initiative:

1. Obtain board and executive commitment to Mega-level strategic planning.
2. Obtain planning team commitment.
3. Develop a shared Ideal (Mega-level) Vision. In doing this, the planning partners will have the opportunity to do values clarification and change their beliefs and values, including those related to change itself as well as change for one's self and others.
4. Transform the existing mission statement to a mission objective (where the organization is headed and how to precisely measure success).
5. Identify needs—gaps in results—through comparing the Ideal Vision with current results and consequences.
6. Prepare a primary mission objective for the entire organization.
7. Identify strengths, weaknesses, opportunities, and threats (SWOTs) through internal and external scanning.
8. Prepare building-block mission objectives for distant and closer-in results to be achieved in specified years in order to move continuously closer to the primary mission and the Ideal Vision.
9. Derive functions and specific performance indicators required to meet the mission objective.
10. Identify roles for accomplishing the products of Steps 6 and 8.
11. Identify and select ways and means to accomplish Steps 6 and 8, including costs/results, or costs-consequences, analyses.
12. Manage implementation, including a serious and consistent continuous improvement process.

13. Determine met and unmet objectives—based on the needs met and those still unmet—and revise/continuously improve as required.

Linking Strategic Plans to Operations

Because everything an organization uses, does, produces, and delivers should be vertically integrated through the Micro, Macro, and Mega levels, the following internal actions steps are suggested. These steps should be applied after the selection of an Ideal Vision along with an associated primary mission objective that clearly details which parts of the Ideal Vision the system is willing to help achieve:

1. Conduct a needs assessment—identifying and prioritizing gaps between current results and desired ones—and placing the needs in priority order. The needs assessment should begin at the Mega level. A needs assessment may be completed, in turn, for the Macro and Micro levels.
2. Develop strategic objectives at the Mega (societal) level and then for the Macro (organizational) and Micro (individual employee/associate) levels.
3. Devise and implement a continuous improvement monitoring procedure to maintain and improve the qualitative level desired by ensuring that what is to be produced is what is actually produced and that what is assessed and continuously improved is data based. The objectives are the "what should be" dimensions of the needs selected for closure, including the measurable performance standards that form the objectives.
4. Ensure vertical and horizontal linking and integration of what is planned and accomplished so that the Mega, Macro, and Micro levels are achieved.
5. Institute a quality management/continuous improvement process that assures continuous improvement of the entire system as it moves constantly toward the mission objective and the Ideal Vision.
6. Design and develop processes, tools, procedures, and methods that will efficiently and effectively deliver quality results. The methods and techniques of systems[32] design and development are valuable for this. This is the step in which HRD, training, and development methods and means are produced based on the contributions each will make to the higher levels of results.
7. Consider the use of technologically driven methods to ensure efficient delivery and continuous improvement.
8. Model, with the methods and procedures we ourselves use, what we want our associates to master and apply.
9. Implement and conduct formative (enroute) evaluation, changing that which is not being successful and continuing that which is. A "quality system" that includes useful and valid data for decision making is imperative. Provide modified methods and means where what is being used has not been effective.
10. Evaluate the effectiveness and efficiency of the methods, means, and processes and decide what to change and what to continue, using the performance data for improving, not for blaming.

11. Revise as required so that you continuously improve as you move toward your mission objectives and the Ideal Vision.

Mistakes Often Made by Strategic—But Not Mega—Planners

Following are some of the most frequent mistakes that conventional strategic planners commit. Avoiding them could mean the difference between just another document gathering dust and a revitalized, productive, successful, and continuously improving organization.

1. **Plan at the department, section, or program level, not at the societal—Mega—level.** Increasingly, organizations are chartered to provide quality and cost-effective Outputs that will allow all to be successful in an ever-changing world. Society is changing, and our organizations must be responsive and responsible or they will vanish or be replaced. If we do not define the future societal and external clients' success that our organization commits to deliver, then we are assuming that what we do will be useful. How successful is our current organization? Can it simply be patched and mended by adding a process here, tougher requirements there?[33] All three levels of results (Mega, Macro, and Micro) must be vertically integrated.

2. **Prepare objectives in terms of means, not results.** Objectives tell us where to head and how to know when we have arrived. If we only set our sites on processes (hold quality meetings, buy new equipment) or resources (higher spending), we put the "process cart" before the "results horse." Objectives must identify ends, not means and/or resources.

3. **Develop a plan without the contributions and cooperation of representative organizational and external partners.** Even though a plan will be put together more quickly when done by a small group, others who don't feel they contributed will not likely accept the product. Besides, the partners who actually develop the plan will be able to contribute to it, and thus make it better, representative, and adopted.

4. **Select solutions before identifying destinations.** Just about every group, good or bad, has a favorite solution, or quick fix. Resist picking a solution (or resource) until you know where you are headed and why. Often, ineffective HRD and training initiatives are selected without previous steps and relation to the Mega-level strategic plan. Doing so risks using interventions that are not successful.

5. **Set objectives based solely on the perceptions of the planning partners, not also anchored in performance realities.** Although people know what they want, they don't often know what they should have. They also don't know much about gaps between current results and required ones. Provide planning partners with the realities of future trends, opportunities, and consequences. By starting with the collection of "core values," you risk "air hardening" old frames of reference that are not functional in today's and tomorrow's world. By starting with the development of an Ideal Vision, you allow the partners to grow, develop, and change.

6. **Define and identify needs as gaps in resources, methods, or techniques.** Although popular usage has "need" used as a verb ("we need more money," "we need less money," "we need more technology," "we need computers," etc.), this is a sure way to select solutions that really aren't responsive to the basic problems. If you first identify gaps between current results and desired ones (needs), you are then free to select the most efficient and effective ways to meet the needs.

7. **Skip some of the steps of strategic planning.** Even though there are a number of steps, leaving out just one will diminish the quality and usefulness of the plan. Review the model (Figure 5.1) and the questions (Table 5.1). Which steps and questions can really be omitted?

8. **Assume that all strategic planning approaches (a) are basically the same and/or (b) are nothing but common sense/intuition.** All models are not the same. Most are reactive *and* start at too low a level—by attempting to improve efficiency, or increasing worker skills, not with turning out deliverables that will be useful and appropriate. And if intuition were sufficient enough, organizations would be wonderful just as they are.

9. **Develop training programs on the basis of producing efficient delivery without questioning the validity and usefulness of the learning objectives.** Many current organizational improvement initiatives assume that the current objectives are correct and useful and go directly to improving the efficiency of delivery and production. We can make operations more efficient without making it effective. Efficient is not the same as effective.

10. **Fail to integrate strategic planning with other improvement initiatives such as quality management, needs assessment, benchmarking, and reengineering.** Even though most organizations are appropriately moving into strategic planning and quality management (or total quality management), they are splintering the efforts instead of integrating them. Quality management and strategic planning use the same databases and also must involve all partners in their pursuit and accomplishment. Integrating these thrusts, including using the same partners, can better assure continuous improvement toward the mission and Ideal Vision.

Benchmarking and reengineering[34] can be powerful, and they also can be deceptive.[35] If one is benchmarking another organization, it is vital to ensure first that the other organization has the right objectives—doing the right thing as well as doing things right—and your organization cannot leap over the competition and create a new reality.[36] All too often, benchmarking and reengineering do not first link to the Mega level and thus result in improving a process, operation, or even an organization that is a solution to no current or future problem or opportunity.

Summary

Mega Planning (and thinking) better ensures that useful and justifiable missions, goals, values, and needs are identified, reconciled, and used in selecting strategies and tactics. Built upon societally useful—Mega-level—objectives, an appropriate, useful, and valid strategic and tactical plan may be fashioned. This Mega Planning framework identifies the necessary components and associated tools for defining and achieving organizational success.

There are critical differences and relationships among Mega,- Macro-, and Micro- levels of strategic planning. These differ in terms of who is the primary client and beneficiary of what is planned and delivered. We identify a generic process for strategic planning for any organization that intends to help (a) fashion the kind of world in which we all wish our children and grandchildren could live and (b) design the organizational and associated performance system that can help make it a reality.

Improvement should be based on the results of a valid and useful Mega-level strategic plan. Strategic objectives should drive operational objectives, and these in turn should be used to develop detailed objectives and related methods and means for delivery. Using strategic thinking and planning, we can have strategy-driven budgets, not the conventional-wisdom budget-driven strategies.

Organizations and their partners can choose to both think and plan strategically. Much of our society's economic and physical health, survival, and future well-being depend upon this conscious and conscientious choice.

EXERCISES

1. Compare your organization's current "strategic plan" and planning process with the framework provide here for Mega planning. What of the 12 elements provided here are present, and what ones are missing?

2. How would you classify your current strategic plan: Mega, Macro, Micro, Process oriented, or Resource/Input oriented?

3. What might you do to get Mega into your next strategic plan? Who are the sponsors you might involve?

4. What are the implications for your organization not focusing first on Mega?

5. How does your organization now prove value added for both the organization and external clients and society? If it doesn't, how will you go about making that demonstration?

Notes

1. Although it is tempting to label most planning as bad planning, I prefer to think of it as incomplete planning. As noted in the first chapters of this book, most planning is more focused on means and resources than on ends, is more concerned with organizational good than it is on external client and societal good, and fails to be precise and rigorous in defining performance criteria.

2. The concept that managers do things right while executives do the right things was, perhaps, first suggested by Drucker in his 1973 classic *Management: Tasks, Responsibilities, Practices* and further suggested by Nanus in 1992.

3. An interesting example of single-issue, or nonsystem thinking, approaches is the organization that only wants to increase market share (simply give the product away) or only increase shareholder value (which can result in driving away clients simply because then they are not well served).

4. Because of its characteristics, it allows the integration of other performance improvement processes, such as quality management, benchmarking, and reengineering, which when each is used alone may stop short of being as powerful and potent as possible.

5. Again, Peter Drucker has shown us the implications for differentiating between ends and means–being well served and not just served well.

6. The primary—Mega-level—focus on society by defining and continuously improving toward the kind of society we want for tomorrow's child—as the primary client and beneficiary—is obtaining increasing support (e.g., Drucker, 1992, 1993a, 1993b, 1994, 1995; Kaufman, 1972, 1988a, 1992b, 1992c, 1992d, 1995f; Kaufman & Grise, 1995; Kaufman, Herman, & Watters, 1996; Popcorn, 1991; Senge, 1990—all referenced earlier).

7. Defining an organization's mission without linking it to societal consequences and payoffs denies the fact that it must make a positive contribution to its external clients as well as society for it to be successful. Organizations are only possible means to societal ends. Any organization (or, indeed, nation) that is not a "good neighbor" has gloomy prospects for its future.

8. Although "evaluation" is the more recognized and conventional term, I use it more in the quality management sense of "continuous improvement." Evaluation identifies the gaps between actual accomplishments and intentions. Continuous improvement takes those data and finds ways to close the gaps. Thus, the data are used for improving and never for blaming.

9. Based on Kaufman (1972, 1992d, 1998b), Kaufman, Herman, and Watters (1996), and Kaufman, Thiagarajan, and MacGillis (1997).

10. Strictly speaking, only Scoping and Data Collecting are concerned with planning. Implementation and Continuous Improvement are the "doing" that comes from a sensible Mega plan.

11. By first defining desired societal consequences and payoffs—such as self-sufficient and self-reliant citizens, a safe environment that does not result in disabling diseases or illness, businesses that legally and ethically prosper—sensible organizational and associated operational decisions may be rationally made and justified. The safest and most practical choice for the starting level for strategic planning is the societal—Mega—level; there *is* life after the delivery of your organization's Outputs to your clients.

12. When the Mega level is included in strategic planning, it becomes *strategic planning plus* (Kaufman, 1992d, 1998b).

13. Based on Kaufman and Grise (1995).

14. The Mega level is vital as well as the safest option.

15. The Mega level is the most practical and pragmatic choice because the simple reality exists that our organizations are means to societal ends. If an organization does not provide external clients with safe, cost-effective, and cost-efficient outputs so that they will be satisfied, successful, and self-sustaining in the world of today and tomorrow then everyone's future is threatened (as noted by Marshall & Tucker, 1992; Naisbitt & Aburdene, 1990; Toffler, 1990). The current demands put on both public and private sector organizations to be responsive and responsible serve as testimony to the fact that we must improve the extent to which we are making useful societal contributions. The U.S. Government Performance and Results Act (GPRA) demands this kind of accountability for results.

16. Some of my earlier frameworks included a step for determining beliefs and values (Kaufman, 1992d). My experience, however, is that this is not required, for beliefs and values are already considered when planning partners define and/or ratify an Ideal Vision. By making it a part of determining the Ideal Vision, a context for changing beliefs and values—often only biases and stereotypes about means and resources—is provided. Bringing it up again simply tends to allow people to return to old paradigms and slows the whole process down.

17. Unfortunately, many popular strategic planning approaches start with harvesting and using the partners' beliefs and values with the naive view that "everyone's values are important and should be included." This is naive because there exist values that are antithetical to democracy, the dignity of human life, and the importance of helping all people to help themselves be successful: There are still people who seek to have others shoulder their disproportionate share of contribution; in other words, they want—and often demand—rights without appropriate related responsibilities.

18. In Step 6, I use this to identify needs in closer-in years, such as the year 2020, 2010, next year, this year.

19. Note that this is a variation of Critical Success Factor 4 that urges that ends and means not be blurred.

20. An example from the public sector: What were the economic, let alone social, costs of not desegregating and integrating in the United States right after the Civil War? What does it cost the nation to continue to have very low and ultra-low birth-weight babies? What did it cost a major baby food company not to recall some defective products rather than "toughing it out" with quality control data that failed to impress most mothers?

21. I use the term "primary" mission objective for this initial and overarching mission objective. The reason for the prefix "primary" is to distinguish it from derivative mission objectives that will identify organizational purposes between the closest-in mission to the primary one.

22. Steven (1951) identified four scales of measurement: Nominal (naming), Ordinal (greater than, less than, or equal to), Interval (equal scale distances with arbitrary zero point), and Ratio (equal scale distances with known zero point). Interval and Ratio measures are more reliable than Nominal or Ordinal. Under these definitions, *everything* is measurable (Kaufman, 1992d, 1998b).

23. Kaufman, Herman, and Watters (1995); also, Kaufman (1998b) previously cited.

24. Such as those identified by Naisbitt and Aburdene (1990), Popcorn (1991), and Toffler (1990).

25. When disagreements occur, they are usually over means and not ends. The products of Elements 1 through 5 provide the common ground: results to be achieved. Use the previous data and information to negotiate to do what is right, not just what is acceptable.

26. Although it is tempting to be "politic" or "capitulating" at this point and move ahead even with some means and resources in focus instead of ends, doing so is an invitation to failure. Ends provide the only rational basis for identifying and selecting means. To allow one or another group to dictate a means, resource, or process before identifying and justifying the needs it will reduce or eliminate is to chance disenfranchising clients and stakeholders—those who deserve the most effective and efficient system possible.

27. Outsourcing and/or privatizing should only be done on the basis of very precise and rigorous objectives and performance specifications. Often, outsourcing is done on the basis of process variables, or price alone, and thus the value added for what is contracted and delivered is likely in question and might be contested. Again, the six critical success factors will serve you well when considering outsourcing or privatizing.

28. See such sources as Deming (1982, 1986, 1990), Dick and Johnson (1993), Joiner (1986), Juran (1988), Kaufman (1991b), and Kaufman and Zahn (1993).

29. U.S. General Accounting Office (1991).

30. Kaufman (1998b), Kaufman and Watkins (1996a), and Muir, Watkins, Kaufman, and Leigh (1998).

31. Scriven (1967).

32. For some time I have attempted to make the distinction between a "system approach," where the emphasis is on delivering external client and societal value added, and a "systems approach" that really starts internally, often at the Micro/Products level. Although subtle, this can be an important distinction (Kaufman, 1968, 1971, 1972, 1992d, 1998b; Kaufman, Corrigan, & Johnson, 1969; Kaufman, Herman, & Watters, 1996; Kaufman, Thiagarajan, & MacGillis, 1997; Kaufman & Watkins, 1996).

33. Change and change management is a vital consideration (Barker, 1989, 1992, 1993; Carnevale, 1991; Conner, 1992, 1998; Handy, 1995-1996; Harless, 1998; Kaufman, 1998b; Kaufman, Watkins, Triner, & Stith, 1998; Kaufman, Thiagarajan, & MacGillis, 1997; Marshall & Tucker, 1992; Naisbitt, 1982, 1996;

Naisbitt & Aburdene, 1990; Nanus, 1992; Nickols, 1990; Peters, 1997; Popcorn, 1991; Senge, 1990; Toffler, 1970, 1980, 1990). I also urge use of proactive "change creation."

34. Hammer and Champy (1993) and Hammer and Stanton (1995).

35. Kaufman and Swart (1995).

36. Hamel and Prahalad (1994).

6

Developing the Mega Plan

From Concept to Plan

Having the concepts and tools for Mega planning, including needs assessment and the important Ideal Vision, it is time to develop the plan from concept to application.

Based on the Mega framework and tools for needs assessment and system planning, this chapter walks you through the steps for developing the Mega-referenced system plan. As you develop the system plan, keep in mind the guides or "templates" provided earlier in the Introduction:

The Organizational Elements Model (Guide 1)
The Six-Step Problem-Solving Model (Guide 2)
The Six Critical Success Factors (Guide 3)

Also recall that we develop a Mega-referenced system plan in order to be able to answer the question "If my organization is the solution, what's the problem?" In this chapter, I provide guidance on how to accomplish the following:

- Identify organizational SWOTs: strengths, weaknesses, opportunities, and threats
- Locate useful information to complete a SWOT analysis
- Select the long and short-term missions
- Develop the management plan: mission and function analysis
- Prepare the mission profile: a management plan that identifies the functions—building-block results—to get from "what is" to "what should be" for results.

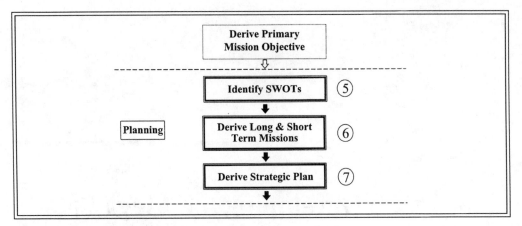

Figure 6.1. The planning phase of Mega Planning.

- Use a discrepancy analysis/needs assessment to prepare the mission profile
- Perform a function analysis
- Relate every level of system analysis to every other level
- Use the function analysis to determine feasibility
- Perform a task analysis (if you require that level of detail)

The part of the Mega Planning framework this chapter deals with is shown in Figure 6.1.

Once we have completed the Scoping phase of strategic planning, we are ready to lay the groundwork for action. In the Planning phase, we map out identified objectives and a development management plan.

To begin this phase, we conduct a SWOT analysis. Based on our Ideal Vision, primary mission objective, and needs assessment data, the SWOT analysis becomes an organization calibration, indicating environmental and operational factors to consider in determining enroute operational requirements and tactics: what tools and methods to use and how we will manage them as we move toward measurable success. The SWOT analysis tells what we have to work with and what we have to overcome in order to be successful.

We continue to use a results orientation. Use the guides provided in the Introduction as we move from strategies developed in the Scoping phase when we determined where we were headed and how to tell when we have arrived:

- The Organizational Elements Model—To keep our focus on linking all the elements as we build the planned bridge from What Is to What Should Be
- The Six-Step Problem-Solving Model—For each time we want to justifiably and systematically get from What Is to What Should Be for results and make certain that we don't select solutions before defining and justifying the problems, and to revise as required any time in the process

- The Six Critical Success Factors—To keep ends and means in perspective, focus on objectives at each and every planning and operational level, use needs (gaps in results) data, and focus on adding value to external clients and society

Even though most people are anxious to get the planning over with and get results, it is vital that the Planning phase does not focus on means but, rather, on ends—not solutions but results. This phase of Mega Planning transitions us from Scoping to the actual plan.

Based on the needs data at the Mega, Macro, and Micro levels (see Chapter 3), our first Planning phase job is the identification of strengths, weaknesses, opportunities, and threats (SWOTs).

Identify SWOTs: Strengths, Weaknesses, Opportunities, and Threats

Based on our Ideal Vision, basic mission, and needs, we may transform our organization to achieve useful results and payoffs rather than merely tinkering with the status quo or "bolting on change"[1] to existing operation.

We now know where we are headed and can justify why we want to get there. We also know that our plan does not begin without history, resources, and a track record. Every organization has many things going for it. There are also many things that can or could get in the way of its being successful. Based on where your organization has decided it is headed, its Ideal Vision-derived primary mission, and the identified needs and their priorities, now is the time to identify objectively the system's strengths, weaknesses, opportunities, and threats (SWOTs).

A SWOT analysis is conducted to determine the strengths and weaknesses, as well as opportunities and threats, that exist both within the organization for which the strategic plan is being developed, and among the external business, political, and economic environment variables (support and restraint elements). The data from both the internal and external SWOT analyses allow the planners to identify and select the yet-to-be-devised and implemented tactics. These, in turn, will increase the probability of achieving the Ideal Vision and missions; all supported by valid data. The SWOT analysis identifies the following:

1. Supports and resources (strengths) that are available to implement tactics—methods, means, resources—in order to meet objectives. Tactics are not selected now but later when actually developing the strategic plan.
2. Weaknesses—obstacles, shortfalls, or detriments that can or should be corrected or neutralized in order to achieve the Ideal Vision and the associated primary mission.
3. Opportunities—possibilities—that are not currently or have not been previously used
4. Threats—things that can block you in achieving the Ideal Vision— that can be avoided, neutralized, or for which tactics can be developed to reduce the negative impact.

The strengths, weaknesses, opportunities, and threats apply to both internal and external environments. Each of these SWOT factors must be objectively identified, carefully analyzed, and seriously considered when developing future action plans. This is no time to be other than brutally objective.

Locating Information to Complete a SWOT Analysis

A strategic planning group has many available sources of information and data.[2] Sources of information may include demographic, political, social, financial, technological, and attitudinal resources. The planners may obtain information from documents, state and national databases, and experts or from valid attitude and organizational climate surveys. Make certain that the data are both valid and reliable. It is wise to compare data from among at least two different sources to make certain their reliability.

Some prime sources of information are these:

- The Internet (but check the validity closely)

- Chambers of commerce: data related to business and industry status and future plans. Note that there are chambers of commerce for communities, states, and nations.

- Local, state, county, professional/organizational, and university libraries: data from historical sources, as well as current study reports dealing with important community, state, national, and international variables, trends, interests, preferences, and attitudes and values

- National, international, state and federal agencies: publications and databases. Many states and countries have central statistical agencies that are rich with data and information.[3]

- Financial institutions and major corporations: demographic projections related to possible future markets; data related to the financial and corporate requirements and markets

- Position statements from associations, political groups, economic groups, and social groups: directional guidelines that may impact tactics to be utilized by the schools or universities

- Information, records and dialogues available through Internet Web sites, bulletin boards, and related electronic databases and interest groups.

- Records of the U.S. and international Census Bureau: all types of demographic variables related to age, sex, race, and other variables beyond education. These data can be retrieved from a single or multiple census tract base to provide specific information related to the geographical area being served by individual school districts, community or junior colleges, and universities.

- Strategic plans that have been developed by organizations such as the United Way, local newspapers, "TaxWatch,"[4] and/or regional, national, international, business and/or government agencies, such as local or state agencies

- Real estate associations: data concerning types of housing and the numbers and categories of adults and children who live in the various types of existing and planned future housing; also demographics of neighborhoods and communities

TABLE 6.1 A Sample SWOT Analysis Format

	Strengths	*Weaknesses*	*Opportunities*	*Threats*
Internal data				
External data				
Analysis				

- State or national bar associations: information related to the impact of recent judicial rulings that may influence the operation of the organization
- Business and Industry plans: information related to current and future projected trends, employee skills, organizational mergers, and the like
- Newspapers: information regarding local, regional, international, and national trends, obituaries, and the like
- Local, county, state, federal, and international government departments of environmental protection: information concerning environmental patterns, changes, and trends

Once collected, data may be placed into a matrix to facilitate its analysis, as shown in Table 6.1. The SWOTs will help guide your decisions, while moving ever closer to the Ideal Vision and accomplishing each of the long and short-term mission objectives, which is the next step within the strategic planning framework. A hypothetical SWOT analysis is shown in Table 6.2.

Selecting the Long and Short-Term Missions

Based on the agreed-on Ideal Vision, identified needs, primary mission objective, and identified SWOTs, select the strategic missions for both the long-term (e.g., the year 2020) and closer-in and related strategic objectives. Figure 6.2 shows the relationship between the (agreed-on and shared) Ideal Vision and the closer-in objectives.

You don't have to achieve Mega right away. The use of building-block strategic mission objectives relieves an organization from having to justify why it will not deliver the Ideal Vision immediately. Unfortunately, some observers (frequently those providing oversight for public service agencies and some shareholders) don't understand the continuous—progress—nature of working toward an Ideal Vision and its related primary mission objective. By showing the building-block missions, one may more easily understand the progressive nature of Mega Planning and associated activities. Mega is the ideal destination toward which we continuously improve or progress.

The "ladder of missions" is derived by determining, based on internal and external organizational realities (strengths, weaknesses, opportunities, and threats—SWOTs), the feasible progression for organizational (Macro) accomplishments. This Mega does not have to be accomplished immediately, but progress toward it must be progressive and deliberate.

TABLE 6.2 A Hypothetical and Incomplete SWOT Analysis

	Strengths	Weaknesses	Opportunities	Threats
Internal data	• Mega Planning endorsed by CEO • All associates commit to planned change • Etc.	• Some growing interesting in unionization by conflicting unions • Education level of new hires decreasing	• Electronic database and support systems getting cheaper and provides better communication • More employees computer facile	• Corporate raiders interested in our better people • Cost of doing business increasing past revenue
External data	• National economy is up each year for 10 years • Trade wars are reducing • The Euro is predicted to stabilize currencies • Etc.	• Unfriendly takeover is possible • Some instability in the Middle East that could overflow • Etc.	• Increasing number of clients desire electronic rather than personal access • Electronic linkages getting cheaper and more reliable • Latin America is considering a shared currency • Etc.	• Confusion among some clients about difference between Mega and "very big" • Clients confused about difference between cost and value • Etc.
Analysis	• The world economic market seems stable for the future • Our organization mobilized for planned change • Etc.	• Professional capabilities have to be strengthened • Conflict among associates has to be eliminated • Etc.	• Virtual contacts and interactions can make our business better for clients and cheaper for us • Etc.	• Costs and return may be made for our associates as well as for the organization • Etc.

From these strategic longer-term and shorter-term mission objectives, tactical objectives may be derived. By aligning with the Ideal Vision and the primary mission objective, eventual selection of methods, means, and resources may be both rationally selected and justified.

Creating a learning organization. By relating strategic objectives to our Ideal Vision we will move systematically and continuously toward creating the world in which we want tomorrow's child to live as well as creating a learning organization that will constantly transform itself to be a responsive and responsible organization. This is a commitment to a defined better future that discourages drifting in the same directions in which we are now heading.

Learning organization:[5] An organization that sets measurable performance standards and constantly compares its results and their consequences with what is required. A learning organization uses performance data related to its Ideal Vision and the primary mission objec-

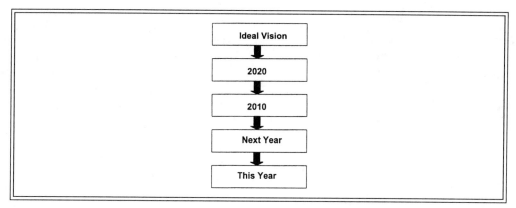

Figure 6.2. The relationship between an Ideal Vision (even though we might not expect to get there in our or our children's lifetime) and related, closer-in objectives.

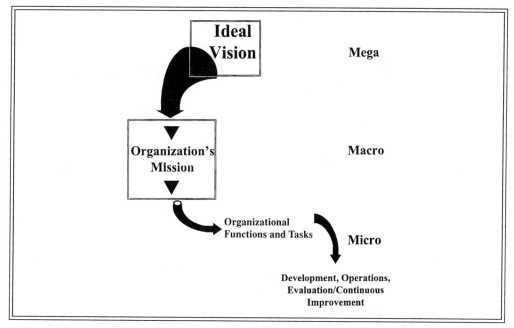

Figure 6.3. The roll-down relationship among the three levels of planning and results. Missions derive from the Ideal Vision. An organization selects what portion of the Ideal Vision it commits to deliver and move ever closer toward. Note that each results level is based on a needs assessment.

tive to decide what to change and what to continue. It learns from its performance and contributions.

Because the basic organizational mission rolls down from the Ideal Vision, it identifies those portions of the Ideal Vision that it intends to take on, as shown in Figure 6.3.[6]

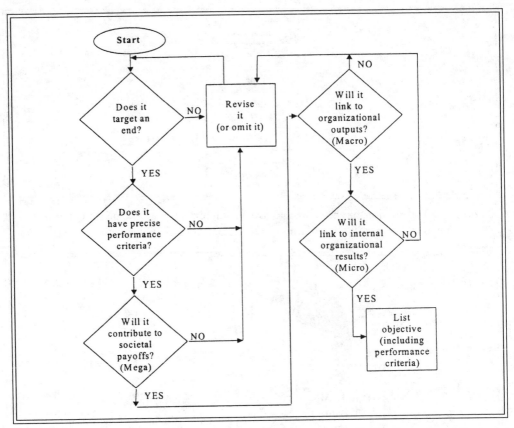

Figure 6.4. Assuring your objective is useful to all three levels of planning and results.

Each of these long- and short-term mission objectives should (a) be based on the now-shared Ideal Vision, needs, and existing missions and (b) precisely identify where the organization is headed and how everyone will know when (and if) they have arrived.

Because measurable criteria[7] are used, progress toward each of the missions and the Ideal Vision may be plotted and reported toward continuous improvement. Appropriate responses, resources, and enroute changes may be related. When developing mission objectives, check to assure that each one will make a contribution to the Ideal Vision. Figure 6.4 provides an algorithm for assuring the linkages between objectives and the chain of results from Mega to Macro to Micro and thus linking what the organization uses, does, produces, and delivers contributes to the primary mission objective as well as to the Ideal Vision.

We have now developed the front end of Mega Planning and have clearly stated where we are headed and provided the criteria for measuring our progress and success. We have further specified our mission objective that was based on our Ideal Vision, needs, and our current mission.

The next part of this Mega Planning phase is to develop a management plan. The management plan identifies the building-block functions—en-route results, or Products—required to get from current results (What Is) to desired ones (What Should Be) and shows the order and relationship among these functions.

Organizational visions and missions: Make them precise and rigorous. The past 20 or so years have seen a boom in organizational "mission statements" or "vision statements."[8] A review of the visions and missions, often posted proudly in lobbies and carried around on cards for pocket or purse, shows that most of them are diffuse, fuzzy, and means oriented. If a statement of organizational purpose does not allow associates and external partners to know exactly what is to be delivered (and to whom), then it isn't very useful. Any statement of purpose should have the same characteristics of any objective: It should state where one is headed and how to tell when one has arrived. And again, I urge the "visions" be the Ideal Visions alone.

Although some of the conventional wisdom about visions and missions is that they should be short and motivational, there must first be a precise statement of destination along with the criteria for success. Rigor, regardless of the level of an objective, is indispensable.

The Management Plan: Identifying the Functions Required to Get From What Is to What Should Be in Terms of Results

A plan provides a road map of results that shows what has to be accomplished, when each must be completed, and all of the necessary elements for getting from current results to required ones. The management plan[9] is made up of several components:

- The *primary mission objective* identifies the parts of the Ideal Vision the organization commits to deliver and move ever closer toward. The primary mission objective is derived from a needs assessment at the Mega level.[10]
- The *mission profile* identifies the top-level—overarching—functions (or results) required to get from current results to required ones for the entire organization.[11]
- The *function analysis* breaks down, or identifies the component Products of, each function in the mission profile.[12]
- The *methods-means* analysis identifies possible tactics and tools for meeting the needs identified in this "system analysis." The methods-means analysis identifies the possible ways and means to meet the needs and achieve the detailed objectives that are identified in this Mega plan. It does not select them but only identifies the alternatives that could be considered along with noting the advantages and disadvantages of each.

Definitions useful for Mega Planning. Some useful tools and their relationships are shown in Table 6.3. Bear in mind that these terms get thrown around a lot, almost always being used loosely and interchangeably.

So? Because this book is about Mega Planning, it is *a systemic approach*. It incorporates a *systems approach, a systematic approach,* and a *system approach.* As noted in Critical Success Factor 3, you must use and link all three levels of planning and results (Mega/Outcomes, Macro/Outputs, and Micro/Products). By distinguishing among these system-related defini-

TABLE 6.3. Definitions Useful for Mega Planning

Term	Definition
System	The sum total of parts, working independently and together to achieve a desired result
System approach	The definition of planned change that uses Mega—external And societal value added—as the primary focus for planning and doing. It is the hallmark of Mega Planning because of the external focus.
Systems approach	Planning and accomplishment based on internal organizational-only purposes. It focuses only on the parts of an overall system, not on Mega but only on Macro or Micro. A systems approach is useful only when you are sure of the external requirements and payoffs; otherwise, it is not holistic and might provide solutions that don't go with the overall "system" problem or opportunities. It is characteristic of Macro and/or Micro planning.
Systematic	Proceeding in an orderly and definable manner
Systematic approach	Planning and doing in an orderly and definable manner. One can be quite systematic and wrong. This focuses on means, methods, and resources (Inputs and Processes).
Systemic	Encompassing and impacting the entire system, or organization
Systemic approach	Planning and doing that involves the whole system, or organization. Because it has a focus on an organization, its effects are at the Macro level.
Deep change	Change that extends from Mega downward into the organization to define and shape Macro, Micro, Processes, and Inputs. It is termed "deep change" to note that it is not superficial or just cosmetic, or even a splintered quick fix.[13]
Planned change	Defining where you want to head, how to tell when you have arrived, and supplying the criteria for determining success and progress
Change management	Assuring that whatever change is selected will be accepted and implemented successfully by people in the organization. Change management is reactive in that it waits until change requirements are either defined or imposed and then moves to have the change accepted and used.
Change creation	The definition and justification, proactively, of new and justified as well as justifiable destinations.[14] If this is done before change management, then acceptance is more likely.

tions, you and your organization can avoid the splintering and fragmentation of planned change. It is meant to define change creation and is a proactive alternative to waiting for things to happen before reacting with change management. It is deep change because it is more than tinkering in the innards of organizational operations.

Mission and Function Analysis

Determining the requirements for getting from our current results (and their consequences) to our desired results (and consequences) are termed mission analysis and function analysis. Both help us define *what* is to be accomplished to meet the needs without selecting *how* we will meet them.

The **mission analysis** provides the requirements for the overall problem resolution[15] to get from current results and contributions to the Ideal Vision and our primary mission. The short- and long-term missions provide the "stepping-stone" accomplishments we are to deliver. The **function analysis** tells about specific detailed building-block results of each part of resolving that problem: the required results (again without selecting any how-to's) to be delivered and when they must be delivered.

The mission analysis supplies the answer to the question "Where are we headed, and how will we know when we have arrived?"[16] The function analysis asks "What has to be accomplished in order to get each part, or Product, of the mission analysis accomplished?" The differences between the two are in degree, not kind.

System Analysis

A mission analysis is one of several tools in a cluster called system analysis. When the mission analysis and the resulting plan links (defines value added) with the Outcome level of results, it is called *Mega Planning*. When it deals only with the Output level, it is termed *Macro planning*. If it begins at the Product level, it is labeled *Micro planning*.

System analysis depends on valid and prioritized needs and purposes having been first identified. The system analysis processs is results oriented and identifies functions, building-block results, to be completed in order to meet the identified needs.

Mission analysis focuses on the overall organizational results to be accomplished.

Function analysis identifies what has to be completed in order to get each element identified in the mission analysis accomplished.

Complicated? Not really. Lock-step and linear? No, since it is understood that we are building a complex performance system where all parts work both independently and together as they are linked to move continuously closer to the Ideal Vision.

System analysis and Mega strategic planning are not linear, lock-step, or inflexible. Quite the contrary.

Some reasonable objections have been leveled at strategic planning in general and flow-charting and system analysis as well.[17] This rigidity and linearity should not exist, and it is not characteristic of what is suggested here.

In addition, the flow charting suggested here, that is based on the six-step problem-solving model, states that the "revise as required" step is required at any point in the problem identification/problem resolution process. Revise as required any time and any place further assures that one will not (and should not) get locked in to premature solutions, methods, and approaches. It is self-correctable and self-correction. Additionally, the revise-as-required step is integral to quality management and continuous improvement that demands that continuous responsive change is part of the corporate culture of planning and change.

A system (Mega) approach to planning, of which mission analysis is a part, has several components. In both planning and doing, organization members must recognize that organizations are complex and that all of its parts interact as parts of a whole. We are building a responsive and responsible system with energizing synergies among its parts.

TABLE 6.4 Steps and Tools of Mission Analysis

Step	Tool
What is the organization to accomplish, and what criteria will be used to determine success?	Mission objective and performance requirements
What are the basic building-block Products, or milestone results, required to be completed in order to get from where one is to where one should be? (management plan)	Mission profile

There are two phases to being successful: *planning,* defining where to head (and justifying why we should get there), and *doing,* defining what it takes to get from current results to desired ones.

A system approach to planning, not surprisingly, has two major functions:

- Planning what to accomplish (results)
- Planning how to get from here to there

Useful organizational system planning consists of identifying and justifying problems[18] and opportunities and identifying what must be accomplished to deliver what is required.

Mission Analysis

Mission analysis is the system analysis step that reveals (1) what results and consequences are to be achieved, (2) what criteria[19] will be used to determine success, and (3) what are the building-block results and the order of their completion (functions) required to move from the current results to the desired state of affairs. The steps and tools of the mission analysis are listed in Table 6.4.

Proceeding from the needs assessment and problems delineation, results of the SWOTs analysis and the selection of long- and short-term missions, the mission analysis states the overall identified missions and the measurable performance requirements (criteria) for the achievement of required results. The primary mission objective and its associated performance requirements state the appropriate specifications for the system being planned and designed (discussed in Chapter 5). The next part of mission analysis is the statement of a management plan, called a mission profile, showing the "major" milestones, or the central pathway, for the building-block results to be accomplished, moving from what is to what should be in solving a given problem.

▓▓ The Mission Profile: A Graphic Management Plan

The mission profile is a graphic presentation of the management plan. The most basic mission profile is used for identifying and resolving problems (the six-step problem-solving process was referenced in the Introduction as one of the basic guides).

The planning effort so far has provided (1) what is to be delivered (the mission objective) and (2) the performance requirements for the mission. Now, plan what to accomplish to get from current results to desired/required ones. This step focuses on what is to be accomplished, not how or who (Step 2 in the six-step problem-solving model). These are the products that must be completed and delivered to accomplish the primary, longer-, and shorter-term mission functions. When the primary and major functions of a mission are identified and placed in logical sequence, they constitute the mission profile. The mission profile is a results-referenced management plan that shows the results to be accomplished to meet the needs.

A mission profile shows, in graphic form, the functional path for achievement of a larger end result. The actual number of individual functions that make up a mission profile can vary, from two to "n"—a higher number that can vary depending on the size of the plan.

Using a Discrepancy Analysis to Prepare the Mission Profile

Identifying needs as discrepancies between what is and what should be is at the heart of doing a needs assessment as well as a systems analysis. Identifying gaps in results is done with a discrepancy analysis.[20] The discrepancy analysis—a needs assessment—process happens over and over in a system analysis. Mega Planning intends to create a better future, and this often involves identifying and eliminating a discrepancy (to meet a need).

A completed needs assessment (see Chapter 3 for the details) tells us where we should be in terms of results: That provides the mission objective, including its performance requirements. Now we can devise the "path of Products" for getting from our current results to required ones. In so doing, we derive the mission profile, a management plan that identifies what is to be completed in order to get us from the "what is" provided by the needs statement to "what should be." A mission profile displays the systematic progression of Products to be completed and delivered.

How is a mission profile derived?

Step 1. Obtain the mission objective and its performance requirements that specify where we will be when we have completed the mission. Next, describe the current results, the status quo. Develop a mission profile that identifies what Products are to be completed in order get us from what is to what is required. The mission profile lists the necessary functions (Products, or results) to be completed and defines the logical order in which they are to be completed. Remember to omit how any of the functions will be done. Identify and list the first function to be completed.

Step 2. When the first major function in the mission profile has been identified, ask "What is the next logical Product to be delivered?" List it as the next function. Continue this process until you have moved from the first function of the mission profile to the last function required to meet and accomplish the mission objective and its performance requirements.[21] The mission profile is graphically presented in a flow chart. Figure 6.5 illustrates the rules for construction of flow charts, including mission profiles.

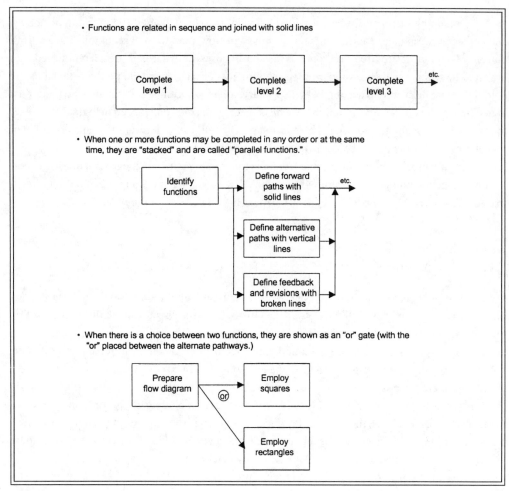

Figure 6.5. Basic conventions in preparing flow charts.[22]

There are seven rules for preparing flow charts:

1. Make all function blocks rectangles or squares and all of equal size.
2. Each function block should contain a statement of a result to be accomplished or delivered.
3. Connect function block with a solid or broken (dotted) arrows (also see Rule 6).
4. Use a decimal system to number the functions. Add a decimal point and begin at zero when moving the analysis to a new level. Number all blocks in the upper righthand corner.
5. When a function cannot be broken down into two or more functions, do not move the analysis to a lower level.

6. Connect the function blocks with solid arrows to show forward flow and with broken (dotted) arrows to show revision pathways. When a choice is to be made along two or more paths, use a circled "or" to show where the choices lie.
7. Show inputs (data from other sources) with an "open" box having two incomplete sides.

Step 3. When all the major functions in the mission profile have been identified, check to make sure that they are compatible with the needs, the mission objective, and the Ideal Vision, that they are internally and externally consistent. This rechecking will also ensure that the functions have external validity and usefulness based on the needs.

This process of check and recheck is performed throughout the entire system analysis process. By reviewing the scope and order of the functions—the building-block results—you can determine if any have been omitted or if unnecessary ones are included, and the planners can make sure that functions are in proper sequence. Some functions can be unified under a larger function, so this checking process will help keep things at the same level of detail. While examining the mission profile, check to see if any performance requirements have been overlooked.

Step 4. Once internal and external consistency have been ensured, arrange the functions in a flow chart. This mission profile is an orderly array of rectangles connected with solid lines and arrows that show the flow of the functions from first to last; from What Is to What Should Be.

A mission profile for completing a mission analysis is shown in Figure 6.6.

An example of a management plan—a possible profile—for preparing instructional materials (a product/Micro-level problem), is presented in Figure 6.7.

The system analysis process in general, and mission analysis in particular, is dynamic. When new data are uncovered, the mission objective and its performance requirements and mission profile might change. Be ready and willing to change the profile at any time.

The overall mission analysis process is shown in Figure 6.8 in the form of a mission profile. The major steps are these:

1. State the (primary) mission objective (based on needs) as well as the performance requirements in measurable, precise—ideally interval or ratio scale—terms.
2. Develop the mission profile/management plan, which shows the major functions required to accomplish the mission.
3. Revise any or all of the previous steps as required—along the way—to maintain consistency among the original requirements and the Products identified in the missions analysis to meet the needs.

A mission profile for strategic planning is shown in Figure 6.9.

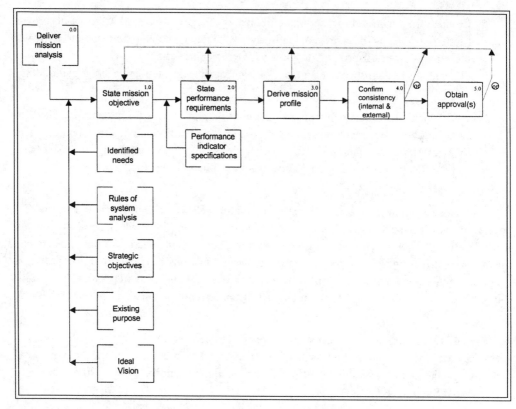

Figure 6.6. A mission profile for the completion of a mission analysis. The dotted, or broken, lines show the major points for revision/continuous improvement.[23]

All mission profiles will be different. The mission profile is a "road map" that graphically shows the basic functions involved in getting from what is to what is required. Not all mission profiles are alike, nor do they have the same number of functions since each shows the functions required to reduce or eliminate a specific need and complete a mission.

Use the basic six-step problem-solving model (Guide 2) for identifying and resolving problems to develop a mission profile. Every profile (regardless of its level of analysis) should have every one of the six steps represented. Usually, there will be several functions for each of the six steps of the problem-solving process. Figure 6.10 illustrates a partial mission profile for a strategic planning effort derived from the Mega level. It also shows the related six steps of the problem-solving process as it relates to this example.

A mission profile identifies, in logical sequence, the major functions that must be performed while meeting the performance requirements. This is the major results pathway for meeting the mission objective.

When the mission objective, performance requirements, and mission profile are completed, the mission analysis is finished. The stage is now set for the second phase of system analysis: function analysis.

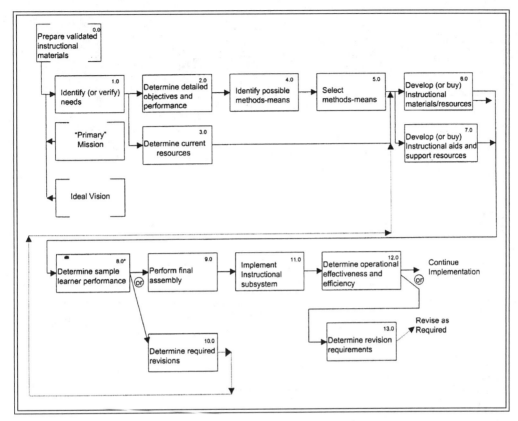

Figure 6.7. A Micro-level management plan for a possible instructional/learning program.

Function Analysis

A function is a building-block result, or product, to be delivered.[24] A function is a product that, along with other products, contributes to the accomplishment of a larger one. It is a collection of delivered results necessary to accomplish an objective. Each function integrates with other functions to accomplish the mission.

Analysis breaks something down into its parts. Analysis identifies what each part of a system contributes and shows how the parts interact. Function analysis identifies the building-block results, the interactions among the parts, and the order in which the results must be accomplished so that a larger objective will be met. Table 6.5 is a checklist for doing a mission analysis.

The Function analysis builds on what has gone before. It proceeds from the original statement of purpose (obtained from strategic planning, needs assessment, and the mission analysis (including the mission objectives and its performance requirements, and the mission profile).

Function analysis defines the "whats" that must be completed in order to achieve the mission objective(s) and its performance requirements. Function analysis, like mission analysis, identifies what has to be delivered as well as the order in which the Products are to be completed.

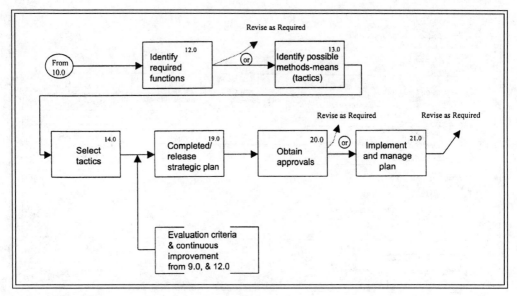

Figure 6.8. A mission profile for the delivery of a mission analysis. Revision of any previous function is possible; the dotted or broken lines show feedback of data for use in revision.[25]

Function analysis is *not* work breakdown structures, job/task analysis, computer flow charts, PERT diagrams, or process charts.

Some examples of functions as they might be stated in a function analysis are the following:

Identify functions

Validate in-service training program

Complete a function analysis

Collect data

Deliver budget

Summarize data

Obtain resources

Derive Ideal Vision

An option for writing functions. Some system planners[26] prefer to write Products in terms of accomplishments to provide the reminder that each is about ends and not means. Under that approach, the above would be stated as follows:

Functions identified

In-service training program validated

Function analysis completed

Date collected

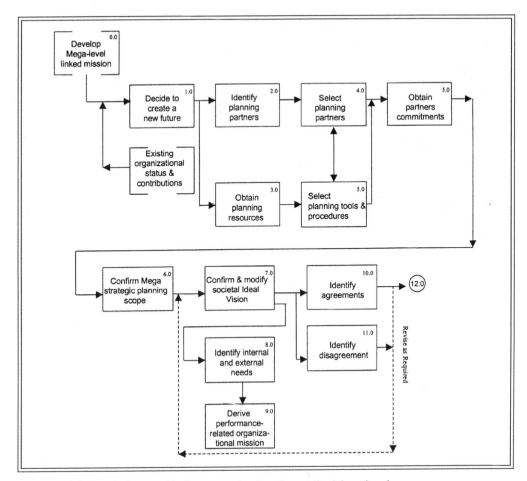

Figure 6.9. A mission profile for strategic planning at the Mega level.

Budget delivered

Date summarized

Resources obtained

Ideal Vision derived

Function analysis proceeds from the top-level (mission profile) functions and breaks them down into lower-level, building-block functions. This process continues until it has identified all the functions down to the lowest level of importance at each level and has determined the interrelations required to achieve the mission.

It is absolutely essential that each function identified (regardless of level)

- state a product (result) to be delivered, not means, methods, or resource.
- be precise, rigorous, and clear about what is to be delivered.

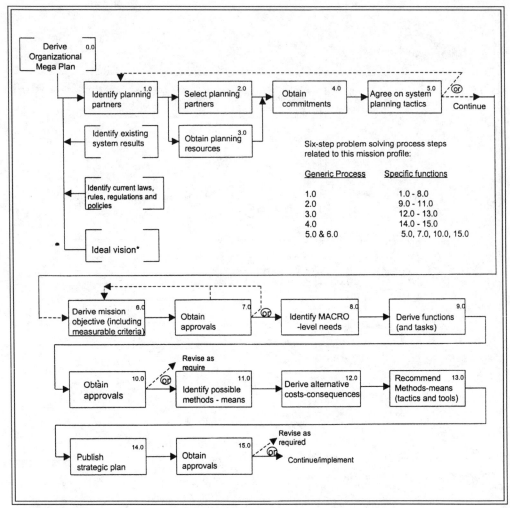

Figure 6.10. An example of a mission profile for strategic planning at the Mega level, showing the relationships to the six-stop problem-solving process[27]
*To remind all planning partners that the mission objective is derived from the Ideal Vision.[28]

- have measurable (best on an interval or ratio scale) performance requirements for each function or group of functions.
- be linked to the Ideal Vision and the primary mission objective.

The function analysis process identifies and analyzes what should be accomplished and gives the proper order of subordinate, lower-order Products (perhaps including jobs or tasks) required to achieve the mission objective and its performance requirements and thus resolve the problem. Function analysis thus identifies, analyzes, and orders.

TABLE 6.5 Mission Analysis Checklist

_____1. Obtain needs data from needs assessment and select problems (selected needs) to be resolved or reduced.

_____2. Derive the mission objective (which includes the performance requirements) so that it is possible to answer, in measurable performance terms, the following questions:
  • What result is to be demonstrated?
  • By whom or what is the result to be demonstrated?
  • Under what conditions is the result to be demonstrated?
  • What criteria, ideally interval or ratio scale, will be used to determine if it has been accomplished?

_____3. Make certain that how—methods, means, resources—the objective will be reached is not included.

_____4. Verify that the mission objective (and the performance requirements) accurately represent the problem selected based on the documented needs.

_____5. Prepare a mission profile that shows the major functions required to get from current to desired results. The mission profile is a management plan graphically displaying the functions (or Products) that will, when completed, eliminate the discrepancy (need) that constitutes the problem. Each function identified will
  • identify a result (Product) to be delivered.
  • show its relative independence from the other functions in the mission profile.
  • be numbered in sequence to show the relationships among all functions.
  • be joined by arrows to show the flow and the relationships among each function and all other functions.

_____6. Assure that all six steps of the problem-solving process are represented at each system analysis level.

_____7. Check the mission analysis to make sure that
  • all functions are present.
  • they are in the correct order.
  • they are consistent with the mission objective and the performance requirements (and will contribute to achieving the Ideal Vision and the primary mission objective)
  • they are consistent with and will meet the needs selected and the associated problem.

_____8. Make any necessary changes based on the Ideal Vision, the primary mission objective, the strategic plan, and justified by the needs assessment data.

Levels of Function Analysis

Because a function is one of a group of results, or Products, contributing to a larger result, a key to the levels of Function Analysis may be found in the term "larger result." Larger results (Outputs or Outcomes) are called higher-level functions. The highest-level function for a system analysis is the mission itself, and all other functions are derived from that overall function.

A useful way of viewing the relation between mission analysis and function analysis is as a matrix, with the mission analysis forming the "width" of the matrix and the function analysis making up the "depth" dimension. In performing a function analysis, we are filling in the "depth" of the mission analysis. Figure 6.11 provides an example of how a breakout from the mission profile keeps breaking out at subsequent levels.

Figure 6.12 shows how the numbering of functions are assigned, starting at 0.0 for the mission objective, and then each level has the next number (1.0, 2.0, etc.), the next level that derives from that showing the number for the function above it (1.1, 1.2, etc.), and so on.

The function analysis is a vertical expansion of the mission analysis. Each element in the mission profile is composed of functions, and it is the role of the planner to identify, for each function in the mission profile, all the subordinate functions and their interrelations.

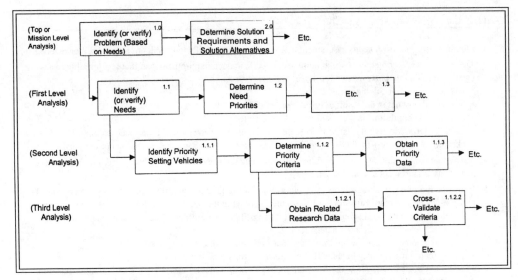

Figure 6.11. An example of a hypothetical function analysis starting from the six-step problem-solving process. Function analysis continues by identifying products (functions) and then identifies the building-block functions for each of the higher-level functions from which it derives.

The function analysis puts flesh on the bones of the mission analysis. It specifies the requirements and interrelations among the subfunctions for each product in the mission profile.

Interactions

An important contribution of function analysis is the identification of the manner in which functions interrelate one to another. The interrelationships are called *interactions*. All systems have interactions, so a vital element of system analysis is identifying interactions and planning for and assuring the successful meshing of parts. Rather than being a rigid, structural, and linear approach, this defines and applies a system network that moves continuously closer to meeting its mission.

Performance Requirements

Mega Planning, and all of its parts, is results referenced. Each function—from the Ideal Vision to the primary mission and long- and short-term missions—and all products in the function (and task) analysis have measurable specifications. These performance requirements (or performance criteria) have all of the characteristics of an objective. They state what result is to be achieved and the criteria for measurement. Performance requirements are listed for each function, and a number—the same as the function for which the criteria pertain—is assigned to each requirement. There might be several pages of performance requirements.

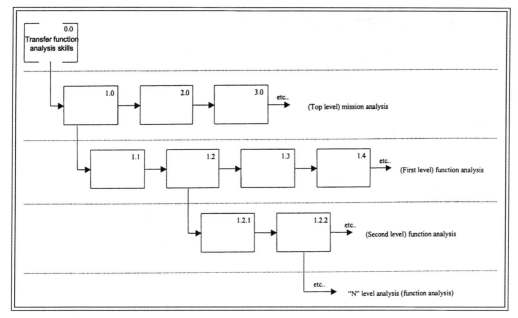

Figure 6.12. The numbering for the function analysis part of mission analysis. In function analysis, each function block would contain the statement of the function and the appropriate reference number. Since the overall in performance terms function is the mission objective, it is labeled 0.0 in a flow diagram.

A performance requirement table may be used. Table 6.6 provides one format.

When Is Enough Enough? Going
Only as Far as You Have To

Function analysis continues to break down the functions necessary to perform higher-level functions to lower and lower levels until there are several "layers" to the function analysis. The process continues until you are confident that functions are defined clearly, precisely, and comprehensively to ensure getting the required results and any further breakdown requires the identifying of processes, or means.

A planner continues a system analysis only to the extent required to answer basic questions. If the analysis relates to strategic planning, then it may suffice to identify the mission objective, mission profile, and their performance requirements. If a planner wants to determine specific product design objectives—Micro-level concerns—it may be necessary to carry the function analysis through two, three, or more levels. While it might be tempting to stop the breakdown analysis after one or two levels, resist the temptation. Taking the analysis down to finer and finer levels will assure you that all parts of the system will be identified in results terms. All of the parts and their relationships are vital, so have patience and persistence.

Functions are products, not processes or means. When a planner first performs a function analysis, it is tempting (because we are trained to be "doers," not planners) to list the means for

TABLE 6.6 A Sample Performance Requirements Table

Page no. 1

FUNCTION (OR TASK) NUMBER	PERFORMANCE REQUIREMENTS
0.0	XXXXXXXXXXXXXXXXXX
0.0a	XXXXXXXXXXXXXXXXXXXXXXX
N.0	Same as 2.0 plus XXXXXX

Page no. 2

FUNCTION (OR TASK) NUMBER	PERFORMANCE REQUIREMENTS
1.0	XXXXXXXXXXXXXXXXXX
2.0	XXXXXXXXXXXXXXXXXXXXXXX
N.0	Same as 2.0 plus XXXXXX

Page no. 3

FUNCTION (OR TASK) NUMBER	PERFORMANCE REQUIREMENTS
N.1	XXXXXXXXXXXXXXXXXX
	Same as n.1.2
N.2	XXXXXXXXXXXXXXXXXXXXXXX
N.N	Same as 0.0a plus XXXXXXXXXXX

performing the function instead of first showing the end product or result. Throughout an analysis, when you find solutions "creeping in," ask yourself, "What is it that this method or means will give me when I am through?" Or, "Why do I want to use that particular method or approach?" Or, "Will accomplishment of this move us closer to the Ideal Vision?" By asking such questions, you will be able to determine the product that you require and avoid locking yourself into a less-than-optimal process or solution.

A critical reason for performing a system analysis in general and a function analysis in particular is to free ourselves to identify and consider new, responsive, responsible, and better ways of doing things, not simply repeat what has helped us in the past. Remember to apply Critical Success Factor 1.

Every level of system analysis is related to every other level. The process of system analysis starts with the statement of the Ideal Vision and then the assessment of needs—the identification of the gaps in results between what is and what is required. What is required is the core of the primary mission objective (and the longer- and shorter-term missions) and the bridge between needs assessment and mission analysis (Figure 6.13).

Recall that the mission analysis identifies the mission objective (including the performance requirements) and the mission profile and interrelates the levels of analysis in a logical, internally consistent manner. The mission profile—the top level of function analysis—thus bridges, or links, mission analysis and function analysis, as shown in Figure 6.13.

Function analysis continues until all the functions have been identified for all the top-level (mission profile) functions. This tells what must be accomplished and delivered to achieve each top-level function.

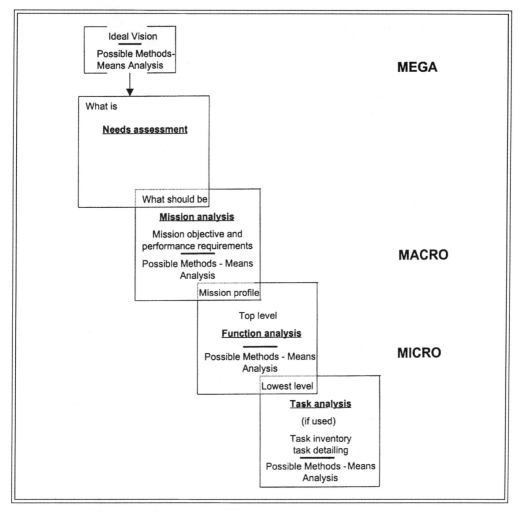

Figure 6.13. The building up and interrelationships among the various phases of a system analysis.[29]

All the functions and subfunctions are identified until vertical expansion of the mission profile is complete. Then all the functions describing *what* has to be accomplished to meet the mission objective and its performance requirements are specified.

Each time a function is identified, performance requirements for it must be specified. That is, one must identify in precise, measurable terms what must be delivered in order to accomplish a given function. This performance requirement identification for each function resembles that which is accomplished in identifying the performance requirements for the mission, except that it occurs at each lowest-level function. Preparing a function is similar to preparing a mission objective, only at a more narrowly defined level: It states both the product to be delivered and the specifications for determining the quality of the product, as if we are to do acceptance testing.

There is a continuous process of determining *what* must be accomplished, as well as the criteria for accomplishment and the kinds of lower-order Products that make up the function.

Remember, the differences among analyses at the various levels are a matter of degree rather than kind; there really is no difference in approach or tools used for a mission analysis, including the mission profile and the function analysis of any one of its functions. That is, the process is exactly the same, only the actual levels of functions differ. Miniature or subordinate "missions" are identified each time a function is "broken out." Performance requirements must be set for each function even if it is the very first one—performance requirements of the mission—or the very last one that can be broken out.

In function analysis, as in mission analysis, a planner's job is to identify the major milestones for completing a function and to know when a function has been successfully performed or delivered.

Function Analysis and Feasibility

A Preview of Methods-Means Analysis

Each time a function (or a family of functions) and its performance requirements are identified, it is time to check to see if one or more reasonable methods-means or "how-to-do-its" exist for achieving those requirements. It is necessary to keep checking back through previous functions and requirements to the needs statement and the Ideal Vision to conform that the "whats" (functions) are both internally consistent and externally valid and useful. All the functions must be compatible with one another as well as the need and the selected problem.

If there is one or more possible methods-means (there should be), we may continue the function analysis to the next level. However, if there is not at least one possible methods-means, we have a *constraint* that must be reconciled before going on to the next level.

For a planner who wants to advise on specific projects, curriculum, or course content, programs, or the design and development of interventions, task analysis is necessary.

▓ Task Analysis: An Option

Task analysis is (depending on your purposes) the lowest level of a system analysis; it is derived from a mission analysis and the related function analysis.[30] It yields the most discrete level of detail required to identify all the "whats" (but not "hows") for problem resolution. Tasks are products at the lowest level of results.

Task analysis can consist of two parts: (1) the identification and ordering of the steps to be taken (task inventory) and (2) the description of the salient characteristics and requirements of successful job and/or task accomplishment (detailed task analysis, or task description). Together, they reveal the units of performance and performance requirements for each task. Frequently, the task listing, along with its performance requirements, will give you all the information necessary.

By and large, task description charts are prepared for task analysis. Many and varied task analysis formats may be used, and selection depends on the required results of the analysis. Such formats vary from a basic and simple one, which utilizes four columns—(1) task number, (2) steps in performing the task, (3) type of performance, and (4) task difficulty—to other quite complex machine interaction formats used in the aerospace field, which might include detailed physiological and psychological considerations and relationships.

The steps for performing such a task analysis description are as follows:

Step 1. List all the tasks and subtasks necessary to accomplish the function being analyzed. This is the same derivation process employed in the breakout of the mission profile and the function analysis. The tasks identified are placed in sequence in the order in which they will occur. In identifying the tasks, we want to make them independent, so there will be no (or minimal) overlap. This is the *task listing* process.

Step 2. List, by tasks, the stimulus requirements (if relevant). These are the "input" requirements, the data required by the "operator" (or "doer" of the task when it is assigned) to perform the tasks. State what form the data must be in to be usable.

Step 3. List the response requirements (the action requirements). These are the operations, the number of times each will occur, and the time necessary to perform the operation if time is a real consideration.

Step 4. By task, list the support requirements. These are the kinds of materials and equipment necessary to support the operation of the task and the types of personnel or equipment required as "operators."

Step 5. List the performance criteria. Here is the specification of the product of the task. Just as a mission will produce a product, and a function will produce a product, so will the task produce a product: a performance result. The performance requirements of the product of the task may be such items as these: (1) no errors, (2) list contains all items, (3) copy is clear and readable by persons without eye corrections, and (4) the form has adequate space for teacher notations—all as certified by the project manager (or other valid performance assessment).

Step 6. Specify the prerequisite knowledge and/or skills the operator must have to perform a given task. If, for example, in the preparation of a proposal there is a necessity for a high skill level of artwork, then advanced art capability may be a critical requirement and as such is a prerequisite that must be noted.

As a matter of practice, the lowest-level subfunction that is being analyzed at the task level is always identified by the function number from which it derives. This function number (e.g., 3.1.5) is usually placed in the upper left-hand corner of the task analysis form. Failure to identify the function being analyzed will confuse just about everyone.

TABLE 6.7 Starting Places for the Phases of System Analysis

Starting System Analysis Phase	Assumed or On-Hand Data Analysis Phase
Mission analysis	Ideal Vision-related needs
Function analysis	Ideal Vision- and primary mission objective-related needs (and performance requirements)
Task analysis	Ideal Vision-related needs
	Primary and longer- and shorter-term mission objectives (and performance requirements)
	Functions (and performance requirements)

The task analysis format selected by the planners should be only as complex as is necessary to supply the data required in the planning process itself. The important thing to remember and include in the task description is that it must specify all requirements for accomplishing the task. Remember that the purpose of performing a system analysis is to identify the requirements for the accomplishment of a given mission. The system analysis process indicates all the parts and the relations between the parts for accomplishing a given mission. Table 6.7 identifies the starting places for the phases of system analysis.

Summary

A SWOT analysis is done to identify the strengths, weaknesses, opportunities, and threats both internal and external to the organization. In a sense, it becomes an organizational barometer by indicating environmental factors beneficial in determining future strategies and tactics toward accomplishing the Ideal Vision.

Once completed, enroute objectives are identified. They are the stepping-stones or results markers as the organization moves toward the Ideal Vision and the primary mission objective. The tools for determining the requirements for getting from where we are to where we should be are termed mission and function analysis. Likened to multiple lenses on a microscope, the mission analysis provides a broader overview, whereas the function analysis magnifies each smaller piece within the overall problem.

All of these pieces are nested, interrelated parts of what is called a system analysis. This analysis depends on priority needs having been identified and selected. It is results oriented—identifying the functions necessary to be completed to meet the needs.

Once the priority functions have been identified within the mission, each function is logically sequenced and becomes a performance map, or management plan. Such a management plan is called a mission profile and only delineates what is to be accomplished. It does not define how the functions will be accomplished.

TABLE 6.8 Questions to Be Asked and Answered in a Mega-Level System Analysis and Steps for Each

Question	Step
Where should we be headed, and why?	Determine Ideal Vision and related needs assessment data
Where is the organization headed, and how do we know when we have arrived?	Determine primary mission objective and associated performance requirements
What are the things that will keep us from where we are headed, and how do we eliminate them?	Determine and reconcile constraints
What are the major milestones—functions— along the way to where we are headed?	Determine long- and short-term mission objectives and their performance requirements Determine mission profile
What are the building-block results that must be completed to accomplish each milestone?	Perform function analysis
What are the possible ways and means for getting the building-block results accomplished?	Perform methods-means analysis

A function analysis builds upon this graphic picture. It further, or more closely, identifies steps (results) to be accomplished within each priority function that link together forming the mission. Task analysis yields the most discrete level of detail required to identify all the "whats" for problem resolution.

System analysis reveals, in layers, the subsystems involved in mission accomplishment. These include the performance requirements for each task or task element in order to provide the detailed information and criteria that would further assure the most relevant and practical possibilities (methods and means) for accomplishing the function being task-analyzed. The results of a task analysis are useful in system design and development, especially having a direct input into learning specifications, perhaps which is determined from a learning task analysis (that is quite different from a job task analysis) as well as to techniques for management and continuous improvement.

Table 6.8 provides a summary set of questions to be answered in a Mega Planning system analysis and the steps for each.

Notes

1. Daryl Conner (1998) has provided a very clear and useful set of "changes" that organizations can or may employ. This "bolt-on change" is his phrase.

2. Data are just facts that, by themselves, are not useful. Information is data useful for making decisions.

3. In a strategic thinking and planning session with the Australian Bureau of Statistics, professional associates were surprised (and mostly pleased) to find out they had data for virtually each of the aspects and items noted in the Ideal Vision (provided in Chapter 4). For some reason, many people are quite willing to assume that data do not exist for Mega Planning, but the reality is that much are available.

4. Florida TaxWatch in Tallahassee has earned an outstanding reputation for conducting and providing data-based reports on the operations and impact of state agencies. Many states have such operations with accessible information.

5. I realize that this is not the strict definition that has been popularized by others. However, it is offered in an attempt to define a learning organization in terms of results and consequences rather than on processes alone.

6. An organization will select what portion of the Ideal Vision it commits to contribute and move ever closer toward.

7. Best on an interval or ratio scale of measurement.

8. Kaufman, Watkins, Triner, and Stith (1998) researched what organizations called their purpose statements and how precise and rigorous they were. None met the criteria suggested in this book for an objective, although there seems to be a migration of purpose statements in the past few years toward Mega.

9. This is actually a plan that people in the organization use to decide what to do or accomplish. It determines or presents the Mega plan.

10. Chapter 4 provides the concepts and tools for this.

11. A needs assessment at the Macro level provides the gaps in results between current and required results for which these functions in the mission profile, when done in appropriate order, will close those gaps. Chapter 4 provides the concepts and process for doing a Macro-level needs assessment.

12. As at each level of planning (Mega, Macro, and Micro), a needs assessment at this Micro level provides the needs to be closed. Chapter 3 provides the concepts and process for doing a Micro-level needs assessment.

13. The term "deep change" was first offered by Kaufman and English (1979). The perils of cosmetic or superficial change are explored extensively by Conner (1992, 1998).

14. Thus, it has a Mega focus and is what is intended to be created through Mega Planning.

15. The general process of "problem solving" also includes the element of "problem identification" and "opportunity finding" as well. Thus, the process, using the six-step process model provided in this book, can be both proactive and reactive.

16. The needs assessment and its linkage to Mega also answers the question of not only "Where are we are headed?" but "Why do we want to get there?"

17. Mintzberg (1994) offers a convincing critique of conventional "strategic planning." Unfortunately, he is correct about conventional varieties that are linear, narrow, and rigid. I contend that his objectives do not hold for Mega Planning.

18. There are important differences between problems and opportunities. Sometimes they are compatible, and sometimes they are different. Problems are "needs selected for elimination or reduction." "Opportunities" are results that would be valuable to deliver. To simplify the discussion, however, I use the term "problem" to mean "problems and/or opportunities."

19. Best on an interval or ratio scale of measurement.

20. This is not a deficiency analysis; too much of something as well as too little might cause a gap in results.

21. In performing a mission (and function) analysis, the planner may, if desired, reverse this top-down, front-to-back process and move from the end to the beginning. In this "back-to-front mode," the mission objective defines the end; it states where you will be when you have accomplished the mission, and this becomes a known. Then the analyst begins with the known and works backward until arriving at the beginning, all the time with a results (not means) orientation.

22. Based on Kaufman (1992d, 1998b) and Kaufman, Herman, and Watters (1996).

23. Based on Kaufman (1992d).

24. In popular language, "function" is often (inappropriately) used to indicate a process. I use it precisely as a result, as do system engineers.

25. Based on Kaufman (1992d) cited earlier.

26. Notably Ryan Watkins of Nova Southeastern University and Doug Leigh of the Office for Needs Assessment & Planning at Florida State University, who constantly harangue me about this option. If you prefer it, use it.

27. Based on Kaufman (1992d).

28. The entire area of performance improvement, or my preferred term "performance accomplishment," is vital for making a Mega plan deliver what is required effectively and efficiently. This is discussed later in Chapter 7.

29. From Kaufman, Herman, and Watters (1996).

30. A task analysis might be useful as a system planning tool if the level of detail requires that you identify very low levels of results—tasks—required to meet the needs. I have dealt extensively with this topic in Kaufman (1992d) and Kaufman, Herman, and Watters (1996). Task analysis is a common topic in the literature (cf. Kaufman, Thiagarajan, & MacGillis, 1997). Other useful references for task analysis include Jackson (1986) and Zemke and Kramlinger (1982). The military services have done extensive work in task analysis, including Branson et al. (1975).

CHAPTER 7

Tactical Planning

From the Mega Plan to Designing and Developing Success

As part of the Implementation and Continuous Improvement phase, one must transition from planning to doing. A key portal is tactical planning that includes the five steps shown in Figure 7.1.

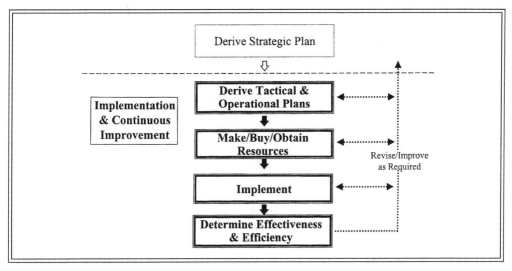

Figure 7.1. The Implementation and Continuous Improvement cluster of Mega Planning.

This chapter deals with deriving the tactical plan:

- Finding out what is available to get from what is to what should be (for results)
- Prerequisites for methods-means analysis
- When methods-means analysis begins
- Locating valid methods-means information
- Matching methods and means to each function (and task)
- Compiling and storing the methods-means data
- Procedure for performing a methods-means analysis
- From system to systems analysis
- Approaches to systems analysis
- Selecting the methods and means

▩ Finding Out What Is Available

Reviewing system analysis, like all of Mega Planning, is a dynamic process. It identifies where to head and defines the requirements for getting there. By applying the six-step problem-solving process, it invites revision at any time; thus it is not a rigid and inflexible process but, rather, an active, holistic tool. A system analysis has several phases, or levels.

Mission Analysis

Based on the Ideal Vision, the primary mission is derived. The primary mission states where the organization is headed and how to measure when it has arrived and how to calibrate its continuous improvement toward that destination. The mission analysis builds on the mission and determines

- where is the organization headed as stated by the mission objectives?[1]
- the mission profile that identifies the building-block results—functions—required to get from current results and consequences to desired and required ones.
- a function analysis that breaks down each function in the mission profile into its constituent component functions (and their performance requirements).
- if done, a task analysis that identifies the lowest level of results required to accomplish each function identified in the function analysis.
- a methods-means analysis that identifies possible ways and means to meet the requirements identified in the earlier system analysis steps and lists the advantages and disadvantages of each (without selecting them).

The overall components and the flow of a system analysis is shown in Figure 7.2.

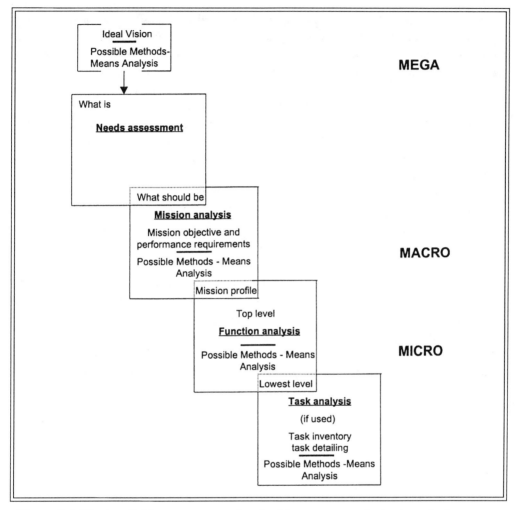

Figure 7.2. The interlinking components involved in a system analysis. A methods-means analysis may be done at any or all levels.

The bridge between planning and doing is the methods-means analysis. It is the system analysis step that allows you to

- determine if there are any ways and means to get the mission and functions, defined by the associated performance requirements, accomplished.
- do a feasibility study, which will reveal when there is no possible way of getting where you have to go based on the performance requirements obtained from the "what should be" part of the identified needs.
- identify the advantages and disadvantages of each of the possible methods and means.

The identification of ways and means for getting required results is based on the previous system analysis data. Mission and function analyses (and task analysis) are used to identify and justify the products to be completed in order to reach a mission objective. Once required products have been identified, it is time to find out whether there are one or more methods and means (solutions, tactics, or processes) to achieve each product or group of products. You want to know not only what to accomplish but also the feasible ways and means to deliver the necessary results. To make the best selection of ways and means for each function, the planning partners compile a list of possible solutions[2] and the advantages and disadvantages of each. This inventory serves as a data bank for later selection and design, development, and application when selected. The process by which the data bank is produced is called **methods-means analysis.**

Before we choose how to meet our mission objectives (and accomplish all of the related functions as we move ever closer toward the Ideal Vision), we build a data bank of the possible techniques and tools (methods and means) for achieving them. A methods-means analysis lets us know if there are any tactics and tools (or ways and means) available to meet our performance requirements.

As part of this analysis, we also identify the advantages and disadvantages of each option. Methods-means analysis not only identifies what methods and means are available but also provides a feasibility study so that we don't try to move ahead if we can't get from here to there.[3] Methods-means analysis identifies what "how-to-do-its" are available to meet our objectives. When doing a methods-means analysis, we do not select how the performance requirements will be met; it only *identifies* the possible ways and means for getting them done. This analysis compiles the necessary data and criteria for actually later selecting how we will do the jobs.

▨ Prerequisites for Methods-Means Analysis

Before starting a methods-means analysis, you should have the following on hand:

- Mission objectives, including related performance requirements, based on the Ideal Vision and the primary mission objective
- Mission profile
- Functions and their performance requirements
- Tasks and their performance requirements (if you have chosen to do a task analysis)

With this system analysis data, you are now ready to

- identify possible ways and means to accomplish each function and task.
- identify advantages and disadvantages of each possible methods and means available to get the job done—meet the performance requirements.
- identify constraints and eliminate them, if possible.

Constraints: Is the Mission, Function, or Task Feasible?

Any plan uncovers obstacles (weaknesses, threats, or constraints). A constraint is anything that will keep you from meeting one or more performance requirements. These are identified in a methods-means analysis. A constraint, although we don't usually welcome it, is a "friend in disguise" because it provides an early warning about obstacles we will likely encounter.

Because they identify possible blockages on our path to success, it is useful to view them as actually being performance requirements. When viewed as a type of performance requirement, they provide criteria for the characteristics or conditions under which the mission (or any other lower-level performance requirement) must be completed. If, for instance, it is given that "no additional funds may be spent," this "obstacle" becomes one of the ground rules: a requirement. Even if a performance requirement is analyzed to be unachievable (a constraint exists), the troublesome requirement must be specified and we have to try to meet it before quitting or changing the mission (or function).

Thus, a constraint arises when it seems that a mission objective, a performance requirement, or a set of performance requirements is not achievable:

A constraint is a condition that makes it impossible to meet one or more performance requirement.

When a constraint appears, planners must select from among several options. The choices include these: (1) Change the objective and/or its performance requirements (and risk not meeting the needs); (2) be creative and develop a new methods-means or combine two or more methods-means that alone would not get the job done; or (if the first two don't work) (3) stop, because it does not make sense to proceed in an attempt to resolve a problem if you now know that the effort will fail. Once a constraint has been identified, we know then that moving on blindly without change will present an unacceptable risk.

If a performance requirement can be met by one or a combination of methods-means, the system analysis continues. If not, then you have a constraint that must be reconciled before you continue.

▓ When Does Methods-Means Analysis Begin?

A methods-means analysis can begin whenever you choose. It can be done each time a function and its requirements, including the Ideal Vision, is identified, or it can be delayed until all the mission, function, and task analyses are complete. At the planners' option, methods-means analysis may be done at any stage of the system analysis process.

Experienced planners often prefer to start the methods-means analysis as soon as the Ideal Vision and/or the primary mission objective and its performance requirements have been identified. As the system analysis continues, the methods-means analysis portion may be done in parallel with each step, with continuous checking to make sure that it is probable that the mission can be accomplished. Thus, continually identifying possible "hows" and the relative advantages

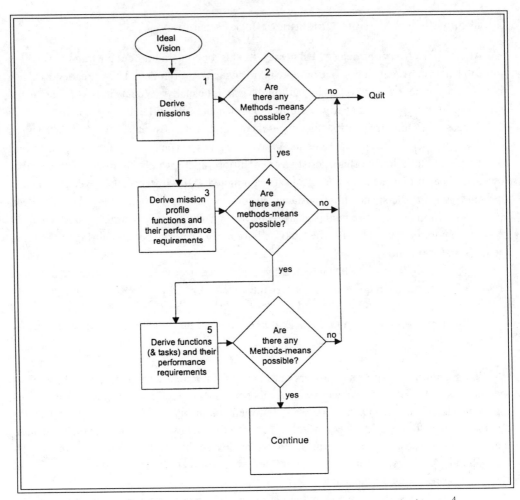

Figure 7.3. A methods-means analysis may be used at each system analysis step.[4]

and disadvantages of each means that an ongoing feasibility study is being conducted, as shown in Figure 7.3.

If there are no possible methods-means (or tactics and tools), STOP! If you cannot get there from here, why push on? If there are some possible ways and means, then go ahead with the assurance, at least at the point in your analysis, that what you want to accomplish is feasible.

For less-experienced planners, choosing to conduct the methods-means analysis after all the functions and tasks have been identified and the performance requirements for each have been determined and listed can be more comfortable:

1. There is less distraction from the process of identifying what is to be accomplished.
2. It avoids the all-too-common temptation to "cheat" the process by prematurely selecting the "how." To avoid this risk, or to avoid the problem of possibly mixing "whats" and

"hows," the methods-means analysis may be delayed until all functions and tasks and performance requirements have been identified.

3. As part of a larger system, each function and its associate methods-means have impact on one another. In the methods-means analysis, a constraint may arise that may have implications for other functions.

However, waiting to do the methods-means analysis until the last part of the system analysis also carries with it considerable risks:

1. You may unintentionally have prematurely let methods-means slip into the objectives.
2. You miss an earlier constraint that had to be reconciled before moving further.

A methods-means analysis provides an ongoing feasibility check. Because of the relative advantages and disadvantages, it is recommended that you conduct parallel methods-means analyses, as shown in Figure 7.4. The figure shows the progression of the overall system analysis (1 to 2 to 3 to 4) and the possible starting places for methods-means analysis (A, B, or C).

Locating Valid Methods-Means Information

Methods-means information is found in many, sometimes unsuspected, places. If you are concerned about the methods and means of successful human resources development, tactical planning, finance, investment, and/or instruction, several texts and journals discuss means at great length and in great detail. If you are interested in other areas, such as facilities construction and management of work incentives or engineering methods and resources, you can consult specialists, vendors, texts, and articles in those fields. Libraries and document search services are good sources for methods-means information. There is much available.

This step of the identification of appropriate tools and tactics is the chance to "brainstorm" and be creative. Here we are not fettered by "the way it's always been done," and thus can explore ideas that might seem extreme, so as to determine if a vehicle and/or a tactic might work to meet the performance requirements. Another piece of good advice from Joel Barker is that you find fascinating new paradigm possibilities by looking outside your discipline or area.[5]

When you have completed your data search, list all the possible methods-means for each requirement and also list the advantages and disadvantages of each. Each performance requirement should be matched with possible methods-means; each and every requirement must be met. Often, performance requirements that are related can be pooled into "families," or clusters.

Compiling and Recording the Methods-Means Data

In a function flow block, diagram each function number: 0.0 for the mission, 1.0 for the first function in the mission profile, 1.1 for a function derived from block 1.0, and so on derived in the

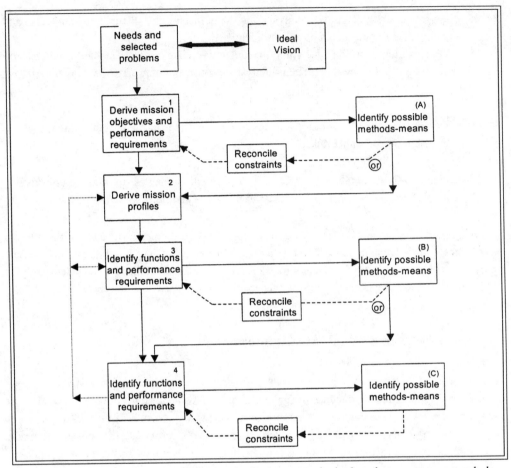

Figure 7.4. An algorithm (job aid) for methods-means analysis that shows a recommended downward progression.[6]

earlier system analysis. These functions and their requirements are used in the methods-means analysis.

Record the function flow block diagram number for each function and list the performance requirements for each function on a methods-means form (Table 7.1). Give each performance requirement a letter (e.g., 1.1A, 1.1B, 3.1A). For each alphanumerically identified performance requirement, list the methods and means that could be used to meet the requirement.

These data are entered for each function and performance requirement (or clusters of performance requirements) as the analysis continues. Recording these data provides a summary of possible methods and means combinations for each function performance requirement (or performance requirement family).

After completing the system analysis, identifying performance requirements at each level, and identifying possible methods-means possibilities for each function, prepare a methods-means summary to use during the design, development, and implementation phases.

TABLE 7.1 Methods-Means Identification Summary Form

Performance Requirement (number)	Current Results	Desired/Re-quired Results	Possible Methods-Means	Advantages (from costs-consequences analysis)	Disadvantages (from costs-consequences analysis)

Procedure for Performing a Methods-Means Analysis

To perform a methods-means analysis, use the following steps:

1. On a methods-means identification form, like the one shown in Table 7.1, record the function number of the function with which you are dealing.
2. Under the "Performance Requirement" column, list the performance requirements that any methods-means combination must meet. Label these requirements alphanumerically to identify them with their appropriate functions.
3. Under the "Possible Methods-Means" column, list any methods-means combination meeting the requirements in the previous list. Number these to match the requirements list. You should have at least two methods-means possibilities for each performance requirement. This encourages you and your planning partners to consider all the possibilities, not just those that have been used before.
4. List the advantages for each methods-means possibility, such as availability, cost, time, reliability, transportability, and ease of use. (Costs-consequences analysis, a tool for estimating return on investment, is presented later in this chapter.)
5. List the disadvantages for each methods-means combination, such as cost, time, or policy law changes.
6. After completing the methods-means analysis for each function, summarize and integrate them into functional families as they relate to top-level (mission profile) functions or as they might relate with other functions from different top-level functions.

Requirements for Methods-Means Analysis

The formality of this process encourages you to be bold, innovative, and creative. Indeed, innovation and creativity are encouraged by a system analysis in general and a methods-means analysis in particular. The methods-means analysis answers the question "What 'how-to-do-its' are possible, and what are the advantages and disadvantages for each?"

When you have completed the lowest level of function (or task analysis) and the final methods-means analysis, there are two products:

- A database and listing of feasible "whats" for problem resolution
- A database and listing of possible "hows" and the advantages and disadvantages for each.

From System to Systems Analysis

The next step after selecting the methods and means is to transition from planning to acquiring the methods-means to implementation.[7] Oddly, this is exactly the point at which most people start their work because they believe they already know the needs and problems and only have to get a solution in operation! Too many planners jump from unwarranted assumptions to foregone conclusions.

Systems analysis is not the same as system analysis. Both are very useful. Fortunately, there are many books and articles on systems analysis that show how to choose methods, solutions, and interventions. There are several different (and often confusing) labels for this process but a convenient one is *systems analysis.*. This is not the same as system analysis.

System analysis focuses on finding out *what* to accomplish, whereas **systems analysis** focuses on *procedures* for selecting the most effective and efficient ways and means. Systems analysis draws upon the products of system analysis, as shown in Table 7.2:

All too often, planners choose methods, means, tools, techniques, interventions, and solutions on the basis of biases, past experience, conventional wisdom ("Everyone else does it that way . . .") comfort, the "hot topic at the recent convention," and/or instinct. Unfortunately, the likelihood is that the quick-fix-of-the-week or the most "mainstream"[8] solution will be picked. It does not have to be that way. You are better off using the appropriate tools and doing the job right the first time. Investing time in both system and systems analysis is wise.

Methods and procedures for rationally choosing among alternative methods and means have been available for many years. These include (but are not limited to) such systems-analysis methods as operations research; planning, programming, budgeting system (PPBS); simulation and gaming; queuing; relevance trees; decision theory; strategic market planning; portfolio analysis; market attractiveness assessment; operational gaming; Delphi technique; nominal group technique; polling; and cross-impact analysis. Also now available is costs-consequences analysis that provides a coarse-grain estimate of return-on-investment.[9] Discussion of such methods occurs later in this chapter.

TABLE 7.2 Comparison of System and Systems Analysis

Tool	Focus
System analysis	Identifies and justifies what should be accomplished based on an Ideal Vision— Results focused
Systems analysis	Identifies the most effective and efficient ways and means to get the required results—Solutions and tactics focused

Following are brief summaries of some of the most straightforward tools and techniques. When you attempt to select methods and means, these will be useful.

Approaches to Systems Analysis

Systems analysis is a way to choose the most effective and efficient solution, or intervention, from alternative possibilities:[10]

1. The systematic examination and comparison of the alternative actions related to the accomplishment of desired objectives
2. The comparison of alternatives on the basis of the resource cost and the benefit associated with each alternative
3. The explicit consideration of uncertainty

Systems analysis is useful once you have identified objectives and requirements (ideally based on needs related to the primary mission objective and Ideal Vision) and when you are ready to define and appraise possible optional methods and means. Systems analysis is best used after you have finished the phases of system analysis: mission, function, (task), and methods-means analysis.

Systems analysis is the generic name for selecting solution strategies/tactics from among alternative possibilities. Following are some systems analysis tools, divided into two general groups: (1) those oriented primarily to numbers and facts and (2) those oriented primarily to people and judgments.

Techniques Oriented Primarily to Numbers and Facts

Operations Research

When we know our purposes, objectives, missions, and requirements, **operations research** can be useful. This approach seeks to find optimum solutions to specific problems where relationships among the variables are known and evaluation criteria are tangible. One representative definition of operations research is

> a method of obtaining optimum solutions to problems in which relationships are specified and criteria for evaluating effectiveness are known. Operations research summarizes alternatives into mathematical expressions and models. It then identifies the set of alternatives that maximizes or minimizes the desired criterion for evaluating effectiveness.[11]

After completing a needs assessment as a part of the system analysis, planners can use operations research to choose the methods-means that will most effectively and efficiently meet requirements.

Planning, Programming, Budgeting System (PPBS)

Most authors agree that PPBS is best used for identifying the alternative courses of action intended to meet the objectives of an organization, project, activity, or intervention and ranking the alternatives (sometimes called *systems*) in terms of their respective costs and benefits. This allows planners to choose among the alternatives on a rational basis and to derive a budget based on the cost of achieving objectives.

Although it makes sense to base the budget on what is planned, the budget is sometimes made up before the planning has been accomplished.[12] After the budget is set, organization members often scurry around to find out what they might do with the dollars they have been allocated. Too often, budgeting systems seem to be more important than planning; this is a serious and usually fatal flaw. The usefulness of PPBS depends on the validity of the original objectives chosen.

Performance-based budgeting. Most states and the U.S. federal government are increasingly interested in relating budget to performance gains. In the Government Performance and Results Act (GPRA),[13] agencies are required to justify everything they use, do, produce, and deliver to an estimate of value added.[14]

Simulation and Gaming

Simulation is a part of everyday life. We "anticipate" future events such as a request for new responsibilities and try out various approaches in our heads. If there is to be an important briefing, we rehearse the presentation and try out—simulate—responses in order to shape our final offering. Whenever we set up a representation of the world and try out something before the fact, we are simulating.

Simulation builds and tries out a model of a predicted or actual event or situation. Simulations range from making a mock-up of a helicopter or a dummy multimedia training room to see how it will work, to holding a dress rehearsal of a play, to running complex, multivariate mathematical models of highway traffic using a computer.

Queuing

Queuing uses a mathematical method to optimize waiting time in a crowding situation (such as customers waiting for fast food, standing in line for refunds, applying for a building permit, or scheduling a concert). Frustration, time expended, and cost are the variables most often studied.

Relevance Trees

Relevance trees[15] are used to identify hierarchies of various levels of complexity of events. Consider the manufacture of an intricate product such as a computer system, where successively lower levels of a complex process emerge like the branches of a tree from a common trunk, each more detailed and/or distinctive. By breaking down a series of sequential components of a system into the processes, tasks, activities, jobs, or actions where problems and/or opportunities might occur, planners can identify the associated difficulties and distinguish the best pathways or alternatives.

Decision Theory

Decision theory[16] determines optimum strategies (or tactics) for reaching a specific goal based on probabilities for alternative pathways and methods. Probabilities are assigned to each option, and the options are examined as branching possibilities (as in relevance trees) and alternative anticipated consequences. Points where decisions are to be made (or the operation of chance) could determine consequences are also included. This approach allows the identification of alternative branch pathways by computing the probabilities of reaching the goal through each action/option.

Market Planning

Many "strategic planning" approaches have evolved that provide ways to choose among alternative market plans.[17] **Market planning** views a business as a system in which different parts (including possible product lines) interact and each can contribute to or detract from corporate health. Various techniques for selecting mixes of businesses (or Products and Outputs) have been offered. One tool, **portfolio analysis**, appraises an organization's products and their differential strengths (plotted as circles of various sizes) relative to the two dimensions of proportion of market share and sales growth rate. From such an assessment, planners can consider differential expansion, reduction, change, and divestment.

A related tool[18] is **market attractiveness-business position assessment**. This technique uses a two-dimensional matrix (market attractiveness and business position) in which an organization's market size is graphically depicted. By examining present and future market possibilities, planners can simulate alternative change strategies in terms of return-on-investment payoffs and penalties.

Most marketing approaches focus on indicators such as market share and/or quarterly profits; an organization-as-primary-client-and-beneficiary orientation. As an alternative, a Mega-
level marketing model offers an approach that places the external clients and society as the primary target and then includes a concern for Macro—organizational—payoffs.[19]

Techniques Oriented Primarily to People and Judgment

Operational Gaming

A variation on simulation and model building is **operational gaming**. Here, people play
such roles as customers or opponents in a political debate in specific situations. For instance,
suppose we faced a court appearance in a lawsuit over our liability due to alleged poor training of
technicians in a nuclear plant. We might set up a "game" in which people played the different
roles of judge, jury members, opposition attorney, witnesses, and spectators. The mock trial will
help us determine what could happen in the courtroom.

Gaming, as well as simulation, can be used during implementation. An executive, manager,
or planning team can stage a simulation or game before moving to the next phase of operations to
test whether it will deliver desired results. If the simulation indicates some possible surprises,
planners have the opportunity to change the approach.

Games. Serious games can be created to get people to understand the relatively complex
variables and relationships. Such games vary from board games to structured discussions.[20]

Game theory has "players" with opposite interests, who are equally knowledgeable and informed and have a known number of options, who are asked to complete their task in a limited
time frame.[21] Game motivations are payoffs (not necessarily monetary), differing value sets, and
a desire to correctly predict the best course of action. Both operational gaming and game theory
attempt to simulate actual, real-world happenings before the fact.

Delphi Technique

The **Delphi technique** stimulates group responses and achieves consensus without getting
the groups together face-to-face. It uses the opinions of expert panelists in a round of questions
targeted to future events and consequences. For each question (e.g., "When will all countries
work toward the progressive documented elimination of environmental pollution?" "When will
AIDS be controlled?"), the respondents provide their expectations. After each set of responses,
the manager reports the median response and the ranges of responses (usually the center 50%)
along with, when appropriate, comments made by the panelists.

By the end of several rounds (usually three or four are sufficient), responses are clustered
into groups that reflect the built-up and integrated considerations of the panelists as they replay
both individually and with knowledge of the responses of other panelists.

Nominal Group Technique

This is a structured problem-resolving process[22] staged to generate ideas and produce group consensus. The **nominal group technique** encourages the participation of everyone in the group, focuses concentration on a specific question, and reaches consensus through voting.

Usually the leader clarifies objectives, illustrates what is desired in terms of response scope and concreteness, prepares the room and environment to encourage participation, and begins. Participants are asked to generate ideas in writing and then share them with the group. Without responding to requests for clarification (so as to not get bogged down in detail), the leader simplifies these inputs in brief phrases or statements. Nominal group protocol provides adequate time for thinking, avoids interrupting others, reduces premature focusing on a single idea or solution, eliminates aggressiveness, and prevents "bosses" from dominating.

Next, there is a round-robin translation of ideas in order to cluster the group's thinking. Each idea is considered, in turn, by each group member, and duplicates are eliminated. Discussion is discouraged until the end of the process. When the process is completed, the group will have reached a consensus of judgments. One potential problem that may arise from using this technique is that "outlying" positions are eliminated by "vote" even though they might be correct.

Polling

Polling entails questioning representative members of a group about their preferences or predications. Sampling methods are crucial. It is important that respondents represent at least a stratified random sample of the group to which the results are to be generalized.

Agreement is not validity. One danger in using consensus-building approaches lies in forcing agreement among participants by leveling responses toward an agreed-on central position. The risk is that the group might not be correct, and an outlying (out-of-the-mainstream) viewpoint that might not be correct will be eliminated because it is not popular or goes against the conventional wisdom.

Cross-Impact Analysis

Our world is not linear. Events happen together—as parts of a system—rather than in isolation from other events. Prediction would be easier if things happened in isolation, but we have to choose alternatives on the basis of the whole, not just a part. **Cross-impact analysis** tries to account for potential interaction effects. In cross-impact analysis, each event is assigned a probability of occurrence and a time frame for likely occurrence. Prior incidents (experience) are used to "guesstimate" the probability of future events happening or not happening. For example, scientific knowledge increases but so does the influence of fundamentalist religious values; pressures against nuclear power increases while the concern over the greenhouse effect demands lower use of fossil fuels; and homelessness is increasing as demands for tax reductions escalate. Given important events, times, and probabilities, a cross-impact analysis examines possible arrays of changes in timing potentials and modifies each of the predicted variables to determine optional possibilities.[23]

Hybrid Techniques

Many of the available tools and techniques overlap and complement each other. One such "hybrid" technique—harnessing and using both hard performance data and personal perceptions and insights—is *quality management.*[24]

▨ Selecting the Methods and Means

Part of Mega Planning is selecting the best ways and means to move continuously closer to the Ideal Vision and the primary mission objective. A **costs-consequences analysis**[25] asks the simultaneous questions "What do you give?" and "What do you get?" for each possible how-to (or cluster of methods and means).

Costs-Consequences Analysis[26]

Using a costs-consequences analysis is one method[27] to estimate a full return-on-investment analysis. Economists often claim to prefer a full analysis of all input costs and all consequences, as shown in the first column of Table 7.3 that identifies possible variables for the Human Resources Development (HRD) department in any organization.[28]

When such data do not exist or cannot be obtained in time for a decision, then some of the variables for a proper return-on-investment analysis may be used to approximate a complete study of all variables. Such critical items for an HRD department are noted in Table 7.3 with a shaded box. Columns 2 and 3 in Table 7.3 identify whether a variable relates to "costs" or to "consequences."

For each variable, the analysis identified the gap between current results and status (column 4 in Table 7.3) and required or desired results (column 5). It should be noted that other interventions and different organizational missions would use a unique and distinctive set of return-on-investment/costs-consequences variables: There would be different variables identified for each costs-consequences analysis. Consequently, a needs assessment—determination of gaps between current and desired results—is performed on each of the variables to determine what is working and what might not be effective.

Among the questions[29] a costs-consequences effort should answer are the following:

1. Who are the participants in the interventions? Who should be?
2. Who are being turned down for the interventions? Who should be?
3. What interventions are the participants getting? What alternative interventions should they get?
4. What are the results of the intervention or interventions (at the Mega, Macro, and Micro levels)?

TABLE 7.3 Approximating a Full Return-on-Investment Analysis: A Costs-Consequences Analysis

Possible Variables	Related to Costs	Related to Consequences	Current Results/ Status	Desired Results/ Status
Current expenditures	X			
Opportunity costs		X[30]		
Societal "spin-offs"		X		
Current departmental or program budget	X			
Costs of interventions (training, continuous improvement, computer-assisted design, etc.) a. Salaries and related benefits b. Facilities c. Equipment d. Expenses	X			
Costs to attend or participate in intervention a. Contributions by participant b. Contributions by others (employers, other funds, etc.) c. Opportunity costs[31]	X			
Change (reduction or increase) in revenue and/or expenditures		X		
Change in productivity of employees		X		
Increase/decrease in employee morale		X		
Drop-out/completion rates		X		
Change in expenditures of participants (include opportunity costs)		X		
Participants enrolled in simultaneous programs	X			
Etc.				

NOTE: The shaded items are the minimum items that should be included in a costs-consequences analysis to provide a coarse-grained identification of the current or anticipated merit of a program, project, or intervention. All the variables would be required of a conventional return-on-investment analysis.

5. What are the completion, dropout, and continuation rates for the participants?
6. What are the performance levels of the completers? Of the leavers and the noncompleters?
7. What value do the participants add for their group, their organization, the external clients, society, and the community?
8. What is the societal condition—levels of self-sufficiency, self-reliance, and quality of life—of the completers? Of the noncompleters? What are the levels of completers' and noncompleters' self-sufficiency and self-reliance (in terms, at least of $C \leq P$)?
9. What interventions and patterns of interventions are making the best contributions in terms of societal (Mega) payoffs and consequences? What is working, and what is not? What are the valid criteria for these?
10. What are the societal (Mega) payoffs and consequences for the various interventions for the various kinds of participants (in terms, at least, of $C \leq P$)?
11. What are the costs for the payoffs and nonpayoffs? Is it worth the expenditures as compared to other interventions that might be made?
12. Have the decisions made not been generalized past the completeness and quality of the data?

Using costs-consequences analysis in any organization. Using the Organizational Elements Model (OEM) and the concept of Costs-Consequences, the following allow for the identification of what was missing for useful evaluation and continuous improvement to occur:

- What data exist?
- What data do not exist?
- What are critical data required by the project/intervention to determine effectiveness, efficiency, and positive costs-consequences?
- What Organizational Elements data exist?
- What Organizational Elements data are missing?
- Are the gaps between what is and what should be identified based on objective data?
- Are all of the Organizational Elements linked? (Does a "flow" from element to element exist, and is the flow justified?)

The selected methods and means—from the systems analysis—will identify what programs, projects, activities, classes, courses, and interventions are working, which ones are missing, and which one(s) should be dropped. Remember, the identification of functions, possible methods and means, and the selected methods and means are the basis for getting from current results to the accomplishment of the missions.

Getting the results first in focus before budget considerations. Using Mega Planning and costs-consequences analysis has several advantages. First, there is a primary concern with results and accomplishments before deriving the budget. Second, decisions about alternative methods-means can be justified before implementing them.[32] Third, and perhaps most helpful, by using Mega Planning you can have strategy-driven budgets instead of budget-driven strategies: results before solutions.

Performance Accomplishment Systems:[33] From Plan to Performance

The transition from Mega plan to performance that delivers success is often the vital missing piece of the performance improvement/accomplishment process. The way in which this transition often fails is in lack of discipline in following the plan either in whole or in part.

There is a systematic progression from Mega to Macro to Micro to Process to Input—a journey from why to what to how. Figure 7.5 illustrates the transition from the Ideal Vision to the organization's missions and functions to implementation and continuous improvement.

Even though it is more comfortable to start in the middle section—missions and functions—of this transition, doing so risks having a well-crafted solution that doesn't meet organizational and external clients' needs. The flow shown in Figure 7.5 (and noted by arrows from phase to phase) has several important parts.

The future we want to create. This is based on the Ideal Vision (discussed in Chapter 4). From a needs assessment that defines the gaps between current societal gaps in results (Mega level), there is a determination of the needs along with estimates of the costs and consequences of meeting or ignoring the needs (discussed earlier in this chapter).

The organization's missions and functions. Based on the selected needs from the Ideal Vision, the mission objectives for your organization are selected (discussed in Chapter 6). Again, a needs assessment is accomplished at the Macro level. A system analysis is completed (again detailed in Chapter 6) based on the needs to define the detailed performance requirements for meeting the needs: moving from current results to desired and required ones.

Implementation and continuous improvement. The reason for the plan lies in the implementation. This is where the organization expends most of its time and energies, but now it has the database to design, develop, and deliver programs, projects, and activities that will lead ever closer to the missions and the Ideal Vision.

There are three major phases and related activities to implementation and continuous improvement:

1. Performance accomplishment system design and development
2. Performance accomplishment system implementation and management
3. Continuous improvement (that is ongoing and not distinct from all other phases)

Performance accomplishment system design and development approaches, by and large, have migrated from isolated sets of concerns and activities—frequently focused on a means, such as training—to being linked formally and measurably to the performance and contributions

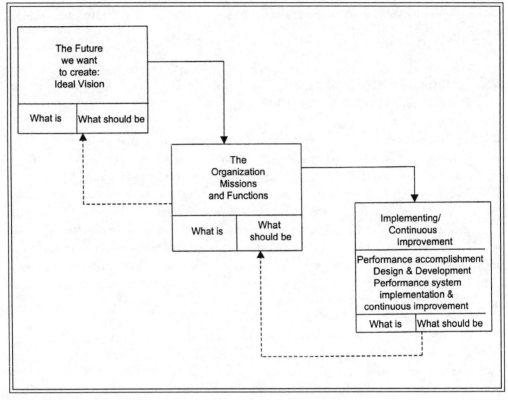

Figure 7.5. The transition from Mega Plan to organizational success: From why to what to how.

of the entire organization. The next generation of these models will increasingly include linkages and contributions to external clients. The evolution of performance accomplishment systems (PAS) is moving from a concern with individual training (a means) to observable performance contributions.[34]

It is interesting to note that most popular models for performance improvement/instructional system design and development are limited. Although models and processes that are widely used for performance improvement should have been substantiated by needs assessment data from the Mega and Macro levels, that is rarely the case.[35] The available models usually assume that performance will be improved by simply using a systematic approach. Conventional practice rarely confirms this assumption. It is important to link the performance improvement models and processes with Macro- and Mega-level planning results and requirements.

Change, Performance Accomplishment, and Performance Systems

Planning is done to identify what an organization should change and what it should keep. Many authors have developed models and processes for change, and most of them will work.

However, most are also incomplete in that they do not usually deal with the three levels of planning—Mega, Macro, and Micro—and not with the associated three levels of results—Outcomes, Outputs, and Products. In fact, most models and processes focus on Products, Processes, and Inputs, such as instructional systems models and conventional performance technology approaches. With such limited scope, they don't make the linkages and required integration among internal (Micro and Macro) as well as external clients (Mega) and consequences. Because there is only a focus on individual and small-group (Micro) performance improvement, important contributions are not considered.[36]

Processes for implementing change initiatives. A process for implementing a decision to change, at any organizational level, is provided in Figure 7.6. Using this suggested process, one first checks to see if a possible change will add value at the Mega, Macro, and Micro levels and if it also will be allowed to proceed based on the current organizational culture. Figure 7.6 shows a progression of functions where the organizational culture (Function 2.0) is considered and possibly revised or modified, based on a change decision for the three levels of results and consequences (Functions 1.0, 3.0, 4.0, and 5.0). In addition, the process includes major considerations of resources and environmental factors involved in useful planned change.[37]

What does one do, when contemplating planned change, if there is a mismatch between the functions to be accomplished and the organizational culture?[38] Rather than charging ahead if there are cultural blocks, identify costs and consequences of not making valid change. Figure 7.7 provides a process for dealing with mismatches between valid change initiatives and a blocking culture. By providing decision makers with the costs and consequences of changing versus not changing, they become aware of variables they might not have previously considered, and/or if they don't accept the change, they become responsible for the consequences of not changing.

The functions for the identification of possible methods-means (tactics and tools) are noted in Figure 7.8. The process, shown as a breakout of Function 5.0 in Figure 7.6, considers again what could be available to meet requirements (or families or clusters of performance requirements) and their costs and consequences.

Taking the system analysis further, Figure 7.9 illustrates the functions for a further breakout of Function 5.1 for the identification of available resources for each performance requirement.

Completing this example of a system analysis for performance accomplishment and change, Figure 7.10 shows the functions for selecting methods-means.

The materials in Figure 7.6 through 7.10 are provided as an example of a performance accomplishment process. This book does not go into the many useful (and usually Micro- and Process-focused) models and approaches, but there continues to evolve many contributions that a series design and development effort should consider.[39]

Management of What Is Planned

The management of programs, projects, and activities and the use of performance data to revise as required are central to "continuous improvement." The currently well-developed literature on this management and continuous improvement is provided in Chapter 8.

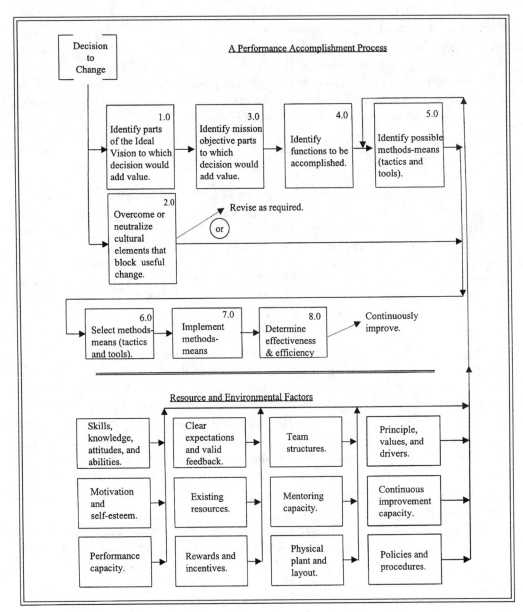

Figure 7.6. A performance accomplishment process, including resources and environmental factors to be considered.

Although this book does not go into the details of many useful models and approaches to performance accomplishment system design and development nor into performance accomplishment system management and control, many of the variables and functions are identified in Figure 7.5. This book does, however, provide the front end to design, development, and imple-

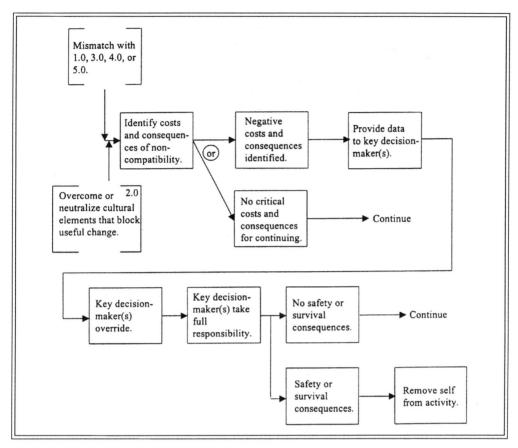

Figure 7.7. Reconciliation of organizational cultural blocks to change.

mentation of performance accomplishment systems. It is, however, imperative that the alignment be maintained among the elements shown in Figure 7.11.

Summary

Mega Planning concepts and tools enable planners to rationally and logically move from the Ideal Vision, primary mission objective, and long- and short-term missions to developing operational plans. This is done by determining alternative ways and means to achieve the missions and functions, completion of feasibility studies to ensure there are one or more methods-means, and identification of the advantages and disadvantages of each method and means. In performing a methods-means analysis, the primary mission objective should already be in place, along with longer- and shorter-term missions, a mission profile, listing of functions and their performance requirements, and task analysis information (if one has been completed).

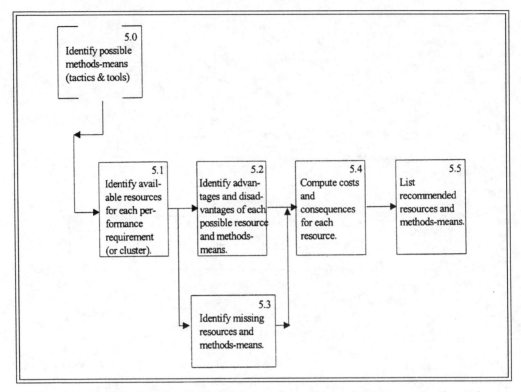

Figure 7.8. The functions for the identification of possible methods-means (tactics and tools).

System analysis will provide a calibration of the advantages and disadvantages of each possible method and means, and it provides a description of the constraints that could interfere with fulfilling the mission.

Methods-means analysis can take place at any point, but conducting the analysis only during mission analysis can lead to the temptation to seek solutions and processes before all possible alternatives have been evaluated. Each performance requirement (or group of performance requirements) must be paired with methods-means through the use of organized structures such as charting and linking each proposed method and means with the appropriate related function and performance requirement.

Systems analysis techniques can be used after mission definition, function analysis, task analysis, and methods-means analysis have been completed. Systems analysis techniques move into the descriptive phase of doing the activities that will reduce the gaps in results.

Systems analysis offers several models, methods, techniques, and procedures for selecting the most effective and efficient tactics and tools. They form, loosely, two groups: one that is oriented to performance facts and one that is oriented to judgment. As both quantitative and qualitative data are important, both approaches are useful. If you have performed the analyses explained in previous chapters, the basic inputs for using these tools are at hand.

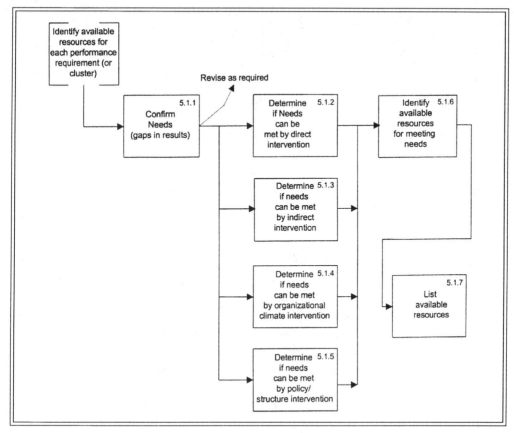

Figure 7.9. The functions for the identification of available resources for each performance requirement or clusters of performance requirements.

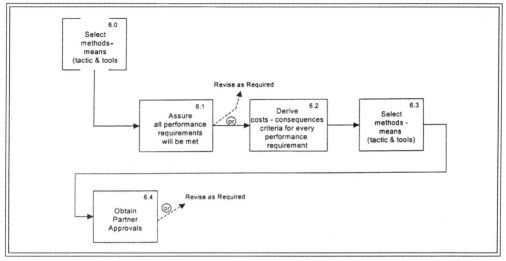

Figure 7.10. The functions for selecting the methods-means (tactics and tools) based on costs and consequences.

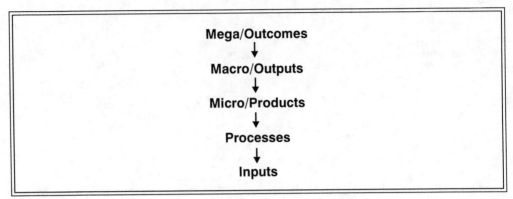

Figure 7.11. Linking three levels of results with Processes and Inputs.

These approaches all relate costs and consequences. Several tools have been only superficially covered. They take us from planning to achievement. The resources cited here should allow you to make the transition to "doer." It is when you choose the actual ways and means for getting required results that the shift from ends orientation to means orientation takes place. All our planning and analyses are simply prologue to doing—where the most energy is spent and the most work occurs.

If you have followed the basics described in this book, you have by now identified

- where you are headed and justified why you want to get there.
- the functions necessary to get from here to there and detailed the performance requirements.
- alternatives and then selected the best methods and means to get from here to there.

You are now ready to put the plan into action. But if it is worth doing, it is worth doing well. Planning provides this quality assurance!

Designing a Response

Putting the Mega plan to work involves (1) developing structures within the organization that will achieve the tactics and tools selected; (2) monitoring the activities and evaluating the activities and the strategies so that continuous improvement will occur; (3) developing an integrated management information system to aid those responsible for management of the strategic, tactical, and operational plans; (4) making in-process adjustments in strategies, tactics, and activities when the performance data indicate that a change is required; and (5) ensuring the effectiveness of the activities and the success of the tactics and methods-means employed.

Costs and Consequences

Review your purposes, objectives, and the precision and rigor of these intention statements—how these are conceived and done at your organization—in terms of the following questions. Answer, for each question, both **What Is** (your current practice) and **What Should Be** (your desired practice; what will best serve your organization).

Each **What Is** and **What Should Be** column—on either side of the questions—has the following dimensions in terms of the relative frequency that something does or does not happen:

Consistently (96-100%)
Quite frequently (85%-95%)
Sometimes (51%-84%)
Not usually (18%-50%)
Almost never (6%-17%)
Rarely, if ever (0%-5%)

My organization focuses

My organization

WHAT IS						Please indicate the frequency (in terms of percentage of times) with which the following statements are happening within your organization. Please provide two responses to each question: **WHAT IS** describes how you see your organization currently operating. — **WHAT SHOULD BE** describes how you think your organization should be operating.	WHAT SHOULD BE					
Rarely, if ever (0-4%)	Almost Never (5%-15%)	Not Usually (16-49%)	Sometimes (50-83%)	Quite Frequently (84-94%)	Consistently(95-100%)		Rarely, if ever (0-4%)	Almost Never (5%-15%)	Not Usually (16-49%)	Sometimes (50-83%)	Quite Frequently (84-94%)	Consistently(95-100%)
①	②	③	④	⑤	⑥	1. On costs	①	②	③	④	⑤	⑥
①	②	③	④	⑤	⑥	2. On time and/or processes and methods	①	②	③	④	⑤	⑥
①	②	③	④	⑤	⑥	3. On costs and time	①	②	③	④	⑤	⑥
①	②	③	④	⑤	⑥	4. On internal/Micro/Products results	①	②	③	④	⑤	⑥
①	②	③	④	⑤	⑥	5. On organizational/Macro/Outputs results	①	②	③	④	⑤	⑥
①	②	③	④	⑤	⑥	6. On external clients/Mega/Outcome results	①	②	③	④	⑤	⑥
①	②	③	④	⑤	⑥	7. First on costs and/or time and then on Micro/Products	①	②	③	④	⑤	⑥
①	②	③	④	⑤	⑥	8. First on costs and/or time and then on Macro/Outputs	①	②	③	④	⑤	⑥
①	②	③	④	⑤	⑧	9. First on costs and/or time and then on Mega/Outcomes	①	②	③	④	⑤	⑥
①	②	③	④	⑤	⑥	10. First on costs and/or time and then on Micro/Products	①	②	③	④	⑤	⑥
①	②	③	④	⑤	⑥	11. First on Micro/Products and then on costs and/or time	①	②	③	④	⑤	⑥
①	②	③	④	⑤	⑥	12. First on Macro/Outputs and then on costs and/or time	①	②	③	④	⑤	⑥
						13. First on Mega/Outcomes and then on costs and/or time						

Suggested patterns:

Items 1 through 3 should be rated low on both What Is and What Should
Be.

Items 4 through 10 should shift increasingly from low ratings on both What
Is and What Should Be. As these items progress, there is an increasing
focus on results but are still both tending toward a reactive and
process-oriented approach.

Items 11 through 13 should be increasingly rated higher on both What Is
and What Should Be as you move from item to item, with Item 13 having
high ratings on both because it is the best situation.

Notes

1. Recall that any objective, including the mission objective, has performance requirements measurable on an interval or ratio scale.

2. Solutions, processes, interventions, activities, initiatives, methods-means, programs, projects, and how-to-do-its are all used in the same way. These all identify possible ways to meet needs and satisfy requirements. It is difficult to choose among these "solutions" in each part of the text, so I ask that you read them as Processes, understanding that they might be an intervention.

3. See Kaufman (1972, 1992d, 1998b) and Kaufman, Herman, and Watters (1996).

4. Based on Kaufman (1992d).

5. Barker (1989).

6. Based on Kaufman (1992d).

7. Moving from Functions 1.0 and 2.0 in the six-step problem-solving process to (Guide 2) 3.0 in that process.

8. See the fable about the Mainstream and Sylvester in the Case Studies chapter.

9. Kaufman (1992b, 1998b), Kaufman and Carron (1980), Kaufman, Thiagarajan, and MacGillis (1997), Kaufman and Watkins (1996a), and Muir, Watkins, Kaufman, and Leigh (1998).

10. Cleland and King (1968a, 1968b).

11. Alkin and Bruno (1970).

12. Mega Planning discourages the usual strategies and encourages strategy-driven budgets.

13. U.S. General Accounting Office (1997).

14. Watkins, Leigh, and Kaufman (1998) based a review and comparison of needs assessment models on the mandate that agency requirements be responsive to the Government Performance and Results Act (GPRA, 1993). The GPRA requires agencies to be accountable for achieving program results, to have the database for justifying objectives based on needs, not wants. The GPRA is based on a new focus on results, service quality, and customer satisfaction. To do this, agencies must set program goals, measure program performance against those goals, and report publicly on their progress.

15. Martino (1983).

16. Rappaport (1986).

17. Abell and Hammond (1979).

18. Abell and Hammond (1979).

19. Kaufman, Stith, and Kaufman (1992).

20. Sivasailam Thiagarajan has built an exemplary business by creating games—serious games. He also edits *Game Newsletter* (published by Pfeiffer/Jossey-Bass) that provides information about the design and use of games.

21. Bell and Coplans (1976).

22. Van de Ven and Delbecq (1971).

23. Martino (1983) and Phi Delta Kappa (1984).

24. This process is covered extensively in Chapter 8.

25. Kaufman (1998b), Kaufman and Watkins (1996a), Kaufman, Watkins, and Sims (1997), and Muir, Watkins, Kaufman, and Leigh (1998).

26. This section is based on Toolkit VIII in Kaufman (1998b) as well as on Kaufman and Watkins (1996), Kaufman, Watkins, and Sims (1997), and Muir, Watkins, Kaufman, and Leigh (1998).

27. Future research and development is required to further clarify and validate this costs-consequences approach. This suggested one is a "work in progress" and should be used only as a guide or preliminary example.

28. Kaufman, Watkins, and Sims (1997).

29. These questions are targeted toward a training/human resources program. These questions should be tailored for other appropriate areas.

30. It could be argued that this is a "cost." However, I argue that because it speaks to results that could be achieved if funds/efforts were expended elsewhere and/or results foregone because of being spent, this is a consequence-related item.

31. As argued above, this could also be a consequence.

32. There are, thus, two different applications for costs-consequences analysis. One is the more conventional, where after-the-fact results are examined for answering "Was what we spent worth it?" The other is proactive, where estimates can be made of alternative methods-means/interventions before they are selected and applied.

33. I coin this term in order to get away from the more popular yet less descriptive terms such as Human Performance Technology (HPT) or Instructional Systems Design (ISD) that seem to focus more on means than on ends and consequences.

34. The International Society for Performance Improvement has been a pioneer in the transition from training to performance.

35. Scott Schaffer of the Office for Needs Assessment & Planning, Learning Systems Institute, Florida State University, has identified major ISD/performance improvement models and their relationship to the Organizational Elements Model. The links to Mega are always missing, and only a few link to Macro.

36. Note that the term "improvement" assumes that what is currently being done and delivered needs only to be improved. Useful change—performance accomplishment—focuses on what to accomplish that is not already being done and already in place.

37. Please see references in note 38 for some of the suggestions for environmental and resource considerations.

38. Again recalling Gary Rummler's observation that if you pit a great performer against a bad system, the bad system will win every time.

39. There are many excellent sources for what is variously called Human Performance Technology (HPT), Instructional Systems Design (ISD), and performance improvement, among other names. What is vital is that all models have some common elements, according to former Wells Fargo Bank Corporate Vice President Roger Addison: Inputs, Processes, results, and a consideration of the environment.

This book, as much as I am tempted, does not go into the rich literature on performance improvement. I thus recommend that the following references, among many other good resources, be considered:

Addison, R., & Johnson, M. (1997). The building blocks of performance. *Business Executive, 11,* 3-5.

Branson, R. K., et al. (1975). Interservice procedures for instructional systems development (Phases I, II, III, IV, V, and Executive Summary, U.S. Army Training and Doctrine Command Pamphlet 350). Fort Monroe, VA: U.S. Army.

Brethower, D. M. (1993a). Strategic improvement of workplace competence I: Breaking out of the incompetence trap. *Performance Improvement Quarterly, 5*(2), 17-28.

Brethower, D. M. (1993b). Strategic improvement of workplace competence II: The economics of competence. *Performance Improvement Quarterly, 5*(2), 29-42.

Brethower, D. M. (1995). Specifying a Human Performance Technology knowledge base. *Performance Improvement Quarterly, 8*(2), 17-39.

Brethower, D. M. (1998). Through an evaluator's eyes: A vision of HRD. In *ASTD training and performance yearbook.* New York: McGraw-Hill.

Brethower, D. M., & Smalley, K. A. (1997). *Performance-based: Linking training to business results.* San Francisco: Jossey-Bass.

Briggs, L. J. (Ed.). (1977). *Instructional design: Principles and applications.* Englewood Cliffs, NJ: Educational Technology Publications.

Briggs, L. J., & Wager, W. W. (1982). *Handbook of procedures for the design of instruction* (2nd ed.). Englewood Cliffs, NJ: Educational Technology Publications.

Corrigan, R. E., & Corrigan, B. O. (1985). *SAFE: System approach for effectiveness.* New Orleans, LA: R. E. Corrigan Associates.

Dean, P. J. (Ed.). (1994). *Performance engineering at work.* Batavia, IL: International Board of Standards for Training, Performance, and Instruction.

Dean, P. J., & Ripley, D. E. (1997). *Performance improvement pathfinders: Models for organizational learning systems.* Washington, DC: International Society for Performance Improvement.

Dick, W., & Carey, L. (1989). *The systematic design of instruction* (3rd ed.). Glenview, IL: Scott, Foresman.

Esque, T. J., & Patterson, P. A. (1998). *Getting results: Case studies in performance improvement.* Washington, DC: ISPI Publications & HRD Press.

Fuller, J. (1997). *Managing Performance Improvement Projects.* Washington, DC: International Society for Performance Improvement.

Gagne, R. (Ed.). (1962). *Psychological principles in system development.* New York: Holt, Rinehart & Winston.

Gagne, R. M., & Medsker, K. L. (1996). *The conditions of learning: Training applications.* New York: Harcourt Brace.

Gilbert, T. F. (1971). Mathetics: The technology of education. In M. D. Merrill (Ed.), *Instructional design: Readings.* Englewood Cliffs, NJ: Prentice Hall.

Gilbert, T. F. (1978). *Human competence: Engineering worthy performance.* New York: McGraw-Hill.

Gilbert, T. F., & Gilbert, M. B. (1989, January). Performance engineering: Making human productivity a science. *Performance & Instruction.*

Glaser, R. (1966, Winter). Psychological bases for instructional design. *AV Communication Review.*

Hale, J. (1998). *The performance consultant's fieldbook: Tools and techniques for improving organizations and people.* San Francisco: Pfeiffer/Jossey-Bass.

Harless, J. (1988). *Accomplishment-based development: Curriculum development.* Newnan, GA: Harless Performance Guild.

Harless, J. (1998). "The Eden conspiracy: Educating for accomplished citizenship." Wheaton, IL: Guild V Publications.

Harless, J. H. (1986). Guiding performance with job aids. In M. Smith (Ed.), *Introduction to performance technology, Part 1.* Washington, DC: National Society for Performance and Instruction.

Hinchliffe, D. R. (1995). *Training for results: Determining education and training needs for emergency management in Australia.* Unpublished doctoral dissertation, Monash University, Clayton Campus, Victoria, Australia.

Jackson, S. (1986). Task analysis. In M. Smith (Ed.), *Introduction to performance technology, Part 1.* Washington, DC: National Society for Performance and Instruction.

Kaufman, R. (1992). *Strategic planning plus: An organizational guide* (Rev. ed.). Newbury Park, CA: Sage.

Kaufman, R. (1995). *Mapping educational success* (Rev. ed.). Thousand Oaks, CA: Corwin Press.

Kaufman, R. (1998). *Strategic thinking: A guide to identifying and solving problems* (Rev. ed.). Arlington, VA & Washington, DC: American Society for Training and Development and the International Society for Performance Improvement.

Kaufman, R. (1999). From how to what to why: The handbook of performance technology as the gateway to the future. In H. Stolovitch & E. Keeps (Eds.), *The handbook of performance technology* (2nd ed.). San Francisco: Jossey-Bass.

Kaufman, R., Herman, J., & Watters, K. (1996). *Educational planning: Strategic, tactical, and operational.* Lancaster, PA & Basil Switzerland: Technomic Publishing.

Kaufman, R., & Keller, J. (1994). Levels of evaluation: Beyond Kirkpatrick. *Human Resources Quarterly, 5*(4), 371-380.

Kaufman, R., & Thiagarajan, S. (1987). Identifying and specifying requirements for instruction. In R. M. Gagne (Ed.), *Instructional technology: Foundations.* Hillsdale, NJ: Lawrence Erlbaum.

Kaufman, R., Thiagarajan, S., & MacGillis, P. (Eds.). (1997). *The guidebook for performance improvement: Working with individuals and organizations.* San Francisco: Pfeiffer/Jossey-Bass.

Kaufman, R., & Watkins, R. (1999a). Needs assessment. In D. Langdon (Ed.), *Intervention resource guide: 50 performance improvement tools.* San Francisco: Jossey-Bass.

Kaufman, R., & Watkins, R. (1999b). Strategic planning. In D. Langdon (Ed.), *Intervention resource guide: 50 performance improvement tools.* San Francisco: Jossey-Bass.

Kaufman, R. A. (1972). *Educational system planning.* Englewood Cliffs, NJ: Prentice Hall.

Kearny, L. (1995). *The facilitator's toolkit: Tools and techniques for generating ideas and making decisions in groups.* Washington, DC: HRD Press.

Kirkpatrick, D. L. (1994). *Evaluating training programs: The four levels.* San Francisco: Berret-Koehler.

Langdon, D. (Ed.). (1999). *Intervention resource guide: 50 performance improvement tools.* San Francisco: Jossey-Bass.

LaFleur, D., & Brethower, D. (1998). *The Transformation: Business strategies for the 21st century.* Washington, DC: International Society for Performance Improvement.

Mager, R. F. (1988). *Making instruction work: Or skillbloomers.* Belmont, CA: David S. Lake.

Mager, R. F. (1992). *What every manager should know about training: Or "I've got a training problem" and other odd ideas.* Belmont, CA: Lake Publishing.

Mager, R. F. (1997). *Preparing instructional objectives: A critical tool in the development of effective instruction* (3rd ed.). Atlanta: Center for Effective Performance.

Mager, R. F., & Beach, K. M., Jr. (1967). *Developing vocational instruction.* Palo Alto, CA: Fearon.

Mager, R. F., & Pipe, P. (1983). *CRI: Criterion referenced instruction* (2nd ed.). Carefree, AZ: Mager Associates.

Mager, R. F., & Pipe, P. (1984). *Analyzing performance problems* (2nd ed.). Belmont, CA: Pitman.

Merrill, M. D. (1983). Component display theory. In *Instructional design theories and models: An overview of the current status.* Hillsdale, NJ: Lawrence Erlbaum.

Merrill, P. F. (1987). Job and task analysis. In R. M. Gagne (Ed.), *Instructional technology: Foundations.* Hillsdale, NJ: Lawrence Erlbaum.

Morgan, R. M., & Chadwick, C. B. (1971). *Systems analysis for educational change: The Republic of Korea.* Tallahassee: Florida State University, Department of Educational Research.

Phillips, J. J. (1997). *Return on investment training and performance programs.* Houston, TX: Gulf Publishing Company.

Reigeluth, C. (Ed.). (1983). *Instructional design theories and models. An overview of their current status.* Hillsdale, NJ: Lawrence Erlbaum.

Reiser, R. A., & Gagne, R. M. (1983). *Selecting media for instruction.* Englewood Cliffs, NJ: Educational Technology Publishing.

Robinson, D. G., & Robinson, J. C. (1995). *Performance consulting: Moving beyond training*; San Francisco: Berret-Koehler.

Rosenberg, M. J. (1990, February). Performance technology: Working the system. *Training.*

Rossett, A. (1998). *First things fast.* San Francisco: Jossey-Bass.

Rothwell, W. J., & Kazanas, H. L. (1998). *Mastering the instructional design process: A systematic approach.* San Francisco: Jossey-Bass.

Rummler, G. A., & Brache, A. P. (1990). *Improving performance: How to manage the white space on the organization chart.* San Francisco: Jossey-Bass.

Silvern, L. C. (1968, March). Cybernetics and education K-12. *Audiovisual Instruction.*

Sleezer, C. M., & Gradous, D. B. (1998). Measurement challenges in evaluation and performance improvement. *Performance Improvement Quarterly, 11*(4), 62-75.

Stolovitch, H. D., & Keeps, E. J. (1992). *Handbook of human performance technology: A comprehensive guide for analyzing and solving performance problems in organizations.* San Francisco and Washington, DC: Jossey-Bass and the National Society for Performance and Instruction.

Swanson, R. A. (1994). *Analysis for improving performance.* San Francisco: Berrett-Koehler.

Tosti, D. T. (1986). Feedback systems. In M. Smith (Ed.), *Introduction to performance technology, Part 1.* Washington, DC: National Society for Performance and Instruction.

Watkins, R., Leigh, D., Foshay, R., & Kaufman, R. (1998). Kirkpatrick plus: Evaluation with a community focus. *Educational Technology Research and Development Journal.*

Watkins, R., Leigh, D., & Kaufman, R. (1998). Needs assessment: A digest, review, and comparison of needs assessment literature. *Performance Improvement, 37*(7), 40-53.

Wedman, J. F., & Graham, S. (1998). Introducing the concept of performance support using the performance pyramid. *Journal of Continuing Higher Education, 46*(3), 8-20.

CHAPTER 8

Putting Mega Planning to Work

Integrating Mega Planning, Needs Assessment, and Quality Management

Planning usually suffers from not being seriously put to work or because it is incomplete. A fine Mega plan does little good if it sits on a desk or coffee table. A main feature of successful planning is continuous improvement—using performance data to revise whenever required. This chapter provides the rationale and tools for making certain that what gets planned gets delivered and covers all the required concerns using the power of quality management and continuous improvement. Integrating needs assessment and quality management with Mega Planning will better assure that planning has the required impact.

This chapter examines these aspects:

- Releasing the power of knowing where to head and continuous improvement (the basis of which came from the Mega plan)
- Making quality management (QM) a reality in your organization
- Applying needs assessment for QM initiatives
- The Mega Planning framework and how it relates to QM
- Shifting the QM paradigm: Quality management plus (QM+)
- Why most QM programs do not go far enough
- What is to be gained by using QM+
- Relating planning and QM/continuous improvement
- Delivering synergy
- Integrating QM+, Mega Planning plus, and continuous improvement

▨ Releasing the Power of Knowing Where to Head and Continuous Improvement

Mega Planning and quality management (QM)[1] are two useful and related processes that when applied correctly will consistently lead to organizational and individual success. They should be integrated. Combining and operating QM and Mega Planning, using the same database and with the same partners, they are more powerful than when applied independently. QM is recognized as a vital means for achieving organizational success.[2] Mega Planning, as described in this book, defines the most justifiable organizational direction. This chapter briefly reviews the basics of Mega Planning and QM and defines conventional quality management. It then goes on to identify how (and why) they should be used together rather than as individual Processes. Unfortunately, many organizations are not getting all of the potential power from Mega Planning and QM because they (1) employ incomplete approaches that don't target big-picture societal (ideal) visions and purposes, and/or (2) view QM and Mega Planning as distinct efforts and run them on parallel tracks. To get the best contributions from both, apply them rigorously, fully, and together. If you do, it will once again prove what sociologists have observed for years: that the whole is more than the sum of its parts. Let's define each and then relate how Mega Planning and QM can work together as well as use the same needs assessment database.

Definitions (and Some Review)

Building on what was provided in earlier chapters—and adding some definitions for quality management—you may use QM to increase the measurable value added both within and outside your organization. Mega Planning (discussed in the Introduction and Chapters 1 through 5) defines and justifies where to head, why you want to get there, and how to tell when you have arrived (see Figure 8.1). With Mega Planning, new objectives may be set and old ones modified or thrown out. It is direction finding and direction justifying.

Tactical planning (discussed in Chapter 7) identifies and selects the best ways and means to achieve valid existing or already selected objectives. It is achieving direction; if you want to get someplace, it is sensible to find the most effective and efficient ways and resources to get there. Naturally, if you don't have the right objectives, increasing the efficiency and effectiveness of methods are a waste, and this is a potentially fatal flaw in most existing models of Mega Planning, needs assessment, quality management and continuous improvement, benchmarking, and reengineering.[3]

Quality management (QM) and **continuous improvement** (CI) involve all organizational members—everyone—in delivering client satisfaction[4] and quality. Everyone in the organization strives to identify the gaps between current and desired results and then continuously improves everything that each person uses, does, and delivers. Individuals and organizations learn from mistakes and use performance data to improve, not blame.[5, 6] The quest to achieve quality[7] is prudent and timely.

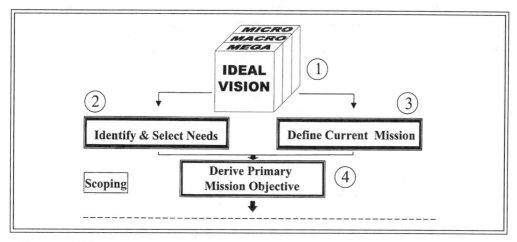

Figure 8.1. The Mega Planning framework.

Quality Management (QM)

Quality management (QM) is a continuous process that intends to deliver to clients what is defined in the Mega plan: what they want, what they can really use, and deliver it when they should have it. Quality and client satisfaction constitute the continuing QM purpose. QM relies on all the factors of production, including the most valuable one: people. Quality-focused people "do it right the first time and every time," so much so that the client is satisfied. QM operates as if each person in the organization were the actual customer, making things the way clients would themselves.[8]

Properly used, QM creates an organizational climate that provides continuous improvement toward perfection: toward Mega.[9] It encourages, but does not demand, all employees to constructively participate in the process and contribute to the overall purpose. QM provides each employee with the opportunity to become a full partner in defining and creating success; it enlists everyone to achieve, minute by minute, day by day, and week by week total quality and client satisfaction. Everyone is supported, aided, encouraged, and empowered to make one's own unique contribution to the total quality effort.

Quality and management cannot be delegated. All senior people must serve as both active participants in, and role models for, quality. It is better to continue operations as usual than it is to "fake" total quality by having the executives and/or board "looking down" on the quality process without being fully committed players. Systemwide commitment and action are vital if an organization is to define and consistently deliver quality. The greater the systemwide commitment to quality, the better it will be achieved. There should be a seamless flow of quality and a value-added quality dimension from one part of the organization to the next. Figure 8.2 shows the conventional upward flow of the elements of QM.

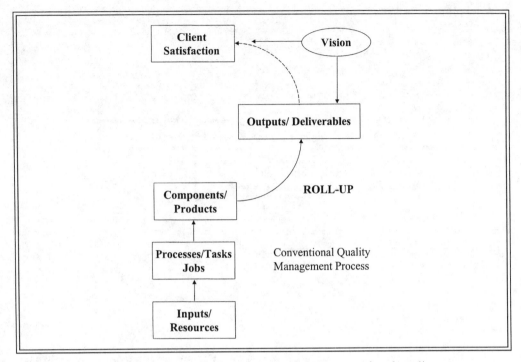

Figure 8.2. The linked components, flowing upward, in a conventional quality management program.

Assuring that the resources, methods, Products, and deliverables are of consistent high quality, QM makes sense. Without QM as part of the corporate culture, conventional organizations don't have a future. How can any organization not realize that external clients must be satisfied and served well? And client satisfaction comes from delivering a quality output time after time after time.

For QM to work, everyone—from security guard to CEO, from human resources technician to board chairperson—must pursue the same purpose: quality to the client. All must also be competent in how to identify and deliver quality, which often requires extensive performance accomplishment development, including education and training.[10]

Good intentions, slogans, and glittering generalities are neither enough nor desirable. We have to be specific: define quality objectives, develop criteria for measuring and tracking accomplishments, and identify what has to be done to get us from where we are to our Ideal Vision and mission objectives.

Many organizations are pursuing QM certification and proudly announce achieving this recognition. However, quality doesn't stop with an award, or even a happy customer. It requires that quality improvement and client satisfaction be continuously pursued. This year's excellent organization can be next year's also-ran. The world changes, and a successful QM process must be continually responsive.

QM involves the entire organization, not simply a part of it. Quality management involves all of the organizational elements—Inputs, Processes, Products, Outputs, and Outcomes—melding to deliver client satisfaction. A QM process includes the integration of ingredients (Inputs), Processes, and organizational results. The Organizational Elements Model (OEM) identifies organizational resources, efforts, results, and consequences.

Frequently missing from usual QM applications are (1) an understanding of the total system, including the organization, to which QM is to be applied, and (2) a balance in application of statistical quality control and decision making, motivation, and a shared and measurable destination.

Defining the "Q" in QM. Usually, client satisfaction, or dissatisfaction, is based on the degree to which Outputs meet specifications—perceived quality. Output quality and customer satisfaction are the "vision" targets for conventional QM. QM emphasizes that it is important for all elements to fit together. They should integrate to smoothly turn raw materials, through competent and caring Processes that add value to the ingredients, into the Products and deliverables (Outputs) that satisfy clients. QM enlists and enrolls everyone in the partnership for quality—suppliers and workers, sellers and buyers—in defining and achieving the vision: delivering quality.

The conventional QM process rolls up to achieve client satisfaction. Figure 8.2 shows the elements of the typical QM process. It starts with the best ingredients and then turns those into Products and Outputs that meet or exceed customer expectations.

Ordinarily, the general purpose of "a satisfied client" is sought, and then a sample of clients is asked to define what it likes and doesn't like about the Outputs currently received. Based on the satisfaction surveys, changes in the Inputs, Processes, Products, and Outputs are determined. Doing so is reactive; there is little consideration of new and different goods, services, and/or deliverables. The typical QM approach, reactively, intends to improve the quality of what the organization already makes or delivers.

QM is essential if we are to transform the organization and move continuously toward achieving our mission.[11] QM can become the engine of continuous improvement, and it will be most successfully implemented when the correct objectives are identified and become our targets.

Making QM a Reality in Your Organization

Basic Steps

Here are eight steps for getting commitment and building the quality partnership. Successful partnerships have the following characteristics:

1. Everyone cooperates toward contribution to a common end.
2. Everyone is important as well as provides support and assistance to others.

3. Everyone is honest with themselves and each other and is committed to improving and never in showing up someone else as wrong.
4. Objectives are stated clearly, concisely, and measurably and are not confusing.
5. Evaluation and feedback are used for continuous improvement, never for blaming. Everyone learns from mistakes and experiences, and so does the organization.
6. A quality system collects and uses performance data and provides them to all so they may identify what works and what doesn't.
7. Means and resources are selected based on the results to be obtained, not the other way around.
8. Constant progress and cooperation characterize everyone's day-to-day efforts and contributions. Everyone looks for opportunities for constructive action. There is constant management and monitoring of performance, and the results are used for improvement. (This is, in reality, an application of needs assessment.)

Deming's 14 Points[12]

These explain the characteristics of QM and the QM process. Deming's 14 points are useful and appropriate for quality and client satisfaction (after all, he is the father, along with Juran, of QM). These points are as follows:

1. Create constancy of purpose.
2. Adopt a new philosophy.
3. Cease dependence on mass inspection to achieve quality.
4. End the practice of awarding business on price alone. Instead, minimize total cost, often accomplishing by working with a single supplier.
5. Improve constantly the system of production and service.
6. Institute training on the job.
7. Institute leadership.
8. Drive out fear.
9. Break down barriers between departments.
10. Eliminate slogans, exhortations, and numerical targets.
11. Eliminate work standards (quotas) and management by objective.
12. Remove barriers that rob workers, engineers, and managers of their right to pride of workmanship.
13. Institute a vigorous program of education and self-improvement.
14. Put everyone in the company to work to accomplish the transformation.

The three clusters of the Deming 14 points: Joiner's triangle.[13] Joiner summarizes and clusters Deming's 14 points into the three angles of a triangle: (a) quality (an obsession with it), (b) scientific approach (data-based decision making), and (c) all on one team. By clustering in this way, it is important to realize that (1) everyone has to define and continuously pursue quality, with every act and decision moving towards its achievement; (2) quality flows from improving the Processes, not relying on inspection; and (3) QM requires a total team culture, with everyone acting individually and together to achieve quality. A way for QM to disappoint us is to allow it to focus efforts on only one or two of these clusters or simply drive toward winning an award—ticket punching—while failing to both delight and serve the the clients well: namely, providing them with what is also good for them and society.[14]

There are unique initiatives involved in moving from Deming's principles to an operational quality process:

- The quality of what gets delivered outside the organization is paramount. No excuses. No deviations.

- The realization that about 80% or 90% of all problems flow from 10% to 20% of the activities (based on a Pareto[15] analysis) and that fixing a Process—making the work right—is essential to delivering quality. Decisions on what to keep and what to change must be made on the basis of valid data and analysis of results, not on bias, intuition, or power—only on scientific decision making.

- Everyone must be headed in the same destination. If everyone is not committed to a common definition of quality and a shared destination, then the results will suffer. Everyone must continuously and consistently act on the basis of a shared destiny. Everyone must be on the same team.

- A quality system—the collection and display of valid and reliable data—has to provide the information for management and continuous improvement, tracking performance, accomplishment, successes, and shortfalls to provide the rational basis for change, continuation, and discontinuation.

Doing a Needs Assessment for QM Initiatives

Any scientific approach requires that decisions be made on the basis of performance data, not on bias, hunches, or popularly held stereotypes or quick fixes. A useful tool for determining what works and what doesn't is needs assessment. Needs, for the sake of QM as well as planning, are best defined as gaps between current results and desired ones (see the discussion in Chapter 3).

For each element in a QM process, the gaps in results between "what is" and "what should be" are determined so that useful ways and means for meeting the needs can be selected. Table 8.1 suggests a format for identifying needs (and quasi-needs) when applying QM.[16]

Evaluating your results and payoffs. Evaluation[17] is finding out what worked and what didn't; identifying which of the objectives were met. Based on the evaluation results, we can tell what to change and what to keep and thus how to continuously improve. The criteria for evaluation comes directly from the "What Should Be column of the needs assessment form. When applying the Deming principles of continuous improvement, the evaluation data are used for fixing and improving and never for finger pointing. So, needs assessment not only provides the objectives for the methods and means of education, teaching, activities, and learning, it also produces the criteria for evaluation and continuous improvement.

TABLE 8.1 Format for Identifying Needs (and Quasi-Needs) When Applying Quality
Management

	Current Results	Current Consequences of the Results	Desired Results	Desired Consequences
Mega level				
Macro level				
Micro level				
Process level (Quasi-needs)				
Input level (Quasi-needs)				

Adding required power to conventional QM: Some suggested changes to the conventional QM process. Quality management should not be isolated from the organization and planning. Mega Planning can and should overlap with a rational extension of QM: adding the Mega level in order to get extra power from conventional QM. By adding Mega—societal value added—the organization can both do things right and do the right things: It can add value as the organization moves ever closer to the Ideal Vision. Mega ensures that the right things are done. This yields quality management plus (QM+). Let's see why this is valuable.

▨ Planning: Where Should We Be Headed? A Brief Review

The Ideal Vision and derived mission provides the front-end alignment for the organization. Everything the organization uses, does, and delivers depends on its heading toward the right destination.

Missions and objectives. Any objectives, including mission objectives, state where we are headed and how we can measure when we have arrived. Objectives may deal with all of these: an entire organization, the missions, functions, and/or tasks. There are three levels, or scopes, for objectives, depending on who is to be the primary client and beneficiary of the Mega Planning and QM efforts. The basic questions that any organization has to ask and answer (unless we choose the short-term "comfortable" deception of ignoring one or more of them) are repeated in Figure 8.3.

The Mega Planning framework and how it relates to quality management. The three-phase framework for Mega planning—Scoping, Planning, and Implementation and Evaluation/Continuous Improvement—was discussed in detail in Chapter 5. QM/continuous improvement is the primary driver, or vehicle, for ensuring that the Mega strategic plan becomes a reality. It better

?	Do you commit to deliver organizational contributions that have positive impacts for society? (**MEGA**/Outcomes)
?	Do you commit to deliver organizational contributions that have the quality required by your external partners? (**MACRO**/Outputs)
?	Do you commit to produce internal results that have the quality required by your internal partners? (**MICRO**/Products)
?	Do you commit to have efficient internal products, programs, projects, and activities? (**PROCESSES**)
?	Do you commit to create and ensure the quality and appropriateness of the human, capital, and physical resources available? (**INPUTS**)
?	Do you commit to deliver (a) products, activities, methods, and procedures that have positive value and worth, and (b) the results and accomplishments defined by our objectives? (**EVALUATION/CONTINUOUS IMPROVEMENT**)

Figure 8.3. Finding direction: The organizational elements noted and related questions.

assures that all means and ends relate and add value for continued progress toward the missions and the Ideal Vision. To do this, all of the organizational elements (Figure 8.3) must be achieved and linked.

Scoping

This first phase of Mega Planning requires a choice among the first three questions in Figure 8.3 to determine the scope of planning. When we commit to start with Question 1, then the conventional Mega Planning scope (which usually limits itself to starting with Question 2 or 3) is expanded to become Mega Planning that adds the Mega level to direction finding. It includes client and societal good and payoffs—both pleasing the client and serving that client well. The first phase requires that an Ideal Vision be derived that will shape and drive everything that follows.

An Ideal Vision identifies the overall result specifications for our shared world. Because we seek to define the future, knowing that if we don't someone else will, preparing an Ideal Vision can be seen as practical dreaming.[18] From the Ideal Vision, next identify the portion that we commit to deliver: the primary mission objective. No single organization is expected to accomplish the whole ideal, but each should contribute to it. By selecting the portion of the Ideal Vision it commits to deliver, an organization may also (a) identify synergies and redundancies with other organizations and (b) reveal blank spaces in the Ideal Vision that are currently unattended in order to identify possible niches for new business.

Identify current mission(s). Most organizational purposes are mission statements: They state the direction in which the organization is heading, but they usually do not provide the planning and evaluation criteria. Conventional mission statements are usually more inspirational than measurable. As previously discussed, turn mission statements into mission objectives by adding "how do we know when we've arrived" to "where are we headed." Provide both direction and measurable criteria for accomplishment:

MISSION STATEMENT + MEASURABLE CRITERIA = MISSION OBJECTIVE
        (Intention)   **(specifics)**   **(Success Statement)**

Identify needs. Need (see Chapter 3) is defined as a gap between current results and desired (or required) ones. Problems are needs selected for resolution or reduction. No need, no problems.

A needs assessment identifies gaps in results and it places them in priority order based on what it costs to meet a need compared to the costs for ignoring it. Defining needs as gaps in results is critical for sensible planning, and for the "data-based decision making" part of QM, and providing us with a powerful QM+.

Planning

The second Mega Planning phase uses the Products from Scoping to map a strategic plan. This phase is results oriented, transitioning from the Scoping phase through to the Implementation and Evaluation/Continuous Improvement phase.

First, within this phase, the identification of strengths, weaknesses, opportunities, and threats (SWOTs) provides indicators of the environment within which the organization is situated. Once the SWOTs are identified, then the long- and short-term missions are derived. By arraying subsequent years' objectives in terms of moving ever closer toward the Ideal Vision, you enter into continuous improvement, an essential ingredient of QM.

The strategic plan itself is next derived. We know where we are headed, can justify why we want to get there, and now can define and plot the building-block objectives and possible resources and methods required to get from here to there.

Implementation and Evaluation/
Continuous Improvement

This third phase is where we put it all to work. The responses and resources are designed and developed: tactical planning. Then the tactics are scheduled and put into action based on our operational plans, and we formatively evaluate (track our progress and revise as required), and then summatively evaluate (compare our accomplishments with our objectives). Finally, we determine what to keep and what to change and revise as required.

The process of formative evaluation is identical to the quality management thrust of continuous improvement. Based on the gaps we identify as we move toward meeting our mission, we change and improve immediately and do not wait to achieve a disaster but improve while in process to assure that we are successful. The Mega Planning process identifies where we should be headed, justifies why we should go there, and provides the criteria for planning, designing, developing, implementing, and evaluating/continuous improvement. It is rational, systemic, and systematic. It also delivers an even greater contribution: It forms the basis of strategic thinking[19]—the way in which we run our lives and make day-to-day decisions. Mega Planning+ also provides a basic database required of QM+. Let's see.

▨ Shifting the QM Paradigm: Quality Management Plus (QM+)

QM, like Mega Planning, can benefit from adding the Mega level—societal and client value added—to the process. When you do, you get QM+. Not only will you do continuous improvement, you will assure yourself that your continuous improvement will lead toward meeting your mission and bringing you ever closer to the achievement of the Ideal Vision.

> **Quality management plus**: Conventional quality management with the addition of Mega—societal value added—used to orient all measurement and continuous improvement.

Adding societal payoffs to the definition of quality. The definition of quality when applying QM+ is not only to deliver to clients what they want when they should have it but also to deliver something that is useful to both them and to society. This definition includes both client satisfaction and usefulness to all external clients.

Why QM+? If we only adopt and apply the conventional QM approach, we could miss being both helpful and ethical. Without the full Mega focus, we could delight our clients while doing things that are not useful for them and our shared world. For example, we could win the Baldridge award even while still making asbestos insulation. We might qualify for an ISO 9000 or ISO 14000 certification (or Deming award) even while building a gene-destroying chemical.

QM+ adds the societal consequences and payoffs to conventional quality processes. We live in a shared world, and we are better off when we all continuously move toward the common good. Organizations that do this adhere to Drucker's advice that doing what's right is more important than doing things right.

When client satisfaction is good, but not good enough. All organizations are means to societal ends, and they all have clients, both internal and external. Internal clients are those who work and operate within the organization. All clients are important. All are stakeholders, and all must be satisfied with what our organization uses, does, and delivers.

To keep the external clients satisfied, organizations must deliver value-added Outputs and services—a continuing positive return on investment. External clients have to be assured that they are at least getting what they pay for, if not something more. Keep in mind that what organizations use, do, develop, and deliver to clients are evaluated on the basis of both customer satisfaction and usefulness of what is delivered.

Conventional quality approaches focus primarily on only one part of the Mega/Outcomes level: client satisfaction. More often than not, the specifications of client satisfaction are informally or loosely defined. Figure 8.2 showed the general rolling up of the typical QM program elements: moving from quality ("We don't have to inspect, we know it's right") to Inputs (resources) to Processes ("Everyone knows their jobs and assures it is done right") to results ("The product is right the first time and every time"). The conventional QM "vision," where we want to be, is focused at the Macro/Output. The "vision" for a conventional QM effort might be "to achieve total acceptance of the quality of what we deliver to our clients and be the organization of choice when a purchase in X is to be made."

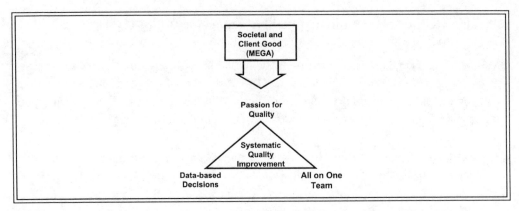

Figure 8.4. Relating Joiner's triangle (clustering Deming's 14 points) and Mega.

Of course, satisfied clients are crucial to a viable organization. But is that enough? Isn't there more?

QM+ takes us beyond client satisfaction. Peter Drucker reminds us that doing things right is not as important as doing the right things. (Total) quality management, as usually practiced, concentrates on doing things right. But what about the contributions and usefulness of what satisfies the clients? We can think of many client-pleasing things that might not be helpful or even safe, such as phosphate brighteners in detergent, DDT, asbestos insulation, and Chlordane. Each of these items could be the subject of a QM program, and each would bring client satisfaction without *quality usefulness* to the client and our shared world.

The missing quality consideration in conventional QM is delivering results that are good for society and that define and create an exemplary safe and satisfying world.

An Ideal Vision defines a shared vision of not just a successful company and/or a satisfied client but of a successful society and community. Nor should it be simply an egocentric vision designed to compete with another agency; rather, it should identify an ideal, even perfect, condition or world. Figure 8.4 shows how Joiner's triangle (data-based decisions, passion for quality, and all on one team) is aligned with Mega—societal and external client good.

A practical and effective Ideal Vision defines a safe and satisfying world where everyone is self-sufficient, self-reliant, and mutually contributing. An Ideal Vision provides the basis of deriving what elements of that Ideal Vision the organization, through its primary mission, will be responsible for providing. The organizational mission rolls down from the Ideal Vision, as shown in Figure 8.5. An extended, or useful, QM process will link the Ideal Vision with conventional QM adding the Mega level.

Figure 8.6 provides a QM+ framework. The QM+ process begins outside the organization by identifying what is required for societal usefulness (the Mega level rolls down to create what should be delivered to the client and then meets with the roll-up contributions of conventional total quality management) and then integrates with conventional total quality management; that is, it takes a good idea and extends it.

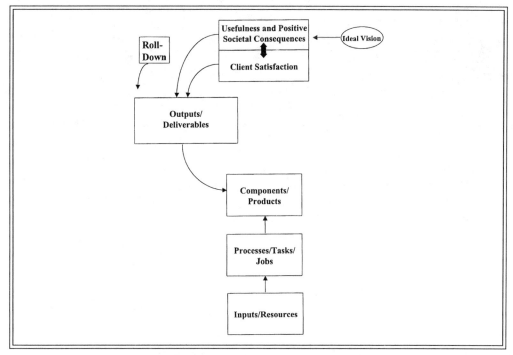

Figure 8.5. The elements of quality management plus (QM+). Mega is added to conventional quality management as it rolls down form Mega to define and align organizational contributions, results, and useful processes and resources.

Extending Mega to benchmarking and reengineering. Just as adding the Mega level to classical QM can make it more realistic and practical, so too may adding it to "benchmarking" and "reengineering" make those more useful. Again, only attending to organizational objectives could only increase your ability to design, develop, and implement a solution to a wrong problem. Although it is useful to set benchmarks—measurable mileposts along the way from current results to desired ones, another related method called benchmarking has been attracting attention. **Benchmarking** is often defined as comparing your process with another leading organization to identify its Processes so you may incorporate them as part of your way of doing business. This might hold some interesting and subtle traps.

If you benchmark another organization you should first assure yourself that

- they have the right objectives (and not heading in a direction that is not appropriate for your organization and clients).
- their Processes you intend to incorporate are, in fact, the most effective and efficient ones.
- they themselves are not also continuously improving, and perhaps you are copying an old and less effective process.

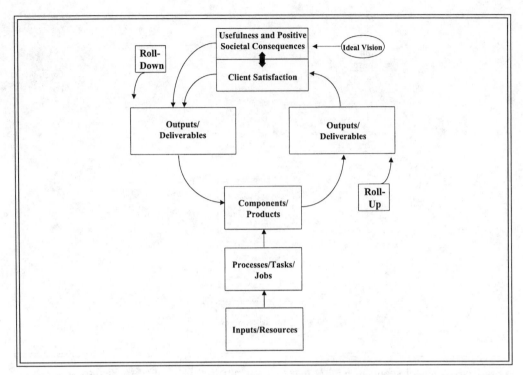

Figure 8.6. The quality management plus (QM+) cycle. Conventional quality management elements are linked with the QM+ after the requirements are rolled down from Mega and Micro to provide continuous improvement.

The most sensible form of benchmarking, as well as reengineering, is to calibrate yourself against the Ideal Vision and continuously improve toward that: **"benchmarking plus."** Thus, you don't have to copy unless you can justify that someone else's Processes will be the best choice for moving you continuously toward your mission and the Ideal Vision.[20] You benchmark perfection.

Relating Planning and Quality Management

When our Mega Planning reveals where to go and how to get there, we must make certain we commit to the plan and continuously improve as we deliver on our promises. QM+ provides the "glue" for achieving our strategic plan. Mega Planning and QM, even used in isolation, are powerful. When combined and integrated, a synergy is developed that makes the organization correctly focused and energized to deliver on its promises.

Integrating the planning and quality partnerships. By integrating planning and quality management, we may, simultaneously, define the right place to head as well as build the team and commitment to get there. Mega Planning best involves the partners who will be responsible for carrying it out. Mega Planning develops the specifications—measurable criteria—for defining where to head. Quality management also uses these data to define what to improve, what to change, and what to eliminate. Both intend to achieve organizational success and contribution. Both use data. Both have a common purpose.

Mega Planning identifies where to head. Quality management provides the engine for change and continuous improvement. They are synergistic, not isolated individual processes. They should be combined and integrated.

By merging the planning team and the quality team, everyone is then on one team to both plan and deliver quality. We thus get both buy-in and commitment from their having defined the Ideal Vision and the mission. Merging the teams delivers two critical quality ingredients: all being on one team and having a passion for (and measurable definition of) quality.

As the partners do the planning, they will begin the data-based decision-making process—another vital QM+ element—by collecting needs (gaps in results) data and preparing all objectives (including mission objectives) that target ends, not means.

Delivering Synergy

What makes more sense than to continuously improve and develop a Mega-level strategic plan to define where to go? What makes more sense than everyone in the organization engaging in and constantly contributing to delivering on the Ideal Vision and missions? What makes more sense than making decisions on the basis of performance data, not on just hunches, intuitions, and biases? QM+ allows everyone to participate in contributing, each in one's own way, to both serving the clients well and satisfying them. Further, by agreeing on the Mega level for the Ideal Vision and missions, the planned effort is not only profitable but ethical and socially responsible. Figure 8.7 shows how Mega Planning and QM+ integrate. Under this integration, QM+ becomes the driver for the smooth transition from Mega Planning, or tactical planning, to operational effectiveness.

Our world has a global economy and a shared destiny, and simple appeals to be competitive again will not suffice. We have to define and create an ideal and then develop leaders, thinkers, integrators, and contributors who can and will lead us there. To do this, we have to be creative, innovative, and inventive, for what must be done is not currently on the drawing board. We have to add to our current models, techniques, and approaches that will identify and create what will be required.

We have a choice. We can concentrate on process and resources—efficiency—and do what we are already doing but attempt to do it at lower cost, or we may define quality management to include the "plus" factor and define and create what will be useful in today's and tomorrow's world. Our world has changed, and so extending today's realities will once again leave us playing catch-up. If tomorrow's world is going to be closer to ideal, then today's successful organization has to define new horizons and new ways to get from here to there and continuously improve.

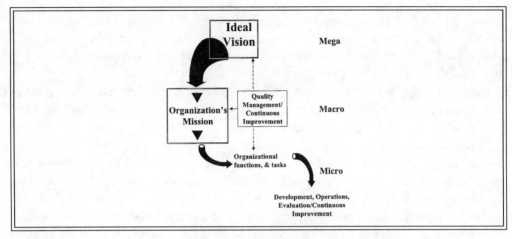

Figure 8.7. Quality management (when stretched to QM+) should be the driver for Mega Planning that links Mega, Macro, and Micro to Processes and Inputs.

EXERCISES

1. Reactive and Proactive

Each **What Is** and **What Should Be** column—on either side of the questions—has the following dimensions in terms of the relative frequency that something does or does not happen:

> Consistently (96%-100%)
> Quite frequently (85%-95%)
> Sometimes (51%-84%)
> Not usually (18%-50%)
> Almost never (6%-17%)
> Rarely, if ever (0%-5%)

Review your corporate culture and the current processes and methods—how these are conceived and done at your organization—in terms of the following questions. Answer, for each question, both **What Is** (your current practice) and **What Should Be** (your desired practice; what will best serve your organization).

My organization

WHAT IS							WHAT SHOULD BE					
Rarely, if ever (0-4%)	Almost Never (5%-15%)	Not Usually (16-49%)	Sometimes (50-83%)	Quite Frequently (84-94%)	Consistently (95-100%)	Please indicate the frequency (in terms of percentage of times) with which the following statements are happening within your organization. Please provide <u>two responses</u> to each question: ⟵ **WHAT IS** | **WHAT SHOULD BE** ⟶ WHAT IS describes how you see your organization currently operating. WHAT SHOULD BE describes how you think your organization should be operating.	Rarely, if ever (0-4%)	Almost Never (5%-15%)	Not Usually (16-49%)	Sometimes (50-83%)	Quite Frequently (84-94%)	Consistently (95-100%)
① ② ③ ④ ⑤ ⑥						1. Responds/reacts when a problem arises	① ② ③ ④ ⑤ ⑥					
① ② ③ ④ ⑤ ⑥						2. Responds/reacts when competition threatens	① ② ③ ④ ⑤ ⑥					
① ② ③ ④ ⑤ ⑥						3. Looks 1 or 2 quarters in the future	① ② ③ ④ ⑤ ⑥					
① ② ③ ④ ⑤ ⑥						4. Looks 2 or 3 years in the future	① ② ③ ④ ⑤ ⑥					
① ② ③ ④ ⑤ ⑥						5. Looks 4 to10 years in the future	① ② ③ ④ ⑤ ⑥					
① ② ③ ④ ⑤ ⑥						6. Looks beyond 10 years in the future	① ② ③ ④ ⑤ ⑥					
① ② ③ ④ ⑤ ⑥						7. Both responds/reacts and looks 2 or 3 years in the future	① ② ③ ④ ⑤ ⑥					
① ② ③ ④ ⑤ ⑥						8. Both responds/reacts and looks 4 to 10 years in the future	① ② ③ ④ ⑤ ⑥					
① ② ③ ④ ⑤ ⑥						9. Both responds/reacts and looks beyond 10 years in the future	① ② ③ ④ ⑤ ⑥					

Suggested patterns:

Item 2 is best rated low in both What Is and What Should Be.

Items 3 and 4 ratings should be higher on both What Is and What Should Be than for Item 2.

Items 5 and 6 should be rated higher on both What Is and What Should Be than for Items 2 through 4. They show a proactive trend.

Items 7 and 8 should be rated increasingly higher (higher on 8 than on 7) on both What Is and What Should Be. They show willingness to continuously improve when the requirements to do so are evident and also look to create a better future.

Item 8 is the best choice among these options and adds more value when both What Is and What Should Be are rated as high.

2. Making Decisions

My organization

WHAT IS							WHAT SHOULD BE					
Rarely, if ever (0-4%)	Almost Never (5%-15%)	Not Usually (16-49%)	Sometimes (50-83%)	Quite Frequently (84-94%)	Consistently(95-100%)	Please indicate the frequency (in terms of percentage of times) with which the following statements are happening within your organization. Please provide <u>two responses</u> to each question:	Rarely, if ever (0-4%)	Almost Never (5%-15%)	Not Usually (16-49%)	Sometimes (50-83%)	Quite Frequently (84-94%)	Consistently(95-100%)

⟵ **WHAT IS** | **WHAT SHOULD BE** ⟶

WHAT IS describes how you see your organization currently operating.

WHAT SHOULD BE describes how you think your organization should be operating.

WHAT IS							WHAT SHOULD BE					
①	②	③	④	⑤	⑥	10. Doesn't use any other group or performance criteria	①	②	③	④	⑤	⑥
①	②	③	④	⑤	⑥	11. Benchmarks internally against successful standard operating procedures	①	②	③	④	⑤	⑥
①	②	③	④	⑤	⑥	12. Benchmarks other organizations in our market area, including competitors	①	②	③	④	⑤	⑥
①	②	③	④	⑤	⑥	13. Benchmarks perfection	①	②	③	④	⑤	⑥

Suggested patterns:

Item 10 is best rated low on both What Is and What Should Be.

Items 11 and 12 are best rated low on both What Is and What Should Be and higher than the ratings for Item 10. Item 12 should be rated higher than 11 but still suffers from no external reality checks.

Item 11 is best rated high on both What Is and What Should Be. It is seeking not to copy others but to identify the ideal and pursue it.

▨ Notes

1. I use quality management (QM) and total quality management (TQM) interchangeably here. I defer to reports that Deming did not like the term TQM, preferring instead "profound knowledge." QM communicates that there is a formal and continuous improvement process to be realized. Also, the term TQM smacks too much, I suggest, of being a splinter activity and not an integral part of strategic thinking.

2. Cf. U.S. General Accounting Office (1991) and Kaufman and Swart (1995).

3. Kaufman and Swart (1995).

4. Cf. Zemke and Bell (1990).

5. Nordstrom's department stores make a convincing case for this approach (Peters, 1997).

6. This also characterizes a "true" learning organization.

7. The definition of quality is important. A standard one is fitness for use as judged by the user. Adding Mega to the definition of quality adds societal value as well.

8. The giant banking and financial services organization First Union has an interesting way to get from satisfaction with the status quo: to have clients really target important issues for their own financial survival and self-sufficiency. First Union noted that when clients were asked "Are your financial program in order?" the answer was usually "yes." The clients seemed satisfied, but the dialogue about helping them stopped there; they were content with the status quo. When they were asked, instead, "What financial concerns do you have?" there was an opening of a dialogue about concerns for future survival and self-sufficiency. This shift from satisfaction to concerns for future survival opened the door to identifying and solving "Mega" problems before they occurred.

9. Leon Lessinger, Distinguished Professor at the University of North Florida, points out that engineers strive for perfection all the time. No engineer sets out to design an average machine but, rather, a perfect one (zero friction, no use of energy, etc.). This same type of inspiration can and should be used by all people, regardless of their discipline or their organization.

10. Training is for specific and known identified skills, knowledges, attitudes, and abilities; education is more about transfer and generalization to unknown situations.

11. As will be seen shortly, conventional QM doesn't go far enough, for it omits or assumes that there will be value added for external clients and society.

12. Quoted in Joiner (1985) as well as by Galagan (1991).

13. Joiner (1985, 1986).

14. Joiner (1985, 1986), Kaufman (1991b), and Kaufman and Zahn (1993).

15. A Pareto analysis, usually shown in diagram form, indicates which of several problems is most severe and shows the relative severity of all of the problems (Kaufman & Zahn, 1993).

16. Later in this chapter, I show how adding Mega contributes to a more powerful quality management process, called QM+ because of the added societal value-added dimension.

17. Sleezer and Gradous (1998) provide useful nuances concerning evaluation.

18. Kaufman (1992b, 1995f) and Roberts (1993).

19. Kaufman (1998b).

20. Kaufman and Swart (1995).

CHAPTER 9

From Mega Plan to Organizational Success

A Mega plan has to be implemented, consulted, and applied if it is to meet its potential: to bring about useful results. This chapter deals with the following:

- The Mega plan report and its elements
- Putting the Mega plan to work
- Selecting the methods and means—the how-to's to meet the objectives
- Obtaining the methods and means
- Management and continuous improvement
- What will be different as a result of Mega-level strategic planning
- Making operational decisions that will build from the Mega plan

Let's see what it takes to implement the Mega plan (developed using what was provided in Chapter 7) (see Figure 9.1).

Remember, any plan, including a Mega plan, is only as good as the results it delivers. All too often a strategic plan is developed and sits on a reception table to impress visitors. Such a table-top plan does not meet the basic criteria for usefulness: When decisions are made, is the Mega plan retrieved and used?

The Mega plan, when developed as suggested here, provides the criteria for successful implementation and proving that the consequences added value for internal and external clients.[1] Because Mega Planning insists on deriving and using measurable criteria—rigorous perform-

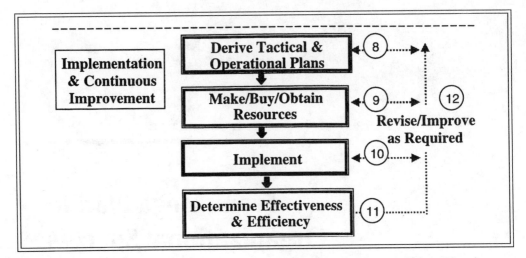

Figure 9.1. The Implementation and Continuous Improvement cluster of Mega Planning.

ance objectives—for implementation and evaluation/continuous improvement, and because each objective is linked to the Ideal Vision, the organizational missions, and the building-block functions, the requirements and processes for implementation are both clear and justifiable.

The Mega Plan Report

To use the results of the Mega plan, a report must be made. The report serves as the blueprint for the design, development, implementation, and continuous improvement. The Mega Planning report is basically a communications document that provides decision makers, including everyone in the organization, with the rationale and information to move forward and continuously improve.

The Mega plan report should do the following:

- Provide a useful guide[2] to implementation
- Allow the organizational partners—associates, administrators, supervisors, executives, external clients, neighbors, and politicians—to understand what is to be accomplished and the basic building-block results necessary for getting from what is to what should be in terms of results and consequences
- Provide the basis for continuous improvement

How long the report should be. The final Mega plan report should be long enough to provide guidance for what to change and what to continue. It should be relatively short, concise, and clear enough to encourage its actual use. Its length may vary, but certainly less than 20 pages will make the document usable.

Elements of the Report

Introduction. This should contain the title of the report, the name of the organization, names of the authors and their positions, and the date of the document.

The Ideal Vision. The statement of the Ideal Vision describes in measurable terms the world that the planning partners wish to help create, with others, for future generations. An option is to provide the Ideal Vision without indicators on the title page, perhaps boxed, with the detailed performance indicators inside the report or as an appendix.

The mission objectives. The mission objectives,[3] including all performance indicators, are provided. An option, if the nature of the readership seems more responsive to tangible purposes first, is to provide the mission objective before the Ideal Vision in the report. In this "tangible option," the closer-in organizational mission objectives provide a more familiar concrete direction before requiring the audience to consider the bigger picture. Each mission objective describes the overall organizational purpose statements of where it is headed and how it will measure (with valid indicators) when it has arrived.[4]

Needs. The gaps in results selected for closure (and anticipated gaps in results and opportunities) are listed. These provide realistic[5] data concerning the realities of current results and desired/required ones. The needs at the Mega/Outcomes, Macro/Outputs, and Micro/Products levels provide the objective and data-based rationale for the mission objectives. Because they identify gaps between current and desired results, the needs provide

- criteria for planning to get from "what is" to "what should be";
- precise criteria useful for selecting how to get from current results and their consequences to desired and required results and consequences;
- the basic criteria for continuous improvement; and
- the rationale and data for justifying what is to be done and spent on the basis of what it costs to meet versus the costs not to meet the needs: the costs-consequences information.

The detailed databases for the needs might be too extensive for some readers. If the data concerning the gaps in results are quite extensive, they might be provided in an appendix.

Policies. Basic policies identify the decision rules that should be used as the Mega plan is being implemented. The decision criteria are listed in this section. Each time a decision is to be made, these policies should guide the decision. Policies should be provided for the Mega, Macro, and Micro levels.

Roles, responsibilities, budgets, and time lines. Individual and group responsibilities for each of the results and missions are provided. These are based on the functions identified during system analysis. This section could include specific programs, projects, and activities as well as when they begin and end.

For each function or role (to achieve one or more of the functions), a precise measurable objective[6] should be prepared and provided. Time lines, perhaps using Gantt charts, for the accomplishment of major functions should be reported. Budgets for each mission objective element, major initiative, or program are provided. This material might be part of the appendix.

Other elements to be included in this section are management and continuous improvement information. How will all of the projects, programs, and support activities be monitored? What will be done with the performance results? This management plan may be shown by using organization charts and flow diagrams. Often, a circular organization chart can show how the parts and functions of the operation are functionally related one to another instead of just reporting hierarchical chains.

Continuous improvement/evaluation. This plan element describes what will be evaluated and the criteria to be used for continuously moving toward the mission objectives and the Ideal Vision. Remember that the criteria have already been identified in the Ideal Vision and the related primary mission. It is now used to move ever closer toward the Ideal Vision. A continuous improvement plan should include the use of both "hard" and "soft" data points and proper assurances that the results and recommendations will be objective and used for fixing, never for blaming.

Appendix. Any required justifications and rationale for the Ideal Vision, the mission objectives, and each of the unique interventions or programs may be provided here. Also, frequently useful may be the detailed presentation of the data-based needs (gaps in results) to show the magnitude of the discrepancies between current status and desired condition. Graphics are very helpful.

If approval of the plan is required, these additional elements should be included:

- The cost to meet each identified need
- The cost not to meet each need
- Alternative costs and consequences for the mission objectives and derived programs, all related to the Ideal Vision.

The cost-consequences analysis tools discussed in Chapter 7 are helpful for determining these costs.

To assure that mission objectives are appropriate and useful, do an objective check to make sure they have the required characteristics of a useful statement. Figure 9.2 illustrates one process for determining a mission objective's usefulness.

Missions: Are They Appropriate?

Mission Elements	Target		Results/Ends Level		
	Ends	Means	Mega	Macro	Micro
a)					
b)					
c)					
Etc. . .					

Steps:
1. List each element of the mission.
2. For each element, determine if it relates to an end or a means
3. If an element relates to an end, determine if it is focused at the Mega, Macro, or Micro level.
4. If an element is related to a means, or to a Macro or Micro result, ask "What results and payoffs would I get if I got or accomplished this?" Keep asking the same question until an end is identified. If you continue this questioning, you will ultimately get to Mega.

Figure 9.2. A format and procedure for assuring that a mission objective has the required characteristics, deals with ends and not means, and has Mega-level consequences.

Putting the Mega Plan to Work[7]

Selecting the Methods and Means—the How-To's to Meet the Objectives

Based on the alternative methods and means identified in the methods-means analysis, the actual selections of methods, means, resources, programs, projects, activities, and initiatives are all made on the basis of costs/consequences analysis: What does it cost to meet versus ignore the need?[8] Remember, it will be a challenge to restrain your organizational partners from pushing to use a particular favorite solution without (a) using the measurable objectives derived from the needs and/or (b) identifying alternative methods and means for meeting the objectives. Once again, the planning partners' group ensures that the most initial selection of representative holistic thinking has been considered.

Obtaining the Methods and Means

Based on the specifications of what each methods-means must deliver, decisions are made concerning who is to do what, and when, as outlined in the Mega plan report. Allocations should be made objectively on the basis of competence to deliver rather than on historical relationships. In addition, to get what Drucker calls "transfer of ownership,"[9] those who will make and/or deliver the methods-means should be integrated into the continuous improvement team of the organization. The "seamless" development, from Inputs to Outcomes, is an imperative quest. It is

TABLE 9.1 A Form for Linking Alternative Activities, Programs, or Interventions to Mega Planning Intentions

[1] Item Being Considered	[2] Ideal Vision Element to Which Related	[3] Primary Mission Element to Which Related	[4] Function to Which Related	[5] Alternative Methods-Means Considered
1. Quality management (plus)				
2. Reengineering				
3. Benchmarking				
4. Distance learning				
5. Self-directing teams				
6. Needs assessment on a continuing basis				
7. Performance-based budgeting				
8. Etc.				

vital to recognize that the organizational results-chain orientation used in planning is not forgotten in the implementation/continuous improvement phase.

When making any decision concerning a program, project, activity, or intervention, continuous reference to the results chain will assist planning partners in their decisions that will result in useful methods-means selection on the basis of what each contributes. To formalize this consideration, Table 9.1 provides one possible form that might be used.

By using this type of check-results-and-requirements-at-all-levels approach, any selection or changes to methods and means will more likely make a contribution to what the organization commits to deliver. For example, if planning partners suggest implementing a "quality management" process, the planning partners might go through the following steps, using the form in Table 9.1:

1. List the item, such as "continues improvement" in column 1, then
2. determine if the objective would successfully move the organization measurably closer to the Ideal Vision (column 2) and identify the element in the Ideal Vision it will contribute toward, then
3. identify the element of the primary mission objective it relates to in column 3, then
4. identify the related function this intervention relates to in column 4.

This procedure will better assure that any means, program, project, or initiative considered will answer the question "If this process were successful, what results would it deliver at the

Mega/Ideal Vision level (column 2), and at the missions and functions levels (columns 3 and 4). This question should be asked and answered until a clear set of results and consequences is provided to assure that, if adopted and implemented, positive results—continuous progress toward the Ideal Vision and derived missions and functions—will occur. Then

5. define alternative methods and means (column 5) and determine the advantages and disadvantages of each.[10] Then
6. recommend the item being considered if it meets all the criteria for adding value at all planning and results levels and will provide continuous improvement toward realizing the Ideal Vision.

By always checking to assure that any means, process, activity, or program makes a contribution in terms of moving the organization toward the Ideal Vision and its missions, there will be an increase in effectiveness and efficiency.

Management[11] and Continuous Improvement

Management is a do-it-yourself kit. Remember, build the organizational team that will continuously improve what the organization uses, does, and delivers. Each team member should have the opportunity to develop or buy in to the Ideal Vision and the missions. If someone does not want to be part of the adventure, don't force the person but don't allow anyone to sabotage or undermine it. If someone doesn't want to be part of the success, don't allow anyone to get in the way of it either.

Obtaining buy-in. It is important that everyone in the organization—the team—agrees on what Mega Planning is to do and deliver. Figure 9.3 shows an agreement table that can be used with all partners to ensure there is agreement.

When using the agreement table, ensure that everyone actually commits—by one's signature or initials on each answer—to either "Yes" or "No" for each question. If anyone has any doubts (e.g., "I don't know what 'client' means," "I don't know what 'quality of life' means") or doesn't agree, ask the person to check the "No" column. No "Maybe" "or "I want to think about that . . ." responses should be allowed.

This agreement table can be very effective in getting people to systematically think about results and consequences. Use it for all clients, internal and external.

Proactive and Reactive Approaches to Mega Planning and Implementation

When considering ways and means, there are two tactics that may be employed: proactive and reactive.

Ideally, you identify and select methods and means as you roll down from Mega to Macro to Micro to Processes to Inputs. A flow for proactive implementation is shown in Figure 9.4.

Strategic Thinking and Planning Agreement Table	Commitment			
	Clients		Planners	
	Y	N	Y	N
1. The total organization will contribute to clients' and societal survival, health, and well-being.				
2. The total organization will contribute to clients' and societal quality of life.				
3. Clients' and societal survival, health, and well-being will be part of the organization's and each of its facility's mission objectives.				
4. Each organizational operation function will have objectives that contribute to #1 through #3.				
5. Each job/task will have objectives that contribute to #1, #2, #3, and #4.				
6. A needs assessment will identify and document any gaps in results at the operational levels of #1 through #5.				
7. Human resources/training and/or operations requirements will be based on the needs identified and selected in #6.				
8. The results of #6 may recommend non-HRD/training interventions.				
9. Evaluation and continuous improvement will compare results with objectives for #1 through #5.				

Figure 9.3. A Mega Planning agreement table.

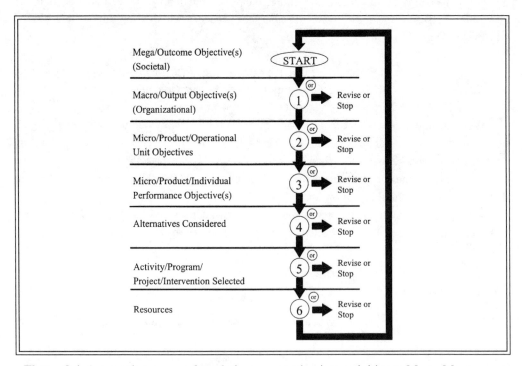

Figure 9.4. A proactive process for relating program/project activities to Mega, Macro, and Micro objectives.

Showing the way. Encourage and model continuous improvement where everyone is on the same team, has a commitment to the Ideal Vision and missions, and makes data-based decisions (on the basis of the gaps between current and required results). Thus, the process of quality management plus (Chapter 8) provides the practical bases for humane and rational management. Everyone, really, is one's own manager.

Report progress and results, and ask teams to identify what should be changed and what should be continued. Those who are doing the work should make decisions. This leads to being active in capturing the expertise of associates, building trust, and better assuring that all are moving toward Mega.

Continuous improvement uses performance data to compare results with intentions and decide what to continue, what to modify, and what to discontinue. Evaluation, in its conventional use, is retrospective, or reactive. It is an important yet after-the-fact determination of successful accomplishment. By comparing accomplishments with intentions (results with objectives), the implementers are able to determine whether or not the methods-means and resources were appropriate. Unlike Mega Planning and its before-the-fact questions, evaluation and continuous improvement are only done after interventions have been put into action. Using a results orientation, including defining needs as gaps in results, evaluation and continuous improvement are both easier and rational because the criteria have already been derived as part of Mega Planning.

Figure 9.5 shows an algorithm to help make the decision to do evaluation and continuous improvement focused on Mega.

Managing the organizational system is not telling people what to do or how to do it. It is not closely supervising them. Management and leadership/stewardship[12] are getting closer together. They are moving from supervising to networking, from an authoritarian hierarchy to finding a common destination and each contributing toward reaching it.[13]

Figure 9.6 illustrates an algorithm for evaluation and continuous improvement that "forces" a Mega focus.

As previously stated, an advantage of being strategic and thinking strategically is that everyone knows and uses

- the Ideal Vision in terms of the society we want for tomorrow's child;
- the mission objectives and the performance indicators for telling both direction and destination;
- the policies (and rules) for decisions; and
- what each person and group within the organization has committed to deliver.

The elements of leadership, stewardship, and management include commitment to a common destination and to the people, individually and together, contributing to get there.

Management may be done by exception. Instead of micromanaging, conduct of the organization's business can be done, often with self-directing teams, by each person or group tracking one's own progress toward known and agreed-on objectives, identifying where and when needs

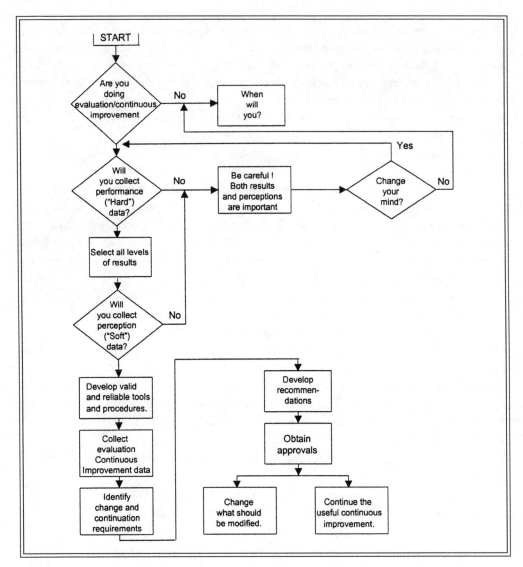

Figure 9.5. An algorithm for evaluation and continuous improvement that links with Mega.[14]

appear or might occur, and knowing precisely where and when to make responsive and responsible changes.

Leaders identify where to go. Managers assure that we get there.[15] Stewards look after everyone in the organization as they move toward a shared destination.[16] The new paradigm for Mega Planning is a shared Ideal Vision to serve as a "guiding star" and ways in which each individual may make one's unique contributions toward shared worthy (Mega level) ends.

Under this shared-destination/teamwork approach, "accountability" now is redefined as agreeing on common destinations and measurable results; developing the most effective and ef-

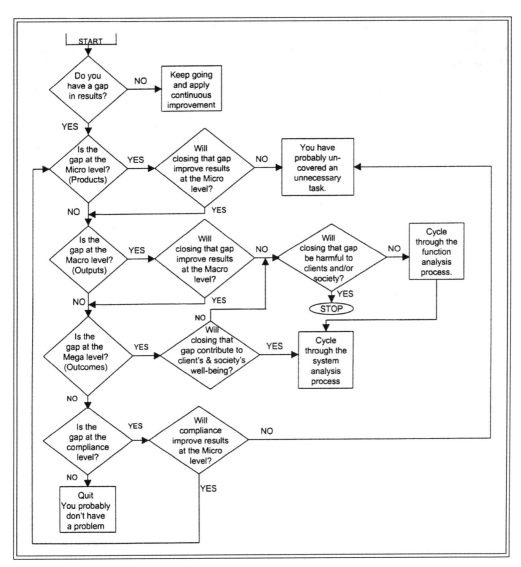

Figure 9.6. Asking the right evaluation and continuous improvement questions to assure a Mega orientation.

ficient ways of getting the required results; finding what works, what doesn't, and fixing it without blame; and getting continuously closer to the missions and Ideal Vision.

Quality management plus (Chapter 8) is the basic implementation "engine" that drives the move from current results and consequences to desired results and consequences. Using a QM+ approach as part of a Mega strategic approach is both sensible and practical. Doing so will initially, for some, require a shift in our paradigms and perceptions about organizations for the corporate culture.

TABLE 9.2 A Business Plan Format for Linking to Mega[17]

What We Will Achieve	What Element of the Ideal Vision Does It Link To?	What Corporate Mission Element Does This Link To?	What Alternative Activities Will Allow Us to Reach Our Objectives?	Our Performance Milestones (functions)	Our Performance Criteria	Our Resources • Physical • Financial • Staff • External Partners

Relating the Mega plan to a business plan. Many organizations develop business plans that describe their intended achievements for the near future. Table 9.2 suggests a business plan format that links the Mega plan and the business plan.

1. Ideal Vision
2. Corporate mission objective(s)
3. Business unit objectives
4. Why we add value by achieving (1) and (2) above

Applying the Three Mega Planning Guides

Three guides, provided first in the Introduction and then along the Mega Planning journey (Figures 9.7. 9.8, and 9.9) will help you as you move from what is to what should be to achieve useful success.

Mega Planning: Creating Success

Mega Planning and tactical planning can help you define and then create, operationally, a better world. Each and every organization, public and private, is a key to that better world, and the application of the concepts and tools just provided will help.

The journey has not been an easy one. If there were one or two simple steps for instant organizational success, they would have been provided. Organizations and society are not simple, nor are the individuals we work with and for every day. Multiply the complexity of individual human differences together and then congratulate all who dare to help associates and organizations be successful in today's and tomorrow's world. Human beings are complex, and to be responsive so must be the methods of Mega strategic, tactical, and operational planning. Who among us would say we ourselves are simple and easy to understand? Why then, should anyone insist on simplistic methods for organizational success? That would only be self-delusion.

CRITICAL SUCCESS FACTOR 1
USE NEW AND WIDER BOUNDARIES FOR THINKING, PLANNING, DOING, AND EVALUATING/
CONTINUOUSLY IMPROVING: MOVE OUT OF TODAY'S COMFORT ZONES.

CRITICAL SUCCESS FACTOR 2
DIFFERENTIATE BETWEEN ENDS AND MEANS—FOCUS ON "WHAT" (Mega/Outcomes, Macro/Outputs,
Micro/Products) BEFORE "HOW."

CRITICAL SUCCESS FACTOR 3
USE ALL THREE LEVELS OF PLANNING AND RESULTS
(Mega/Outcomes, Macro/Outputs, and Micro/Products).

CRITICAL SUCCESS FACTOR 4
PREPARE OBJECTIVES—INCLUDING IDEAL VISION AND MISSION OBJECTIVES—THAT HAVE
MEASURES OF HOW YOU WILL KNOW WHEN YOU HAVE ARRIVED
(Mission statement plus success criteria).

CRITICAL SUCCESS FACTOR 5
DEFINE "NEED" AS A GAP IN RESULTS
(not as insufficient levels of resources, means, or methods).

CRITICAL SUCCESS FACTOR 6
USE AN IDEAL VISION AS THE UNDERLYING BASIS
FOR PLANNING (don't be limited to your organization).

Figure 9.7. The six critical success factors for Mega Planning.

?	Do you commit to deliver organizational contributions that have positive impacts for society? (**MEGA**/Outcomes)
?	Do you commit to deliver organizational contributions that have the quality required by your external partners? (**MACRO**/Outputs)
?	Do you commit to produce internal results that have the quality required by your internal partners? (**MICRO**/Products)
?	Do you commit to have efficient internal products, programs, projects, and activities? (**PROCESSES**)
?	Do you commit to create and ensure the quality and appropriateness of the human, capital, and physical resources available? (**INPUTS**)
?	Do you commit to deliver (a) products, activities, methods, and procedures that have positive value and worth, and (b) the results and accomplishments defined by our objectives? (**EVALUATION/CONTINUOUS IMPROVEMENT**)

Figure 9.8. The basic questions every organization must ask and answer, the levels of planning (Mega, Macro, and Micro) and the levels of results (Outcomes, Outputs, and Products).

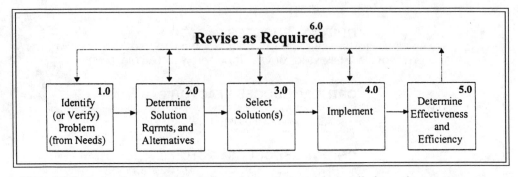

Figure 9.9. A six-step problem-solving process that may be applied any time you want to identify and resolve problems.

For the creation of organizational success, it is important to set ourselves in the context of the larger world in which we all live. To create success we must first define the world we wish to help create and then align everything we deliver, do, and use to that ideal place. We can take our lead from environmentalists who advise "think globally and act locally."

A summary of Mega Planning's 18 steps for achieving organizational success is given in Figure 9.10.

The line between fact-oriented and judgment-oriented approaches is not always clear. You will notice that, regardless of the approach, model, or technique used, human judgment plays an important role. There is no clear line between facts and opinions in planning, management, and evaluation. There is no substitute for rational, sensible human contribution. Ideally, methods and techniques are as much a way of thinking as they are rules and procedures.

Use any tool, including these, as a guide, never as your master. Mega Planning focuses on the big picture of creating, continuously, a better world for all.

Above all, think and act Mega.

EXERCISE

Evaluation and Continuous Improvement

Each **What Is** and **What Should Be** column—on either side of the questions—has the following dimensions in terms of the relative frequency that something does or does not happen:

Consistently (96%-100%)
Quite frequently (85%-95%)
Sometimes (51%-84%)

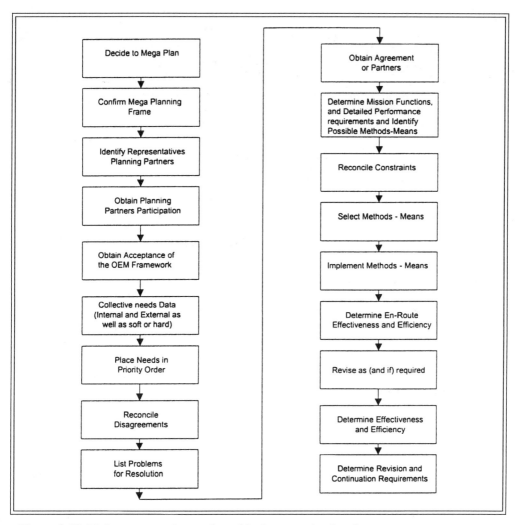

Figure 9.10. Eighteen general steps for achieving organizational success.

Not usually (18%-50%)
Almost never (6%-17%)
Rarely, if ever (0%-5%)

Review your evaluation and continuous improvement processes and methods—how these are conceived and done at your organization—in terms of the following questions. Answer, for each question, both **What Is** (your current practice) and **What Should Be** (your desired practice; what will best serve your organization):

In my organization

WHAT IS							WHAT SHOULD BE					
Rarely, if ever (0-4%)	Almost Never (5%-15%)	Not Usually (16-49%)	Sometimes (50-83%)	Quite Frequently (84-94%)	Consistently(95-100%)	Please indicate the frequency (in terms of percentage of times) with which the following statements are happening within your organization. Please provide two responses to each question:	Rarely, if ever (0-4%)	Almost Never (5%-15%)	Not Usually (16-49%)	Sometimes (50-83%)	Quite Frequently (84-94%)	Consistently(95-100%)

⟵ **WHAT IS** | **WHAT SHOULD BE** ⟶

describes how you see your organization currently operating.

describes how you think your organization should be operating.

WHAT IS							WHAT SHOULD BE					
①	②	③	④	⑤	⑥	1. Evaluation is done after something has happened	①	②	③	④	⑤	⑥
①	②	③	④	⑤	⑥	2. Evaluation is based on perceptions and opinions	①	②	③	④	⑤	⑥
①	②	③	④	⑤	⑥	3. Evaluation data are used for finding faults with individuals and/or small groups	①	②	③	④	⑤	⑥
①	②	③	④	⑤	⑥	4. Evaluations is used for finding organizational faults	①	②	③	④	⑤	⑥
①	②	③	④	⑤	⑥	5. Evaluation is used for finding external and client faults	①	②	③	④	⑤	⑥
①	②	③	④	⑤	⑥	6. Evaluation is used for finding what to improve for individuals and/or small groups	①	②	③	④	⑤	⑥
①	②	③	④	⑤	⑥	7. Evaluation is used for finding what to improve for the entire organization	①	②	③	④	⑤	⑥
①	②	③	④	⑤	⑥	8. Evaluation is used for finding what to improve to add value for external clients and society	①	②	③	④	⑤	⑥

Suggested patterns:

Items 9.1 through 9.5 are best both rated low on What Is and What Should Be.

Items 9.6 and 9.7 are best rated low on What Is and What Should Be, but it is better to be higher on What Should Be than Items 9.1 through 9.5.

Item 9.8 is best rated high on What Is and What Should Be.

▨ Notes

1. As an old adage tells us, a problem well defined is more than half solved. Another advises us that failing to plan is planning to fail.

2. The emphasis is on "guide." There is a tendency for strategic plans in general to be Micro plans and provide too much in terms of procedures, activities, methods, and processes and miss the opportunity for creative and committed organizational members to select the best ways and means to meet the primary mission, the long- and short-term missions, and thus move everyone closer to the Ideal Vision. A Mega plan should not be a vehicle for micromanagement.

3. Recall that there is the primary mission objective and long-and short-term missions that provide a chain of missions linking this year and next year to a succession of missions moving ever closer toward the Ideal Vision.

4. Recall Critical Success Factors 2 and 4 and make certain that rigorous performance indicators/criteria are included for the mission objectives.

5. Both hard and soft data.

6. In interval or ratio scale terms.

7. The major focus of this book is on Mega-level strategic and tactical planning. This section only provides a brief introduction to the delivery of the plans since there are a number of excellent books on management and administration. I don't attempt to duplicate these resources but only provide the basic data to be used by them.

8. See Chapter 8 for these tools and approaches.

9. Drucker's insight is that by involving people in the decision to do or use something, they shift from seeing it as "your plan" to seeing and accepting it as "our plan."

10. The uses of costs-consequences analysis and/or other systems analytic tools, described in Chapter 7, are useful here.

11. I am not going into program management. The literature is full and useful, so I suggest that you review the models and techniques available, remembering that almost all of them stop at a Macro focus.

12. Block (1993).

13. Bennis and Nannus (1985), Block (1993), Deming (1986, 1990), Drucker (1973, 1985, 1988), Joiner (1985, 1986), Kanter (1989), Kaufman and Zahn (1993), Naisbitt and Aburdene (1990), Peters (1987), Popcorn (1991), Roberts (1987), Senge (1990), and Toffler (1990).

14. Based on Kaufman (1992d).

15. Bennis and Nannus (1985) and Drucker (1973).

16. Block (1993) has a powerful concept, and I suggest that it be extended to include the Mega level of concern. Block seems to stop at the Macro level.

17. This is based on the result of a workshop on strategic thinking and planning with professional staff of the Australian Public Service.

Applications and Case Studies of Mega Planning

Many people want to know if Mega Planning really works. Can it really be done, or is it academic and theoretical? Will public and private organizations accept and apply it, or are they only interested in improving the efficiency of current operations and rely on the profound hope that doing things right will result in doing the right things?[1] This section deals with these questions.

It works when applied fully and consistently. Mega planning has been applied. And it works. It works best when people apply it completely and with integrity. Partial attempts don't serve us well. After all, why should there be detours on our way to making our world measurably better instead of a direct path?

In this section of the book, I offer (1) some simulated case studies—to make major points about Mega planning clear—and (2) some brief summaries of cases where Mega planning has been successfully applied in operational situations.

Not every application has been totally successful. Why? Because when even partially successful cases are objectively analyzed to find out why they "failed," it usually turns out that there are one or more reasons for most: (1) Only part of the process has been applied; that it has been inserted[2] in one part of an operation without taking account of the fact that every organization (and its context) is a system; (2) good intentions were overcome by quick fixes; (3) there was a change of ownership or executive management,[3] where the new players acted to replace existing initiatives with their own in an effort to "take control" and have no vestiges of the old regime; (4) there was not sufficient sponsorship by senior management who often jumped on a newer and more fashionable bandwagon; (5) internal politics took precedence over adding value to all partners; (6) turnover of key personnel revealing lack of depth of competence and commitment; and/or (7) planners lost the discipline about the six critical success factors of Mega planning and shifted back to more comfortable (and acceptable) tools and methods. We can learn from both successful and unsuccessful applications, however.

The context of Mega planning is important, and often people don't understand why one would want to think in terms of societal value added instead of simply improving current processes and procedures. Let's look as some stories that answer the question "Why do Mega planning?"

Hypothetical Scenarios Based on Reality

First, a fable about a fish, conventional wisdom, and planning. It speaks to the requirement to change paradigms in order to be successful at Mega Planning.

The Mainstream (a Fable)[4]

Ever since he was spawned, Sylvester seemed different. He didn't even care for his name—he thought it sounded more devious than smart. Although he was a fairly good student in school (he was often in school, for fish tend to live in schools), Sylvester was always thinking, questioning, and seeking alternatives.

The teachers, it seemed to him, were preparing everyone for life in the Mainstream. There were courses on water temperature, bottom characteristics, velocity, the sociology of fish, turbulence, plankton, predators, and cooperative swimming. Students were told it was their destiny to learn their lessons, grow up, and take their preordained place in the Mainstream.

Sylvester wasn't completely convinced. He continued to think, puzzle, and question. Why were all of these courses being taught? What *was* the Mainstream? Where was it going? Why should he want to go where it was headed? His teachers were, at first, amused and patronizing. They told him that such foolish questions would pass. "Just study your lessons," they advised.

As Sylvester got older (he developed a fine set of gills that was the envy of many of his classmates), his questions were still unanswered. Typical of his inconsistent high school career, he didn't make the high school swimming team. He even tried, unsuccessful, to institute a swimming-upstream event.

Going to college. Sylvester graduated from high school with grades good enough to get himself into a decent college—Aquarian University, right in his home creek. The courses were all about living, and "making it," in the Mainstream. Fish who were experienced in the "real world" came to class and lectured on life there. Still, Sylvester asked, "Isn't it easier to find the Mainstream than to know where it is going? Are there any alternatives?" The professors at Aquarian were less amused than his high school teachers. They told him that to get along, he had to go along. The business of fish, they said, was like politics: It was the art of the possible. They advised him to think about change—if he had to be concerned with it at all—as incremental. "Take small, deft slithers lest you displease the bosses or even your associates." "Be 'practical. Be 'real world.'" Sylvester grappled quietly with his heretical questions, studied, and passed his courses. Still, he thought about purpose, destination, rationality, and goal setting, not just goal seeking.

He devoured the literature on planning and management, and most of it, regardless of the rhetoric, sounded, well, basically "Mainstream." The "in" books had a few punchy phrases and were occasionally peppered with some innovative-sounding words. But at closer examination they were simply suggesting more *efficient* ways to swim in the Mainstream.

On to work in the "real world." After graduating, Sylvester took a job in a large and prestigious Mainstream company. The pay was good (with lots of extra plankton as bonuses). One of his coworkers, Fred, was more conventional and thought that planning was best done by building on what was known and accepted. Fred and Sylvester argued. A lot. After months of wrangling passed, their mutual boss decided that research should resolve their conflict; both of them were to pursue a major project, each following his method of planning. There was to be a competition based on results, not talk!

Sylvester's boss was astute. She allowed him to pursue his "curious" type of strategic planning. (He called it "Mega Planning" because it took a very wide-angle view as compared to the conventional methods that Fred quoted.) It was time to go from theory to results.

A different perspective. While most fish just worked on improving their technique, swam in circles, drifted in the current, and headed downstream in unquestioning unison, Sylvester wanted to find out where the Mainstream was headed and what was there where it ended. His approach depended on finding the gaps between the payoffs waiting at the end of the Mainstream and what would be good for fishdom. He wanted to identify the current results and compare those to the best possible payoffs before selecting solutions, such as swimming styles and swimming teams.

One day, while doing research at the edge of the Mainstream, Sylvester came upon a variety of fish he had never seen. (He thought it might be something called a salmon, but he was too discreet to ask.) The stranger told him about a new (for Sylvester) technique that would allow a fish to swim both up- and downstream, to venture to the side, and to go into new waters. Sylvester picked this "radical" method, which would allow him to venture all the way downstream—and to come back! With this technique, he could find out the real consequences of following the Mainstream. Fred, on the other fin, selected the traditional tail extenders to accelerate his trip downstream, noting that his approach was "practical" and "real world."

Finding the real "real world." Fred and Sylvester set out at the same time, with many supporters cheering for Fred and a very few wishing Sylvester well. Fred was a bit smug as he glided in the Mainstream, for he had called together all of his colleagues and gotten their concurrence on his means and methods. Sylvester was less self-assured, but he told himself that reason was on his side—didn't it make sense to know where you want to go before swimming there? He believed that everyone was so busy doing what fish had been doing for centuries that none realized that they just might be swimming in a river of no return!

Once downstream (which was a long way away from where they started), Sylvester found to his horror that the revered Mainstream led over a waterfall and into a shark pool where all of the Mainstreamers were becoming shark food! He watched helplessly as Fred, tail extenders and all, was swept to his gastronomic fate. Sylvester, seeing the impact of simply following the "tried and true" Mainstream, quickly diverted, using the approach he learned from the salmon, into a different river, there to find a huge, fish-friendly lake with ample food and opportunity. It was a different destination than the one gained by following the traditional current, but it offered much, much more than the conventional and accepted Mainstream. Using his newly acquired technique, he rushed back (upstream, of course) and tried to change the conventional wisdom about swimming in the Mainstream! He told of his experience, the shark pool, the new lake, and pointed out that Fred wasn't back—and wouldn't be.

It wasn't easy to convince others. It was established and conventional fish wisdom that swimming in that Mainstream was destiny. They said that the Big Fish knew what they were doing, and other small fry should just follow the directions and example of ages. Sylvester tried to change their minds. He attempted, for example, to get alternative planning courses in the schools, but the tenured fish resisted.

The payoffs. Fortunately, Sylvester's company was innovative and concerned about both fish and business. It encouraged Sylvester's "big picture" approach to planning and used it to plan a new subsidiary, which prospered. Sylvester now is president of the offshoot (called Fish-Futures) that is making a major contribution from working on the new lake he discovered. Also, his employees are setting up even more new businesses in previously unfamiliar rivers and tributaries—business areas that never would have been thought of without Sylvester's new technique that he based on a new paradigm for fish and swimming.

But to make sure his approach and objectives weren't flashes in the plan (or bait on a hook), Sylvester has just hired another "questioner," an innovator, to head up FishFutures' planning department. She will make certain that any new "mainstreams" they select will not turn out as poorly as did the old, traditional one.

Moral: *The mainstream has a lot of momentum, but you might not want to end up where it is going.*

From Training to Performance[5]

Here is a simulated dialogue between a vice president and an employee of a hypothetical company. It demonstrates how Mega Planning can work to everyone's advantage.

Karen and John:[6] Avoiding the Quick Fix

Karen is Vice President of Personnel for Watkins Industries. She has a small staff of two personnel specialists, two human resource developers, an affirmative action officer, a staff assistant, and two clerk typists. There are over 1,000 people in the company.

Recently, there has been some concern about falling orders, and some informal reports that salespeople "didn't know how to 'sell.'" John, the training specialist, suggested in a memo to Karen that a special training course be offered (even mandated) that would show salespeople how to sell. (In fact, his memo read "We *need* a sales training program.")

Karen sat down with John and carefully and skillfully walked him through some considerations. Karen began, "I appreciate your taking the initiative in helping make Watkins Industries and all of its associates successful. I have read your proposal and would like to explore it and some possibilities with you. Before we move ahead, let's get some of the 'hard' data on sales, selling, and orders." Pulling out the latest computer readouts, she spread them out for both to see. "There does seem to be a decrease in sales, and even corrected for seasonal cycles, we are down 31% over the past two reported years. We do have a gap in our results, don't we?"

John smiled and nodded.

"Does this mean that we ought to be training?" Karen asked.

John seemed puzzled; he was a trainer, and training had always been *the* solution around Watkins Industries. Karen suggested, "Let's dig into the data a bit more, OK?"

They poured over the data, and John noticed that sales were down across the board in all product lines and among all salespeople.

"That's strange, come to think of it," he said. "If it were a training problem, some salespersons might be more successful than others, but there aren't really any major differences, are there? Let me go back and reexamine this area and rethink my proposal."

Five days later, John was back.

"Karen, I think I was jumping into a solution—training—before really documenting the problem. The pattern of sales data got me thinking, and I looked further. It seems that there is also an increase in customers returning our shipments to us. When I looked at the curve of decreased sales, it almost perfectly matched with the increase in returns! He noted that we have a performance problem, not a training problem. It turns out that our manufacturing plant has shifted over to a new set of vendors for materials in order to save money, and most of our customers report that the quality of our outputs has suffered badly. Sales are slipping because our poor quality is turning off even loyal customers. Sales training won't do us any good. We'd better get this information about quality to top management in case they haven't gotten the word."

Karen was dismayed at the news but pleased that she had not squandered resources by going ahead with a large training program before finding that the basic problem was different from that which was first assumed. Means (training), desirable ends (fitness of the output as judged by the user and profits that continue over time, not just one or two fiscal quarters), and their difference-yet-relationship were now clearly in focus at Watkins Industries.

In this example, Karen and John correctly identified an initial problem (by discovering the basic causes of the presenting symptoms) before rushing into a training solution. The *means* was at first thought to be training (remember the prescriptive-sounding "We *need* sales training"), but the real needs were the gaps in quality of the ends, which adversely affected orders, sales, and profits. The training suggested by John could have been the subject of intensive Micro planning and still failed to provide the desirable larger (Mega or related Macro) results.

Mega Planning and Personal Everyday Life

Mega Planning can be applied to one's personal life. Here is a scenario from two people struggling to find happiness and a good life. Note how "need" when used as a verb and not as a gap in results can distort one's thinking—and consequences.

Jim and Katherine:[7] Deciding on Good Mental Health

Jim had just broken up with Katherine. He was really sad—actually quite blue—and often lacked the energy to get out of his apartment or to work up to his capability. He made an appointment with a counselor to get some help and insight into his feelings and future. As the appointment time grew closer, he got more panicky and several times picked up the phone to call Katherine to apologize and attempt to get back together. Then he recalled the vast differences in their values, in what they liked to do, and in what made them happy. She was a nice person, to be sure, but the warmth between them just didn't last. Still, Jim was miserable.

"I don't know what to do," Jim said to the counselor. "I just plain *need* Katherine. I am lonely and desperate without her. I can't seem to think straight or do anything. I just sit around and think about her and how I want to be with her."

Silence.

"I know that we really don't match, but I just seem to *need* her."

More silence.

"What's going on? Why can't I get her out of my head?"

The counselor asked, "If Katherine is the solution, what's the problem, Jim?"

Jim was stunned at first. He pondered the question and started putting Katherine into perspective with his hopes, aspirations, goals, and desires.

"Are you telling me that I have picked Katherine as a solution to my problems and I haven't first identified my goals—where I want to go in life? Who I am, what I want, where I want to go, what makes me happy? Do I have to resolve that and *then* consider whether or not Katherine is the partner with whom to accomplish all of this?"

The counselor responded, "Does that seem to make sense to you?"

Jim wrestled with this "means-ends" issue for a while and then was ready to pursue it some more. At his next appointment, he asked, "Isn't dealing with emotional things like love and desire out of the bounds of formal problem solving? I mean, don't feelings defy 'scientific' analysis?"

The counselor replied, "Why should it be out of bounds to apply rationality to one's own life and future?"

"Hmmm," responded Jim, as he began to realize that one's personal life could be the subject of rational thought and analysis.

Jim's counselor laid out a six-step[8] process for identifying and solving problems and sent him home to see if it could be applied to Jim, his life, Katherine, his feelings, and the future he wanted to create. At first, Jim was uncomfortable and wanted to chuck it all, call Katherine, and get back together. Then he remembered his pain and Katherine's hurt and anguish each time they argued over very basic values and interests. He said to himself, "The problem-solving approach has to be worth a try. I guess if it doesn't really work—if it doesn't allow me to figure this whole situation out—then I can always call Katherine and try to patch things up."

Jim bought a stack of file cards and wrote each of the six steps on a different one and then tried to put onto paper the results of applying each step. After much erasing and throwing away what seemed like a thousand cards (it was really only 12), the results looked like this:

1.0 *Identify (valid) problems based upon needs.* I want to be happy; self-fulfilled; make enough money to live on without hardship or denying myself food, shelter, and transportation, and then retire at an upper-middle-class level; share love with a partner so that I want to come home to her; have two or three children who can go to college if they choose. I want good health, to experience the world—Africa, Asia, Australia, Europe—and finish my master's degree in management.

I am not happy now; I seem to be drifting. My master's program has been ignored for a year and a half. I am in love (I think), but it doesn't make me happy. (Is this the way love should feel?) I don't have children now, and without a wife it doesn't seem likely.

Having written the above, Jim began to realize that he had identified some of his goals, purposes, and the gaps between "what is" and "what should be," but he lacked the specific details to go further. He then turned to the next cards.

2.0 *Determine detailed requirements and alternatives for resolving the problem.* I want to retire at or before age 60 with income from savings and/or investments of at least 40% above the then standard for middle-class comfort. My children, *if they so desired,* will have attended colleges of their choice and graduated and found self-sufficient employment. I will have a wife, and we will stay married (happily, as indicated by my feelings and hers and by our actively being together instead of drifting into isolation). My wife will share the same values as mine while maintaining her personal worth, dignity, and desires—she should share visions with me, not subvert her own. I will have my master's degree in management and will have been promoted to a manager's level, or higher, in a company.

My alternative possible solutions to this include Katherine (although she doesn't seem to match me and these values, does she?), seeking counseling with her, or finding another partner. I could finish my current master's program or shift to another. I could start an investment program, join an investment club, learn the stock market and the economics of investing and risk, or bet all of my savings at the track.

Jim thought that there were some more options to consider, but for now he continued. Thinking in terms of costs (financial and emotional) and associated payoffs, Jim came up with the following:

3.0 *Select solutions from among the alternatives.* Sign up for the remaining courses in my master's program. Date other women and frankly share with them my values and future objectives and determine the extent to which love is discovered *and* they share my future and I share theirs. I will start Monday to review investment options with the licensed investment broker who has been so successful for my Uncle Bill, lay out my financial timetable and resources, and start moving toward my objectives.

4.0 *Implement selected solutions and methods.* Jim wrote down the sequence and schedule for each of these functions, along with major milestones to use for determining his progress (or lack thereof).

Getting into all of this, Jim then wrote down a rough evaluation and continuous improvement plan.

5.0 *Determine effectiveness and efficiency.* Check progress weekly, monthly, and yearly using the criteria from Steps 1.0 and 2.0.

6.0   *Revise as (and when) required.* Based on my criteria and my progress, I commit to changing, as required. I can even change my goals, objectives, and values!

Jim took this back to the counselor, laid it all out, and asked, "How am I doing?"

The counselor replied, "What do *you* think?"

Jim replied, "I'm on my way!"

"Right," said the counselor. "I believe you will do just fine."

"I might ring your bell if I run into trouble down the road. Thanks for your help," said Jim with the first real smile he had shown during counseling. The counselor concluded with "You've done yourself some real favors. Count on yourself."

Thus Jim applied the lessons of Mega Planning and used the six-step problem-solving process: differentiate between means and ends, focus first on Mega–societal and personal survival and well-being—and apply a six-step process in which you identify problems before solving them. Even in our personal lives, being rational, sorting out means from ends, and watching out for solutions that don't go with our real problems can be very constructive—even freeing.

▓▓ Case Studies of Organizations Applying Mega Planning

Organizations, both public and private, have opted to apply Mega Planning. Here are some. First, the Florida Department of Corrections.

Benchmarking Perfection to Obtain Best Practices and Add Value to Floridians[9]

In the 1990s, the Florida Department of Corrections (DC) responded to a challenge from citizens and the governor to deliver and demonstrate value added for the taxpayers of Florida. The literature and accomplishments from "total quality management" inspired a self-direction to continuously improve. The DC has developed and is continually improving a quality program called "Corrections Quality Management Leadership" (CQML). The DC is additionally addressing several elements missing from conventional quality management processes by benchmarking not only externally, against other "industry leaders," but internally, against definitions of the kind of results it wishes to achieve for the kind of society it desires to co-create.[10] Doing so required rethinking assumptions that had been made about quality and including some additional directions as the quality team and management enlarged the quality management/continuous improvement envelope.

Benchmarking: A solution in search of a problem? One source of possible misdirection (despite the best of intentions) was a popular notion that public sectors should always benchmark private sector organizations, often without first defining the desired end results and consequences.[11] This practice is usually not productive. For one thing, private sector organizations often tend to pay less attention to societal value added than do public ones. A second problem might come from a tendency for private sector organizations to optimize in the short term (quarterly profits) and not look after the middle and longer runs in terms of value added for external clients (including society).

To expand their paradigm to Mega, the consideration of societal/health/well-being was added before indiscriminately adopting other organizations' "best practice." For the DC, then, best practices and benchmarks combined that which was developed internally with that which was discovered externally from both the public and private sectors.

To apply societal payoffs–where inmates go to after release and realizing that the same society pays for crime and criminality created by any failures of a corrections system to prepare inmates for life—the DC decided to identify society as the primary client and beneficiary of any and all organizational activity, including itself. It adopted a new organizational paradigm, where there are two "bottom lines:"

Conventional bottom line: Short-term profits (for profit-seeking organizations), continued funding (for public sector organizations)

Societal bottom line: Measurable value added to society

An example of applying Mega-level concerns to quality and planning is the Florida Department of Corrections' *operational mission* (informal, but part of the culture) to do the following:

Put ourselves out of business through success: reduce recidivism to zero and, working with others, help create a society where no one goes to prison.

Sadly, this mission is not likely to be achieved in our lifetime, but it gave a focus to all that the DC uses, does, produces, and delivers: the improvement of society and all who live there. By focusing on an ever-improved society, the DC could make operational and tactical decisions based on societal value added. Also, it used this societal bottom line to enlarge the conventional quality management envelope to one that added societal value added to internal organizational performance improvement.

As a cooperative venture with Florida State University, the DC developed a self-assessment instrument that collected basic benchmarks of DC understanding and performance relative to quality management so that the organization and its associates could gain performance data on which to base its continuously improving. Mega-level indicators were added to the conventional 14 points of Deming's to assure that linkages would be made between what the DC uses, does, produces, delivers, and societal value added.[12]

The Florida Department of Corrections used this database to answer organizational questions most important to its quality managerial leadership processes. Based on a representative sample of the DC's 28,000+ employees' opinions regarding CQML, the aggregated data from the survey were used to determine the discrepancy between current and desired states of quality managerial leadership for different demographic groups within the DC. Based on the magnitude of these discrepancies, decisions regarding the closure of these gaps (in terms of prioritization and importance) are better facilitated. Additionally, data obtained from the initial survey effort can be used to establish a baseline against which the DC can track future progress. This database will continue to be part of the way in which the DC continuously improves as it adds value to its associates, to the agency, and to the people of Florida.

It developed and used a holistic and Mega-focused system approach to quality management and continuous improvement. The continuous improvement concept and process are vital for any organization and its associates to add value to themselves, their organization, and to their external clients as well as society to be served. By adding the focus of the societal bottom line to strategic planning, needs assessment, and quality management, the DC can now better assure that it not only does things right but also does the right things—advice long ago given by Peter Drucker. In addition, it provides solid measurable justification for improvement and demonstrating to others what return they have received for the expenditures. This approach is one the DC has successfully applied to the continuous improvement of its continuous improvement process.

A Major International Energy Company Applies Mega Planning

Another example of applying Mega planning is Refinor, a very large petroleum products division of Perez Companc, an Argentinean based industrial giant.

Refinor, being the leader in the production and distribution of combustible products in North Argentina, Bolivia, and Paraguay, is dedicated to reaching the full potential of its area of influence, Mercosur (south market) of Latin America. This recognized potential extends beyond natural resources onto its people, employees, customers, and the community.

Refinor produces liquid combustibles such as propane and butane as well as kerosene, gas oil, light oil, and so on. The first destination of all condensed crudes in the Northeast is the distillery, dominating the local market as it is the only one in the region. Local storage plants throughout the region satisfy demand. It also commercializes its products through the operation of many full-service retail stations in the region.

Under the guidance of Buenos Aires-based management consultant Mariano Bernardez, the company, community, and stakeholders pursued applying Mega Planning. They started by setting a Mega-related Ideal Vision[13] that was used to drive organizational performance improvement:

> Refinor's social end is the development and delivery of a better standard of living for the people in their communities. Create self-sufficiency and self-reliance, generate jobs and professional advancement for employees, clients, and vendors.

From Mega to Macro. The Refinor planning partners derived Macro-level objectives (based on the Ideal Vision) in order to derive their mission:

> Increase to at least 35% in Refinor's gasoline sales based on brand recognition and preference among the people in the northwestern region of Argentina who are in its market and in its regional home office.

From this Ideal Vision and primary mission, they derived differential business factors:
1. *With its clients,* increase sales by
   - developing new service centers that integrate quality and quantity, thus generating a positive trademark image and reflecting the prestige of its shareholders.

- developing superior sales tactics based on their comparative advantage.
- including independent service stations and clients with Refinor in a chain of solid service, united by the same commercial philosophy.

2. *With its business partners,* create strategic alliances and communication channels that will permit Refinor to
- participate in and develop common business interests.
- continuously identify convergent points of interests.

3. *With the communities,* as a "good neighbor," to recognize its responsibilities to preserve the environment and commit to minimizing/eliminating the effects caused by its products and services to avoid adverse effects on its employees, clients, the community, and the environment.

Policies. After the purposes had been derived, the planning team developed policies to achieve the above:

- Full compliance with all environmental rules and regulations.
- Optimize the use of energy, natural resources, and other materials.
- Raise awareness and respect for the environment and how to maintain and improve it toward zero pollution and resulting illness or disability.
- Monitor compliance with policies and objectives, guaranteeing a commitment to continuous improvement and health and well-being.
- Constant collaboration with educational and sanitary organizations to achieve the Mega objectives.

To operationalize the mission and commitment to survival and self-sufficiency of all members of the communities it served, Refinor made a commitment to meet ISO 14000 environmental standards and then met them. The parent company also learned from this Mega example and applied it to other parts of its operation, including Peru where it stopped production of a newly acquired company until environmental quality standards were met.

The development of human resources. All Refinor personnel participated in continuous improvement programs and/or workshops. Workshops consisted of a three-day activity with cross-sector, cross-level teams composed of management, labor force, and vendors, directed at creating and developing solutions to problems previously identified by the company and/or the community.

Refinor's investment in its people sets it apart from its competitors. At this time, the company is going through a stage of consolidation with its people and their values that should be reflected by

- high professionalism of jobs and training/education.
- formation of multidisciplinary, multilevel work groups to achieve a common goal of societal survival, self-sufficiency, and well-being for all.

- high commitment and enthusiasm to each other and Mega objectives.

- management locations close to its clients, processes, and markets.

- norms and procedures created by a genuine consensus among all involved.

- encouragement of employees by empowering them with the capacity and responsibility to make decisions and take the initiative.

- positive mental attitude.

Process for implementing Mega Planning. A key process for Refinor's Mega Planning implementation was the "workout." As the organizational consultant and change facilitator, Bernardez formed partnerships with management, the communities, and other service providers and used a General Electric-developed process—the "workout"—for linking individual and organizational activities to the mission and the Ideal Vision. The workout is a participative process that involves all planning partners in defining and achieving the company's future and its contributions to the shared future.

The workouts revealed some very interesting things. One area was concern about losses of petroleum as it went from refinery to distribution points. With a Mega orientation, they observed that "if we don't leverage the real income of the local population, they will rather steal than buy our fuel at a cost of $5M a year for a $50M total sales company." Instead of investing heavily in pipeline repair and maintenance, they investigated other possible sources of loss and found that some locals along the pipelines were "tapping" into the lines as a source of cheap (free) energy. Instead of a focus on repair and maintenance, Refinor dealt with how to get people, who could be clients and not thieves, to be able to acquire its products legitimately. The standard fix was maintenance; the Mega approach identified an entirely different solution as being required.

The workouts also found that another source of losses was from ill-maintained tanks. These maintenance problems were directly related with the perceived former employees of YPF (the former Argentinean government-owned petroleum company) who felt disempowered. This perception resulted in a loss of interest in their regular tasks. Again by being concerned with performance instead of means and activities, the realistic focus for improvement was uncovered. The workouts provided the vehicle for a commitment to adding value for self and others, not just "licking their wounds." The workouts, by focusing on Mega, resulted in participants being actively concerned with adding value to themselves, their organizations, and the communities in which they all lived. The workout process raised commitment to performance and results.

Refinor's Mega Planning has a lasting effect. The initiative was so successful that the communities decided, when the company was put on the market by its parent organization, to continue this program on their own resources so that it would be independent of any organizational support.

The Niagara Wires Case: Its Mega Approach

The management of the Niagara Wires[14] plant in Quincy, Florida, wanted to improve quality and productivity. They had read about the success of "Japanese-style management," "excellence," "involvement groups," and "quality circles." Management wanted to find a way to harness the human potential of all of their workers, from hourly employees to executive staff.

Niagara Wires, located in a town of about 9,000 people, is one of the largest employers in the area. The plant makes forming fabrics that are sold directly to paper manufacturers who use the fabric to make paper items such as bags, cartons, and writing pads. It does not have a direct retail market but supplies those who do; in other words, Niagara Wires' customers have customers. Niagara's clients are very exacting about the quality of the forming fabric. Not only must it perform well, it also must look perfect.

Because the company didn't have a retail clientele, it would have been tempting for some at the plant to forget about delivery quality, to forget their customers' concerns about how the forming fabric worked as part of a larger, complex manufacturing process assembly for those who bought the forming fabric from them. Management was having none of this attitude and launched an ambitious (but realistic) program to improve quality. They were insightful enough to realize that all employees, from top to bottom, had to share in the quality vision and then, together, make it a reality.

Niagara Wires hired a needs assessment and planning consultant who laid out all three planning scales and urged the Mega option. The discussions were lively. Some managers wanted to focus on production and each point along the production line as the point for improved quality. (This was, it was explained, a Micro-level, or Product-level, concern.) Others argued for out-the-door quality as the basic unit of concern (the Macro level). A few lobbied for the Mega frame of reference, noting that all of the pieces and products within Niagara Wires had to integrate with other pieces and products within their plant as well as at the customers' plants. Without successful integration, they argued, there would be little business in the future.

The Mega scale won out (upper management liked this option). Workshops on needs assessment and planning, quality circles (termed "involvement teams"), and quality were held for executives, managers, supervisors, and lead personnel.

Soon it was time to get the hourly workers involved and committed. Some planners expressed concern about the ability of the on-the-job workers to understand the "big, big picture." Even the consultant cautioned that workers who never completed high school might not be able to conceptualize the three kinds of results, let alone a results chain. The vice president of manufacturing was resolute: "If we are going to define a better future, we all have to know and share the same vision. I have confidence in these people, and even if they don't understand it all, at least we gave them the opportunity. Each person, from hourly employee to the president of the company, gets the same information."

As a result, the hourly production workers not only were to be involved in discussion about the product (the Micro-level concern) but were to receive full disclosure of the company's Mega-level intentions. Briefings were scheduled for the hourly workers, one for each of the shifts. The consultant was a bit wary. Could the hourly workers understand the big picture? According to the conventional wisdom, such people were literal, tangible, and "practical"—perhaps they couldn't handle abstractions!

In spite of the apprehensions, the briefings went quite well. The hourly workers were pleased that management seemed to be interested both in them and in their ideas. At the night shift briefing, the Mega perspective was presented (as it was in the previous two meetings). The consultant, attempting to determine the level of understanding, asked, "Does this make sense to you? Is it practical?" One worker answered, "Sure, it's like the sign over the parking lot that says 'Our next quality inspection is made by our customers.' "

Management knew then and there that their quality program was going to be a "winner." Not only did everyone care about the results of their own work, they understood how it all had to "add up" for everyone outside their plant. It was obvious to the hourly employees as well as supervisors and management that there was a results chain that reached from the raw materials to their production floor, from inspection to the loading dock, from their plant to Niagara Wires customers, and from the retail customers back to them. All employees applied Mega Planning concepts and tools. It was a team quality improvement effort.

The payoffs. With a few months after the plan was implemented, indicators supported the initial optimism: Rejections were down, the number of accidents had been reduced, production schedules for making and shipping forming fabric were being met better than ever before, and customers were noticing the better quality.

Using a Mega unit of analysis was really very sensible and practical. If Niagara Wires had limited its concern for quality to production and productivity at each production stage alone, without considering the whole results chain, it might not have met the requirements of its clients and its clients' clients and failed to facilitate the flow of benefits from consumer to producers to workers.

A Community Does Mega Planning[15]

Under the inspiration of its futures-oriented mayor, Tallahassee, Florida, and its host Leon County decided to provide the criteria and basis for decision making and accountability of its citizens and elected officials. A 21st Century Council was born, and citizens representative of the communities set out to define the "vital signs" of quality of life for all who lived there. It was to be nonpolitical; in fact, its policy was to have no elected politician on its board.

After much discussion, they derived "quality of life" indictors that were reviewed and approved by citizens and published yearly. The public reported on progress toward or away from the indicators. In graphic form, it reported in such areas as premature deaths, low-birth-weight babies, infant mortality, suicide rates, violent and nonviolent crime rates, traffic fatalities, homelessness, child abuse, and people in poverty, among other indicators.[16] These quality-of-life indicators provided the basis for doing studies on juvenile justice and human services effectiveness.

Interestingly, by using Mega planning criteria, the Council found that current human services organizations did not know, or would not reveal, their impact on citizens; they were funded in terms of numbers of people served and frequency of services but did not "keep score" on impact and value added. This flaw was not universally well received by conventional human services agencies (some were outright hostile), some of which initially tried to get the study killed. Thanks to a courageous County Council Chair and Council, the report was accepted and released.

The 21st Century Council continues as a community force and resource. It still publishes its independent quality-of-life indicators yearly and special reports whenever it feels it can help the community to improve its responsiveness to its citizens, regardless of color, race, creed, sex, religion, location, or national origin.

▨ Notes

1. This distinction has been clearly made by Peter Drucker in a number of his writings. The concept is so useful that it is often used by other authors, frequently without attribution.

2. See Daryl Conner's 1998 book *Building Nimble Organizations* for some useful advice on change management.

3. Including changes in political parties for public agencies.

4. Based on the original version I wrote for *Strategic Planning Plus* (Kaufman, 1992d).

5. Major professional organizations concerned with helping people and organizations to be successful have started the transition from training to performance. First, perhaps, was the International Society for Performance Improvement, which started out as a programmed instruction society, and then the American Society for Training & Development. This is a trend that should be nurtured, encouraged, and accelerated.

6. Again, this is modified from Kaufman (1992d).

7. Again, slightly modified from Kaufman (1992d).

8. The same six-step problem-solving process discussed in this book.

9. This is based on a longer report prepared by Harry Singletary, former Secretary, Florida Department of Corrections, Tallahassee; Doug Leigh, Graduate Research Assistant, Office for Needs Assessment & Planning, Florida State University, Tallahassee; Bernard Cohen, Assistant Deputy Secretary, Florida Department of Corrections, Tallahassee; Roger Kaufman, Professor and Director, Office for Needs Assessment & Planning, Florida State University, Tallahassee, and Research Professor of Engineering Management, Old Dominion University, Norfolk, Virginia.

10. By benchmarking perfection, they are skipping over "copying" others who may or may not have the same objectives or who might be continuously improving so that what is referenced is out of date. This was suggested by Kaufman and Swart (1995).

11. Cf. Kaufman (1998a, 1998b).

12. A generic version of this instrument can be found in the 1998 *Team and Organization Development Sourcebook* (pp. 173-184).

13. Slightly modified for this report.

14. Now acquired by another global organization and thus no longer uses this name. This case is earlier reported in Kaufman (1992d).

15. Reported by the 21st Century Council in a paper and CD report titled "Human Services Interactive: Executive Summary." More information may be obtained by contacting 21st Century Council, P.O. Box 10312, Tallahassee, Florida 32302.

16. Because the indicators were derived and approved by nonplanners—citizens—there were indicators included that were Input, Process, Product, and Output related. The extent to which groups did not strictly develop Mega criteria for planning and accountability is an indicator of the failure to transfer their paradigms to Mega. It did, however, provide the data for possible continuous improvement for the future.

Glossary

ABCD model: A four-step guideline for developing objectives: audience, behavior, conditions, and data.

Benchmarking: The procedure of comparing one's means and ends with that of others.

Change creation: The definition and justification, proactively, of new and justified as well as justifiable destinations. If this is done before change management, acceptance is more likely.

Change management: Assuring that whatever change is selected will be accepted and implemented successfully by people in the organization. Change management is reactive in that it waits until change requirements are either defined or imposed and then moves to have the change accepted and used.

Comfort zones: The psychological areas, in business or in life, where one feels secure and safe (regardless of the reality of that feeling).

Constraint: A condition that makes it impossible to meet one or more performance requirement. A constraint may only be identified after it is determined that there are no methods-means available to meet performance requirements.

Corporate culture: How "we do things around here"; the social norms and communication protocol associated with a particular organization.

Costs-consequences analysis: The process of estimating a detailed return-on-investment analysis before an intervention is implemented. It asks two basic questions simultaneously: What do you expect to give, and what do you expect to get?

Criteria: Those precise and rigorous specifications that allow one to prove what has been or has to be accomplished.

Critical Success Factor 1: Use new and wider boundaries for thinking, planning, doing, and evaluating/continuous improvement. Move out of today's comfort zones.

Critical Success Factor 2: Differentiate between ends and means—focus on "what" (Mega/Outcomes, Macro/Outcomes, Micro/Products) before "how."

Critical Success Factor 3: Use and link all three levels of planning and results.

Critical Success Factor 4: Prepare objectives—including those for the ideal vision and mission objectives—that have indicators of how you will know when you have arrived.

Critical Success Factor 5: Define "need" as a gap between current and desired results.

Critical Success Factor 6: Use an Ideal Vision as the underlying basis for all planning and doing (don't be limited to your own organization).

Cross-impact analysis: Examines possible arrays of changes in timing potentials and modifies each of the predicted variables to determine optional possibilities. Cross-impact analysis tries to account for potential interaction effects.

Decision theory: Determines optimum strategies (or tactics) for reaching a specific goal based on probabilities for alternative pathways and methods.

Deep change: Change that extends from Mega downward into the organization to define and shape Macro, Micro, Processes, and Inputs. It is termed "deep change" to note that it is not superficial or just cosmetic, or even a splintered quick fix.

Delphi technique: Stimulates group responses and achieves consensus without getting the groups together face-to-face. The Delphi uses the opinions of expert panelists in a round of questions targeted to future events and consequences. For each question, the respondents provide their expectations. After each set of responses, the manager reports the median response and the ranges of responses (usually the center 50%) along with, when appropriate, comments made by the panelists. By the end of several rounds (usually three or four are sufficient), responses are clustered into groups that reflect the built-up and integrated considerations of the panelists as they replay both individually and with knowledge of the responses of other panelists.

Discrepancy analysis: Identifying needs as discrepancies between what is and what should be. This is not a deficiency analysis.

Ends: Results, achievements, consequences, payoffs, and/or impacts.

Formative evaluation: Checking of progress toward an objective to assure that means and methods are contributing to move ever closer toward an objective. It is the process of comparing your progress toward an objective in terms of getting closer to and finally achieving the intended result(s).

Function analysis: Breaks down and accurately identifies the component Products (building-block results) required to meet a higher-level objective, such as a mission.

Game theory: "Players" with opposite interests who are equally knowledgeable and informed and have a known number of options are asked to complete their task in a limited time frame.

Hard data: Performance data that is based on objective observation and is independently verifiable.

Ideal Vision: The measurable definition of the kind of world that one, together with others, commits to help deliver for tomorrow's child.

Implementation and evaluation/continuous improvement: Third phase of strategic Mega Planning; has five steps, or elements: (1) derive the tactical and operational plans, (2) obtain resources, (3) implementation—and simultaneously—(4) continuous improvement/formative evaluation, and (5) determine effectiveness and efficiency. While not strictly planning, this is the part that puts all of the previous planning to work to achieve positive results.

Inputs: The ingredients, raw materials, physical and human resources that an organization can use in its processes in order to deliver useful ends.

Interactions: The interrelationships between or among functions.

Interval: Measurement scale that has an arbitrary zero point and equal scale distances (e.g., degrees in Fahrenheit— 34° is the same distance from 35° as 81° is from 82°).

Learning organization: An organization that sets measurable performance standards and constantly compares its results and their consequences with what is required. Learning organizations best use performance data, related to an Ideal Vision and the primary mission objective, to decide what to change and what to continue; it learns from its performance and contributions.

Macro level of planning: Planning focused on the organization itself as the primary client and beneficiary of what is planned and delivered.

Market attractiveness-business position assessment: Uses a two-dimensional matrix (market attractiveness and business position) in which an organization's market size is graphically depicted.

Market planning: Views a business as a system in which different parts (including possible product lines) interact and each can contribute to or detract from corporate health.

Means: Processes, activities, resources, methods, or techniques used to deliver a result.

Mega level of planning: Planning focused on external clients, including customers/citizens and the community and society that the organization serves.

Mega Planning: Planning where the primary client and beneficiary is society, now and in the future. Mega Planning views individuals and organizations as means to societal ends; planning at the Outcomes level of results.

Mega thinking: Thinking about every situation, problem, or opportunity in terms of what you use, do, produce, and deliver as having to add value to external clients and society. Same as *Strategic thinking.*

Methods-means analysis: Identifies possible tactics and tools for meeting the needs identified in a "system analysis." It does not select them but only identifies the alternatives that could be considered along with noting the advantages and disadvantages of each.

Micro level of planning: Planning focused on individuals or small groups, such as desired and required competencies of associates or supplier competencies.

Mission analysis: The system analysis step that reveals (1) what results and consequences are to be achieved, (2) what criteria (in interval and/or ratio scale terms) will be used to determine success, and (3) what are the building-block results and the order of their completion (functions) required to move from the current results to the desired state of affairs.

Mission profile: Identifies the top-level—overarching—functions (or results) required to get from current results to required ones for the entire organization.

Need: The gap between current results and desired or required results.

Needs analysis: Taking the determined gaps between adjacent Organizational Elements and finding the causes of the inability for delivering required results; also identifies possible ways and means to close the gaps in results—needs—but does not select them.

Needs assessment: Identifies gaps between current results and desired (or required) ones and places them in priority order for resolution based on the cost to meet the need as compared to the cost of ignoring it.

Nominal: Measurement scale that simply names, such as bad/good, hot/cold, on/off.

Nominal group technique: A structured problem-resolving process staged to generate ideas and produce group consensus; encourages the participation of everyone in the group, focuses concentration on a specific question, and reaches consensus through voting.

Objective: Precise statement of purpose, or destination (Where are we headed, and how will we be able to tell when we have arrived?), having four parts: (1) what result is to be demonstrated, (2) who or what will demonstrate the result, (3) where will the result be observed, and (4) what interval or ratio scale criteria will be used.

Operational gaming: People play such roles as customers or opponents in a political debate in specific situations.

Operational results: Results at the Micro/Products level.

Operations research: A method of obtaining optimum solutions to problems in which relationships are specified and criteria for evaluating effectiveness are known; it summarizes alternatives into mathematical expressions and models and then identifies the set of alternatives that maximizes or minimizes the desired criterion for evaluating effectiveness.

Ordinal: Measurement scale that rank orders, such as first, 13th, greater than, less than, and equal to.

Organizational Elements Model (OEM): Identifies and links everything any organization, public or private, uses, does, produces, delivers, and the resulting payoffs for external clients and society.

Outcomes: Results at the external client and societal level. Outcomes are results that add value to society, community, and external clients of the organization.

Outputs: The results that an organization can or does deliver outside of itself to external clients and society.

Paradigm: The framework and ground rules people use to filter reality and understand the world around them.

Performance accomplishment systems: Any of a variety of interventions, such as "instructional systems design and development," quality management/continuous improvement, benchmarking, reengineering, and the like that are results oriented and are intended to get positive results; usually focused at the Micro/Products level.

Performance indicators: Data points that give information regarding a specific objective, or that we agree on represents the result; often, an agreed-on approximation, such as accepting the temperature measured at the airport as an indicator of the temperature in the city adjacent.

Planned change: Defining where you want to head, how to tell when you have arrived, and supplying the criteria for determining success and progress.

Planning phase: Second phase of strategic Mega Planning; has three steps, or elements: (1) identify strengths, weaknesses, opportunities, and threats; (2) derive long- and short-term missions; and (3) derive the strategic plan. The products from the Scoping elements provide the basis for building the Mega-referenced strategic plan.

Polling: Entails questioning representative members of a group about their preferences or predications. Sampling methods are crucial. It is important that respondents represent at least a stratified random sample of the group to which the results are to be generalized.

Portfolio analysis: Appraises an organization's products and their differential strengths (plotted as circles of various sizes) relative to the two dimensions of proportion of market share and sales growth rate.

Primary mission objective: Based on the part of the Ideal Vision the organization commits to deliver and to continuously move toward; the mission objective serves as the basic direction in which the organization will head. It states the Macro-level results (Outputs) to be delivered.

Processes: The means, activities, interventions, programs, and initiatives an organization can or does use.

Products: The building-block results of individuals and small groups that form the basis of what an organization produces, delivers inside as well as outside itself, and the payoffs for external clients and society.

Quality management and continuous improvement: Involving all organizational members to deliver client satisfaction and quality. Everyone in the organization strives to identify the gaps between current and desired results and then continuously improves everything each uses, does, and delivers. Individuals and organizations learn from mistakes and use performance data to improve, not to blame.

Quality management plus: Conventional quality management with the addition of Mega—societal value added—used to orient all measurement and continuous improvement.

Quasi-need: A gap in a method, resource, or process.

Queuing: Uses a mathematical method to optimize waiting time in a crowding situation, such as customers waiting for fast food, standing in line for refunds, applying for a building permit, or scheduling a concert.

Ratio scale measurement: Measurement scale has both a known zero point as well as equal scale distances (e.g., temperature in Kelvin, where matter stops moving, my bank account now)

Relevance trees: Used to identify hierarchies of various levels of complexity of events.

Results: Ends, products, outputs, outcomes—accomplishments and consequences.

Results chain: Linking Mega, Macro, and Micro results together and also with Inputs and Processes.

Scoping: First phase of strategic Mega Planning; has four parts: (1) select the Mega level of planning; (2) identify and select needs; (3) define current mission; and (4) derive the primary mission objective.

Simulation: Builds and tries out a model of a predicted or actual event or situation.

Six-step problem-solving model: Used to (1) identify (or justify) problem based on needs, (2) determine solution requirements and identify solution alternatives, (3) select solutions from among alternatives, (4) implement, (5) determine performance effectiveness and efficiency, and—at each and every step—(6) revise as required.

Social spin-offs: Organizational contributions made over and above individual and/or organizational payoffs and consequences.

Soft data: Perceptions of reality that are personal and are not independently verifiable; also termed "needs sensing" data.

Strategic alignment: The linking of Mega/Outcomes, Macro/Outputs, and Micro/Product level planning and results with each other and with Processes and Inputs.

Strategic thinking: Approaching any problem, program, project, activity, or effort with noting that everything that is used, done, produced, and delivered must add value for external clients and society.

SWOT (strengths, weaknesses, opportunities, and threats) analysis: Indicates environmental and operational factors to consider in determining enroute operational requirements and tactics: what tools and methods will be used and how to manage them while moving toward measurable success.

System: The sum total of parts working independently and together to achieve a desired result.

System analysis: Identifies and justifies *what* should be accomplished based on an Ideal/Mega Vision and is results focused.

Systematic: Proceeding in an orderly, definable manner; not to be confused with *Systematic approach, Systems approach,* or *System approach.*

Systematic approach: Planning and doing in an orderly and definable manner; focuses on means, methods and resources (Inputs and Processes).

Systemic: Encompassing and impacting the entire system, or organization.

Systemic approach: Planning and doing that involves the whole system, or organization; effects observed at all organizational levels, including the Mega, Macro, and Micro levels.

Systems analysis: Identifies the most effective and efficient ways and means to get the required results; solutions and tactics focused.

Systems approach: Planning and accomplishment based on internal, organizational-only purposes. It focuses only on Macro- or Micro-level results and contributions and is useful only when one is sure of the external requirements and payoffs; otherwise, it is not holistic and might provide solutions that don't go with the overall "system" problem or opportunities.

Tactical planning: Finding out what is available to get from what is to what should be at the organizational/Macro level. Tactics are best identified after the overall mission has been selected based on its linkages and contributions to external client and societal (Ideal Vision) results and consequences.

Tactical results: Results at the Macro/Outputs level.

Task analysis: The (depending on your purposes) lowest level of a system analysis; has two parts: (1) identification and ordering of the steps to be taken (task inventory) and (2) description of the salient characteristics and requirements of successful job and/or task accomplishment (detailed task analysis, or task description). It is derived from a mission analysis and the related function analysis and yields the most discrete level of detail required to identify all the "whats" (but not "hows") for problem resolution. Tasks are products at the lowest level of results.

Type I indicators: Implementation-oriented/process-oriented indicators that identify fidelity of activity and compliance in the application of methods, means, resources, and/or approaches.

Type R indicators: Results-oriented indicators that identify measurable performance, consequences, payoffs, or ends. Results targeted may include individual contributions as well as organizational results and consequences and external client and societal value added. This type of results indicator is urged.

What is: Current operational results and consequences; these could be for an individual, an organization, and/or society.

What should be: Desired or required operational results and consequences; these could be for an individual, an organization, and/or society.

Bibliography

Cited works and related readings basic to Mega Planning are noted with a "•" preceding each.

Abell, D. F., & Hammond, J. S. (1979). *Strategic market planning: Problems and analytic approaches.* Englewood Cliffs, NJ: Prentice Hall.

Ackoff, R. L. (1972). *The second industrial revolution.* Philadelphia: Wharton School of Business, Fordyce House.

Adams, S. (1996a). *The Dilbert principle: A cubicle's-eye view of bosses, meetings, management fads & other workplace afflictions.* New York: HarperBusiness.

Adams, S. (1996b). *Dogbert's top secret management handbook.* New York: HarperBusiness.

Addison, R., & Johnson, M. (1997, November). The building blocks of performance. *Business Executive,* pp. 3-5.

Alkin, M. C., & Bruno, J. E. (1970). System approaches to educational planning. In *Social and technological change: Implications for education* (Part 5). Eugene, OR: ERIC/CEA.

Alliger, G., & Janek, E. (1989). Kirkpatrick's levels of training criteria: Thirty years later. *Personnel Psychology, 42*(3).

American National Standards Institute. (1992). *Quality systems: Requirements for using quality principles in education and training* (American National Standard draft document: ANSI/ASQC Z-1 .11). Milwaukee, WI: Author.

American Society for Quality Control. (1987, June 19). *American National Standard: Quality systems—Model for quality assurance in design/development, production, installation, and servicing* (ANSI/ASQC Rep. Q91). Milwaukee, WI: Author.

Anderson, L. G., & Settle, R. F. (1977). *Benefit-cost analysis: A practical guide.* Lexington, MA: Lexington Books.

Argyris, C. (1991, May-June). Teaching smart people to learn. *Harvard Business Review.*

Argyris, C., Putnam, R., & Smith, D. McL. (1985). *Action science.* San Francisco: Jossey-Bass.

Ayres, R. U. (1969). *Technological forecasting and long-range planning.* New York: McGraw-Hill.

Banghart, F. W. (1969). *Educational systems analysis.* Toronto, Ontario: Macmillan.

• Barker, J. A. (1989). *The business of paradigms* [Videotape]. Burnsville, MN: ChartHouse Learning.

259

- Barker, J. A. (1992). *Future edge: Discovering the new paradigms of success.* New York: William Morrow.
- Barker, J. A. (1993). *Paradigm pioneers* [Videotape]. Burnsville, MN: ChartHouse Learning.

Beals, R. L. (1968, December). Resistance and adaptation to technological change: Some anthropological views. *Human Factors.*

Bell, C. R., & Zemke, R. (1992). *Managing knock your socks off service.* New York: American Management Association.

Bell, R., & Coplans, J. (1976). *Decisions, decisions: Game theory and you.* New York: Norton.

Bennis, W., & Nannus, B. (1985). *Leaders: The strategies for taking charge.* New York: Harper & Row.

Bertalanffy, L., von. (1968). *General systems theory.* New York: George Braziller.

Bhote, K. R. (1989). The Malcolm Baldrige Quality Award. *National Productivity Review, 8*(4).

Blalock, C. (1992, March 24). Four grocers tell how they created environmental programs that work. *Grocery Marketing.*

Blanchard, K., & Peale, N. V. (1988). *The power of ethical management.* New York: William Morrow.

Block, P. (1993). *Stewardship.* San Francisco: Berrett-Koehler.

Boisot, M. (1995). Preparing for turbulence: The changing relationship between strategy and management development in the learning organization. In B. Garratt (Ed.), *Developing strategic thought: Rediscovering the art of direction-giving.* London: McGraw-Hill.

Bounds, G., Yorks, L., Adams, M., & Ranney, G. (1994). *Beyond total quality management.* New York: McGraw-Hill.

Boutwell, C. E. (1997, October). Profits without people. *Phi Delta Kappan,* pp. 104-111.

Branson, R. K., et al. (1975). *Interservice procedures for instructional systems development (Phases I, II, III, IV, V, and Executive Summary).* U.S. Army Training and Doctrine Command Pamphlet 350, Fort Monroe, VA.

Briggs, L. J. (Ed.). (1977). *Instructional design: Principles and applications.* Englewood Cliffs, NJ: Educational Technology.

Briggs, L. J., & Wager, W. W. (1982). *Handbook of procedures for the design of instruction* (2nd ed.). Englewood Cliffs, NJ: Educational Technology.

Bryson, J. M. (1988). *Strategic planning for public and nonprofit organizations.* San Francisco: Jossey-Bass.

Buckley, W. (Ed.). (1968). *Modern systems research for the behavioral scientist.* Chicago: Aldine.

Burton, J., & McBride, B. (1988). *Total business planning.* New York: John Wiley.

Butz, R. (n.d.). En-route social indicators. *Performance & Instruction, 22*(8), 28-31.

Can corporate America cope? (1986, November 17). *Newsweek* (quotation of H. Ross Perot).

Caplan, F. (1990).*The quality system: A source book for managers and engineers.* Radnor, PA: Chilton.

Carnevale, A. P. (1991). *America and the new economy: How new competitive standards are radically changing the American workplace.* San Francisco: Jossey-Bass.

Carnevale, A. P., Ferman, L. A., et. al. (1990). *New developments in worker training: A legacy for the 1990's.* Madison, WI: Industrial Relations Research Association.

Carter, L. F. (1969). *The systems approach to education: The mystique and the reality* (SDC Rep. SP-3921). System Development Corporation.

Carter, R. K. (1983). *The accountable agency* (Human Service Guide No. 34). Beverly Hills, CA: Sage.

Churchman, C. W. (1969). *The systems approach.* New York: Dell.

Churchman, C. W. (1975). *The systems approach* (2nd ed.). New York: Dell.

Cleland, D. I., & King, W. R. (1968a). *Systems analysis and project management.* New York: McGraw-Hill.

Cleland, D. I., & King, W. R. (1968b). *Systems, organizations, analysis, management: A book of readings.* New York: McGraw-Hill.

Collins, J. C., & Porras, J. I. (1997). *Built to last: Successful habits of visionary companies.* New York: HarperBusiness.

Conner, D. R. (1992). *Managing at the speed of change.* New York: Villard.

Conner, D. R. (1998). *Building nimble organizations.* New York: John Wiley.

Corrigan, R. E., et al. (1975). *A system approach for education (SAFE)*. Garden Grove, CA: R. E. Corrigan Associates.

Corrigan, R. E., & Corrigan, B. O. (1985). *SAFE: System approach for effectiveness*. New Orleans, LA: R. E. Corrigan Associates.

Corrigan, R. E., & Kaufman, R. (1966). *Why system engineering?* Palo Alto, CA: Fearon.

Covey, S. R. (1996, March). Principle-centered leadership: Organizational alignment. *Quality Digest,* p. 21.

Critchlow, D. T. (1996). *Studebaker: The life and death of an American corporation*. Bloomington: Indiana University Press.

Crosby, P. B. (1979). *Quality is free: The art of making quality certain*. New York: McGraw-Hill.

Deal, T., & Kennedy, A. (1982). *Corporate cultures: The rites and rituals of corporate life*. Reading, MA: Addison-Wesley.

Delp, R., Thesen, A., Motiwalla, J., & Seshadri, N. (1977). *Systems tools for project planning*. Blooming-ton: Indiana University, International Development Institute, Program of Advanced Studies in Institution Building and Technical Assistance Methodology.

Deming, W. E. (1972). Code of professional conduct. *International Statistics Review, 40*(2), 215-219.

Deming, W. E. (1982). *Quality, productivity, and competitive position*. Cambridge: MIT, Center for Advanced Engineering Study.

Deming, W. E. (1986). *Out of the crisis*. Cambridge: MIT, Center for Advanced Engineering Technology.

Deming, W. E. (1990, May 10). A system of profound knowledge [Personal memo]. Washington, DC.

Det Norske Veritas Industry. (n.d.-a). *Accredited quality system certification*. Houston, TX: Author.

Det Norske Veritas Industry. (n.d.-b). *9000 & 9: Most often asked questions on ISO9000*. Houston, TX: Author.

Dick, W., & Carey, L. (1989). *The systematic design of instruction* (3rd ed.). Glenview, IL: Scott, Foresman.

Dick, W., & Johnson, F. C. (Eds.). (1993). Quality systems in performance improvement [Special issue]. *Performance Improvement Quarterly, 6*(3).

Dow Chemical. (1991, April). Our quality coaches. *Training & Development,* Supplement.

Drucker, P. F. (1973). *Management: Tasks, responsibilities, practices*. New York: Harper & Row.

Drucker, P. F. (1985). *Innovation and entrepreneurship*. London: William Heinemann.

Drucker, P. F. (1988, September-October). Management and the world's work. *Harvard Business Review*.

Drucker, P. F. (1992, September-October). The new society of organizations. *Harvard Business Review,* pp. 95-104.

Drucker, P. F. (1993a). *The five most important questions you will ever ask about your nonprofit organization*. San Francisco: Jossey-Bass.

Drucker, P. F. (1993b). *Post-capitalist society*. New York: HarperBusiness.

Drucker, P. F. (1994, November). The age of social transformation. *Atlantic Monthly,* pp. 53-80.

Drucker, P. F. (1995, February). Really reinventing government. *Atlantic Monthly,* pp. 49-61.

Drucker, P. F. (1998, October 5). Management's new paradigms. *Forbes,* pp. 152-169.

Fink, R. (1993, September 28). Group therapy: That's benchmarking. *Financial World*.

Forbes, R. (1998, August). The two bottom lines: Let's start to measure. *Quality Magazine, 7*(4), 17-21.

Fox, J. F. (1990, September). Applied models in HRD: Maslow and mega planning. *Performance & Instruction*.

Frankl, V. (1962). *Man's search for meaning: An introduction to logo-therapy*. Boston: Beacon.

Gagne, R., & Driscoll, M. P. (1988). *Essentials of learning for instruction* (2nd ed.). Englewood Cliffs, NJ: Prentice Hall.

Gagne, R. M., & Briggs, L. J. (1979). *Principles of instructional design* (2nd ed.). New York: Holt, Rinehart & Winston.

Gagne, R. M., Briggs, L. J., & Wager, W. W. (1988). *Principles of instructional design* (3rd ed.). New York: Holt, Rinehart & Winston.

Galagan, P. A. (1991, June). How Wallace changed its mind. *Training & Development, 45*(6).

Garratt, B. (1987). *The learning organization*. London: HarperCollins.

Garratt, B. (1994). *The learning organization* (2nd ed.). London: HarperCollins.

Garratt, B. (Ed.). (1995). *Developing strategic thought: Rediscovering the art of direction-giving.* London: McGraw-Hill.

Geber, B. (1995, March). Does your training make a difference? Prove it! *Training,* pp. 27-34.

Gilbert, T. F. (1971). Mathetics: The technology of education. In M. D. Merrill (Ed.), *Instructional design: Readings.* Englewood Cliffs, NJ: Prentice Hall.

Gilbert, T. F. (1978). *Human competence: Engineering worthy performance.* New York: McGraw-Hill.

Gilbert, T. F., & Gilbert, M. B. (1989, January). Performance engineering: Making human productivity a science. *Performance & Instruction.*

Glaser, R. (1966, Winter). Psychological bases for instructional design. *AV Communication Review.*

Glaser, W. (1992, May). The quality school curriculum. *Phi Delta Kappan.*

Greenwald, H. (1973). *Decision therapy.* New York: Peter Wyden.

Greenwald, H., & Rich, E. (1984). *The happy person: A seven step plan.* New York: Avon.

Gruender, C. D. (1996, May-June). Constructivism and learning: A philosophical appraisal. *Educational Technology, 36*(3), 21-29.

Hamel, G., & Prahalad, C. K. (1994). *Competing for the future: Breakthrough strategies for seizing control of your industry and creating the markets of tomorrow.* Boston: Harvard Business School Press.

Hanford, P. (1995). Developing director and executive competencies in strategic thinking. In B. Garratt (Ed.), *Developing strategic thought: Rediscovering the art of direction-giving.* London: McGraw-Hill.

Hammer, M., & Champy, J. (1993). *Reengineering the corporation: A manifesto for business revolution.* New York: HarperBusiness.

Hammer, M., & Stanton, S. A. (1995). *The reengineer revolution: A handbook.* New York: HarperCollins.

Handy, C. (1995-1996). *Beyond certainty: The changing worlds of organisations.* London: Arrow Books.

Harari, O. (1992, August). The peg-leg pig and other corporate fables. *Management Review, 81*(8), 28-29.

Harless, J. H. (1975). *An ounce of analysis is worth a pound of cure.* Newnan, GA: Harless Performance Guild.

Harless, J. H. (1986). Guiding performance with job aids. In M. Smith (Ed.), *Introduction to performance technology, Part 1.* Washington, DC: National Society for Performance and Instruction.

Harless, J. (1988). *Accomplishment-based curriculum development.* Newnan, GA: Harless Performance Guild.

Harless, J. (1998). *The Eden conspiracy: Educating for accomplished citizenship.* Wheaton, IL: Guild V.

Hequet, M. (1993). The limits of benchmarking. *Training, 30*(3).

Hersey, P., & Blanchard, K. (1982). *Management of organizational behavior: Utilizing human resources* (4th ed.). Englewood Cliffs, NJ: Prentice Hall.

Hinchliffe, D. R. (1990, September). Implications for using outcome/mega planning referents in military training. *Performance & Instruction.*

Hinchliffe, D. R. (1995). *Training for results: Determining education and training needs for emergency management in Australia.* Unpublished doctoral dissertation. Monash University, Clayton Campus, Victoria, Australia.

Hogan, R., Curphy, G. J., & Hogan, J. (1994, June). What we know about leadership: Effectiveness and personality. *American Psychologist, 49*(6).

Holton, E. F., III. (1996). The flawed four-level evaluation model. *Human Resource Development Quarterly, 7*(1), 5-21.

Howard, P. K. (1994). *The death of common sense: How law is suffocating America.* New York: Random House.

IBM. (1993). *Annual report, 1993.* Armonk, NY: Author.

Imai, M. (1986). *Kaizen: The key to Japan's competitive success.* New York: McGraw-Hill.

Isaac, S., & Michael, W. B. (1971). *Handbook in research and evaluation.* San Diego, CA: Knapp.

Ishikawa, K. (1986). *Guide to quality control.* White Plains, NY: Quality Resources.

Jackson, S. (1986). Task analysis. In M. Smith (Ed.), *Introduction to performance technology, Part 1.* Washington, DC: National Society for Performance and Instruction.

Jaeger, R. (Ed.). (1988). *Complementary methods for research in education.* Washington, DC: American Educational Research Association.

Janson, R. L. (1987). *Handbook of inventory management.* Englewood Cliffs, NJ: Prentice Hall.

Joiner, B. L. (1985). The key role of statisticians in the transformation of North American industry. *American Statistician, 39*(3).

Joiner, B. L. (1986, May). Using statisticians to help transform industry in America. *Quality Progress,* pp. 46-50.

Jones, L. B. (1995). *Jesus CEO.* New York: Hyperion.

Jones, P., & Kahamer, L. (1995). *Say it and live it: The 50 corporate mission statements that hit the mark.* New York: Currency/Doubleday.

Juran, J. M. (1988). *Juran on planning for quality.* New York: Free Press.

Kanter, R. M. (1983). *The change masters: Innovation for productivity in the American corporation.* New York: Simon & Schuster.

Kanter, R. M. (1989). *When giants learn to dance: Mastering the challenges of strategy, management, and careers in the 1990's.* New York: Simon & Schuster.

Kaufman, R. A. (1968). A system approach to education: Derivation and definition. *AV Communication Review, 16,* 415-425.

Kaufman, R. A. (1971). A possible integrative model for the systematic and measurable improvement of education. *American Psychologist, 26*(3).

Kaufman, R. A. (1972). *Educational system planning.* Englewood Cliffs, NJ: Prentice Hall. (Also *Planificacion de systemas educativos* [translation of *Educational system planning*]. Mexico City: Editorial Trillas, S.A., 1973).

Kaufman, R. (1985). Linking training to organizational impact. *Journal of Instructional Development, 8*(2), 23-29.

• Kaufman, R. (1987, May). On ethics. *Educational Technology,* pp. 48-49.

Kaufman, R. (1988a, July). Needs assessment: A menu. *Performance & Instruction.*

Kaufman, R. (1988b, September). Preparing useful performance indicators. *Training & Development.*

Kaufman, R. (1989a, February). Selecting a planning mode: Who is the client? Who benefits? *Performance & Instruction.*

Kaufman, R. (1989b, February). Warning: Being a proactive planner could be hazardous to your "being-loved" health. *Performance & Instruction.*

Kaufman, R. (1990a, June). Performance technology and quality management: Conflict or new partnership? *Educational Technology,* pp. 24-25.

Kaufman, R. (1990b, September). Strategic planning and thinking: Alternative views. *Performance & Instruction.*

Kaufman, R. (1990c, November). Why things might go bump in the night . . . and what to do about it. *Educational Technology.*

Kaufman, R. (1991a, May/June). The mainstream. *Performance & Instruction.*

Kaufman, R. (1991b, December). Relating evaluation and needs assessment. *Human Resource Development Quarterly.*

Kaufman, R. (1991c, December). Some cures for HRD myopia. *Training & Development.*

Kaufman, R. (1991d, December). Toward total quality "plus." *Training.*

Kaufman, R. (1991e). Trainers, performance technologists, and environmentalists. *Performance Improvement Quarterly, 4*(2).

Kaufman, R. (1991f, May). When good bosses ask for bad things. *Training & Development.*

Kaufman, R. (1992a, July). Comfort and change: Natural enemies. *Educational Technology.*

Kaufman, R. (1992b, July). The magnifying glass mentality. *Performance & Instruction Journal.*

Kaufman, R. (1992c, May). 6 steps to strategic success. *Training & Development,* pp. 107-112.

Kaufman, R. (1992d). *Strategic planning plus: An organizational guide* (Rev. ed.). Newbury Park, CA: Sage.

Kaufman, R. (1993a, October). Mega planning: The argument is over. *Performance & Instruction.*

Kaufman, R. (1993b, April). The vision thing: Florida's salvation. *Ideas in action* (Vol. 2, no. 5). Tallahassee: Florida TaxWatch.

Kaufman, R. (1994a, February). Auditing your needs assessment. *Training & Development.*

Kaufman, R. (1994b). Needs assessment and analysis. In W. R. Tracey (Ed.), *Human resources management & development handbook* (2nd ed.). New York: American Management Association.

Kaufman, R. (1994c, February). A needs assessment audit. *Performance & Instruction.*

Kaufman, R. (1995a, August 31). If distance learning is the solution, what's the problem? Beyond DDSS. *DEOSNEWS* (an electronic publication of the American Center for the Study of Distance Education/American Journal of Distance Learning of the Pennsylvania State University).

• Kaufman, R. (1995b, February). Is market-driven good enough? *Performance & Instruction, 34*(2), 16-19.

Kaufman, R. (1995c, November-December). Mega planning: The changed realities. Part 1. *Performance & Instruction.*

Kaufman, R. (1995d, November-December). Mega planning: The changed realities. Part 2 *Educational Technology.*

Kaufman, R. (1995e, November-December). Mega planning: The changed realities. Part 3. *Performance & Instruction.*

Kaufman, R. (1995f). *Mapping educational success* (Rev. ed.). Thousand Oaks, CA: Corwin.

Kaufman, R. (1995g, May-June). Quality management plus: Beyond standard approaches to quality. *Educational Technology.*

Kaufman, R. (1996a, May-June). Ideal visions: A modern imperative. *Educational Technology.*

Kaufman, R. (1996b, September-October). Visions, strategic planning & quality: More than hype. *Educational Technology, 36*(5), 60-62.

Kaufman, R. (1996c, January). What works and what doesn't: Evaluation. *Performance & Instruction Journal.*

Kaufman, R. (1996d, July). Why use a consultant if you already know what's best? *Performance Improvement Quarterly.*

Kaufman, R. (1997a, May-June). Avoiding the "dumbing down" of human performance improvement. *Performance Improvement Quarterly.*

Kaufman, R. (1997b, October). A new reality for organizational success: Two bottom lines. *Performance Improvement Quarterly, 36,*(8).

Kaufman, R. (1998a, February). If benchmarking is the solution, what's the problem? Some informal observations of the Australian reality. *Quality.*

Kaufman, R. (1998b). *Strategic thinking: A guide to identifying and solving problems* (Rev. ed.). Arlington, VA, and Washington, DC: American Society for Training & Development and the International Society for Performance Improvement.

Kaufman, R. (1999). From how to what to why: The handbook of performance technology as the gateway to the future. In H. Stolovitch & E. Keeps (Eds.), *The handbook of performance technology* (2nd ed.). San Francisco: Jossey-Bass.

Kaufman, R., & Carron, A. S. (1980). Utility and self-sufficiency in the selection of educational alternatives. *Journal of Instructional Development, 4*(1), 14-18, 23-26.

Kaufman, R. A., Corrigan, R. E., & Johnson, D. W. (1969). Towards educational responsiveness to society's needs: A tentative utility model. *Journal of Socio-Economic Planning Sciences, 3,* 151-157.

Kaufman, R., & English, F. W. (1979). *Needs assessment: Concept and application.* Englewood Cliffs, NJ: Educational Technology.

Kaufman, R., & Gavora, M. J. (1993). Needs assessment and problem solving: A critical appraisal of a critical reappraisal. *Performance Improvement Quarterly, 6*(2), 87-98.

Kaufman, R., Gavora, M., & James, A. (1993, July 31). *Healthy start evaluation: A study to cooperatively develop a practical evaluation framework and define useful evaluation criteria.* Tallahassee: Florida State University, Learning Systems Institute, Center for Needs Assessment & Planning.

Kaufman, R., & Grise, P. (1995). *Auditing your educational strategic plan: Making a good thing better.* Thousand Oaks, CA: Corwin Press.

Kaufman, R., Herman, J., & Watters, K. (1996). *Educational planning: Strategic, tactical, and operational.* Lancaster, PA: Technomic.

Kaufman, R., & Jones, M. (1990, February). The industrial survival of the nation: Union/management co-operation. *Human Resource Development Quarterly.*

Kaufman, R., & Kaufman, J. (1992). What should high-risk operations evaluate relative to safety and safety training. *Performance Improvement Quarterly, 5*(3).

Kaufman, R., & Keller, J. (1994, Winter). Levels of evaluation: Beyond Kirkpatrick. *Human Resources Quarterly, 5*(4), 371-380.

Kaufman, R., Rojas, A. M., & Mayer, H. (1993). *Needs assessment: A user's guide.* Englewood Cliffs, NJ: Educational Technology.

Kaufman, R., Stith, M., & Kaufman, J. D. (1992, February). Extending performance technology to improve strategic market planning. *Performance & Instruction.*

Kaufman, R., & Stolovitch, H. (1991, February). Planning, perspective, creativity, and control. *Educational Technology.*

Kaufman, R., & Stone, B. (1983). *Planning for organizational success: A practical guide.* New York: John Wiley.

Kaufman, R., & Swart, W. (1995, May-June). Beyond conventional benchmarking: Integrating ideal visions, strategic planning, reengineering, and quality management. *Educational Technology,* pp. 11-14.

Kaufman, R., & Thiagarajan, S. (1987). Identifying and specifying requirements for instruction. In R. M. Gagne (Ed.), *Instructional technology: Foundations.* Hillsdale, NJ: Lawrence Erlbaum.

Kaufman, R., Thiagarajan, S., & MacGillis, P. (Eds.). (1997). *The guidebook for performance improvement: Working with individuals and organizations.* San Francisco: Pfeiffer/Jossey-Bass.

Kaufman, R., & Thomas, S. (1980). *Evaluation without fear.* New York: Franklin Watts, New Viewpoints.

Kaufman, R., & Valentine, G. (1989, November/December). Relating needs assessment and needs analysis. *Performance & Instruction.*

Kaufman, R., & Watkins, R. (1996a, Spring). Costs-consequences analysis. *Human Resource Development Quarterly, 7,* 87-100.

Kaufman, R., & Watkins, R. (1996b). Mega planning: A framework for integrating strategic planning, needs assessment, quality management, benchmarking, and reengineering. In J. E. Jones & E. Biech (Eds.), *The HR handbook* (Vol. 1). Amherst MA: Human Resource Development Press.

Kaufman, R., & Watkins, R. (1999a). Needs assessment. In D. Langdon (Ed.), *The resource guide to performance interventions.* San Francisco: Jossey-Bass.

Kaufman, R., & Watkins, R. (1999b). Strategic planning. In D. Langdon (Ed.), *The resource guide to performance interventions.* San Francisco: Jossey-Bass.

Kaufman, R., Watkins, R., & Leigh, D. (1998). What is your organization's quality management culture? In M. Silberman (Ed.), *The 1998 team and organization development sourcebook* (pp. 173-183). New York: McGraw-Hill.

Kaufman, R., Watkins, R., & Sims, L. (1997). Costs-consequences analysis: A case study. *Performance Improvement Quarterly, 10*(3), 7-21.

Kaufman, R., Watkins, R., Triner, D., & Stith, M. (1998). The changing corporate mind: Organizations, visions, mission, purposes, and indicators on the move toward societal payoff. *Performance Improvement Quarterly, 11*(3), 32-44.

Kaufman, R., & Watters, C. (1992). Future challenges to performance technology: Ethics, professionalism, quality. In *Performance technology handbook.* Washington, DC and San Francisco: National Society for Performance & Instruction and Jossey-Bass.

Kaufman, R., & Zahn, D. (1993). *Quality management plus: The continuous improvement of education.* Newbury Park, CA: Corwin.

Kaufman-Rosen, L. (1994, October 17). Being cruel to be kind. *Newsweek,* pp. 51-52.

Kenyon, V. S. (1990, September). Managing a large-scale public organization while maintaining an outcome/mega orientation. *Performance & Instruction.*

Kirkpatrick, D. (1967). Evaluation. In R. L. Craig & L. R. Bittel (Eds.), *Training & development handbook* (American Society for Training & Development). New York: McGraw-Hill.

Kirkpatrick, D. (1996, Spring). Invited reaction: Reaction to Holton article. *Performance Improvement Quarterly, 7*(1), 23-29.

Kirkpatrick, D. L. (1994). *Evaluating training programs: The four levels.* San Francisco: Berret-Koehler.

Kuhn, T. (1962). *The structure of scientific revolutions.* Chicago: University of Chicago Press.

Kuhn, T. (1970). *The structure of scientific revolutions* (2nd ed.). Chicago: University of Chicago Press.

LaFeur, D., & Brethower, D. (1998). *The transformation: Business strategies for the 21st century.* Grand Rapids, MI: IMPACTGROUPworks.

Langley, P. (1989). Evaluating the economic and social impact of vocational rehabilitation programs in Victoria (Australia). *Performance Improvement Quarterly, 2*(2).

Laswell, H. D. (1948). *The communication of ideas.* New York: Harper & Row.

Lee, C. (1993, February). The vision thing. *Training, 30*(2).

Lenzer, R., & Johnson, S. (1997, March 10). Seeing things as they really are. *Forbes.*

Lessinger, L. M., & Salowe, A. E. (1997). *Game time: The educator's playbook for the new global economy.* Lancaster, PA: Technomic.

Levin, H. M. (1983). *Cost effectiveness: A primer* (New Perspectives in Evaluation series). Beverly Hills, CA: Sage.

Lloyd, B. (1992). Mintzberg on the rise and fall of strategic planning [Interview]. *Long Range Planning, 25*(4), 99-104.

Mager, R. F. (1988). *Making instruction work: Or skillbloomers.* Belmont, CA: David S. Lake.

Mager, R. F. (1992). *What every manager should know about training: Or "I've Got a Training Problem" . . . and other odd ideas.* Belmont, CA: Lake.

Mager, R. F. (1997). *Preparing instructional objectives: A critical tool in the development of effective instruction* (3rd ed.). Atlanta: Center for Effective Performance.

Mager, R. F., & Pipe, P. (1983). *CRI: Criterion referenced instruction* (2nd ed.). Carefree, AZ: Mager.

Mager, R. F., & Pipe, P. (1984). *Analyzing performance problems* (2nd ed.). Belmont, CA: Pitman.

Majchrzak, A. (1984). *Methods for policy research* (Applied Social Research Methods Series, Vol. 3). Beverly Hills, CA: Sage.

• Marshall, R., & Tucker, M. (1992). *Thinking for a living: Education and the wealth of nations.* New York: Basic Books.

Martin, R. (1993, November-December). Changing the mind of the organization. *Harvard Business Review.*

Martino, J. P. (1983). *Technological forecasting for decision-making* (2nd ed.). New York: North-Holland.

Maslow, A. (1954). *Motivation and personality.* New York: Harper & Row).

Mayer, N. (Ed.). (1984). *GAIA: An atlas of planet management.* New York: Anchor.

Maynard, H. B., Jr., & Mehrtens, S. E. (1993). *The fourth wave: Business in the 21st century.* San Francisco; Berrett-Koehler.

McLagan, A., et al. (1983). *Models for excellence: The conclusions and recommendations of the ASTD Training and Development Competency study.* Washington, DC: American Society for Training and Development.

Meals, D. (1967, January). Heuristic models for systems planning, *Phi Delta Kappan.*

Melvin, C. A. (1993). Application of control charts to educational systems. *Performance Improvement Quarterly, 6*(3).

Merrill, P. F. (1987). Job and task analysis. In R. M. Gagne (Ed.), *Instructional technology: Foundations.* Hillsdale, NJ: Lawrence Erlbaum.

Mintzberg, H. (1994). *The rise and fall of strategic planning.* New York: Free Press.

Mintzberg, H. (1995). Strategic thinking as "seeing." In B. Garratt (Ed.), *Developing strategic thought: Rediscovering the art of direction-giving.* London: McGraw-Hill.

Mitroff, I. I., Mason, R. O., & Pearson, C. M. (1994). Radical surgery: What will tomorrow's organizations look like? *Academy of Management Executives, 8*(2).

Muir, M., Watkins, R. Kaufman, R., & Leigh, D. (1998, April). Costs-consequences analysis: A primer. *Performance Improvement, 37*(4), 8-17.

Naisbitt, J. (1982). *Megatrends: Ten new directions transforming our lives.* New York: Warner.

Naisbitt, J. (1996). *Megatrends Asia: Eight Asian megatrends that are reshaping our world.* New York: Simon & Schuster.

Naisbitt, J., & Aburdene, P. (1990). *Megatrends 2000: Ten new directions for the 1990's.* New York: William Morrow.

Nanus, B. (1992). *Visionary leadership.* San Francisco: Jossey-Bass.

Nickols, F. (1990, January). Why those darned "training" problems won't go away. *Performance & Instruction.*

Nolan, T. M., Goodstein, L. D., & Pfeiffer, J. W. (1993). *Shaping your organization's future: Frogs, dragons, bees, and turkey tails.* San Diego: Pfeiffer.

Ohmae, K. (1982). *The mind of the strategist: Business planning for competitive advantage.* New York: Penguin.

Ornstein, R., & Ehrlich, P. (1989). *New world new mind: Moving toward conscious evolution.* New York: Simon & Schuster/Touchstone.

Osborne, D., & Gaebler, T. (1992). *Reinventing government: How the entrepreneurial spirit is transforming the public sector.* Reading, MA: Addison-Wesley.

Pascale, R. T., & Athos, A. G. (1981). *The art of Japanese management: Applications for American executives.* New York: Warner.

Peters, T. (1987). *Thriving on chaos: Handbook for a management revolution.* New York: Knopf.

Peters, T. (1997). *The circle of innovation: You can't shrink your way to greatness.* New York: Knopf.

Peters, T. J., & Austin, N. (1985). *The passion for excellence: The leadership difference.* New York: Random House.

Peters, T. J., & Waterman, R. H., Jr. (1982). *In search of excellence: Lessons learned from America's best run companies.* New York: Harper & Row.

Pfeiffer, J. W., Goodstein, L. D., & Nolan, T. M. (1989). *Shaping strategic planning: Frogs, bees, and turkey tails.* Glenview, IL: Scott, Foresman.

Phi Delta Kappa. (1984). *Handbook for conducting future studies in education.* Bloomington, IN: Author.

Pipho, C. (1991, February). Business leaders focus on reform. *Phi Delta Kappan,* pp. 422-423.

Pomeranz, F. (1978, Summer). Social measurement: A primer for implementation. *Journal of Accounting, Auditing & Finance,* No. 4, 385-389.

Popcorn, F. (1991). *The Popcorn report.* New York: Doubleday.

Quinn, D. (1992). *Ishmael.* New York. Bantam/Turner.

Rappaport, A. (1986). *General system theory.* Cambridge, MA: Abacus.

Renard, P. G., & Sinnock, P. (1990, September). Training needs assessment: Fact or fiction. *Performance & Instruction.*

Ricoeur, P. (1986). *Lectures on ideology and utopia.* (G. H. Taylor, Ed.). New York: Columbia University Press.

Roberts, W. (1987). *Leadership secrets of Attila the Hun.* New York: Warner.

Roberts, W. (1993). *Victory secrets of Attila the Hun.* New York: Doubleday.

Roberts, W. (1997). *Protect your Achilles' heel: Crafting armor for the new age at work.* Kansas City, MO: Andrews & McMeel/United Press Syndicate.

Rodriguez, S. R. (1988). *Needs assessment and analysis: Tools for change. Journal of Instructional Development, 11*(1), 23-28.

Rogers, C. (1964). Toward a modern approach to values: The valuing process in the mature person. *Journal of Abnormal and Social Psychology, 68*(2).

Rojas, A. M. (1988). Evaluation of sales training impact: A case study using the organizational elements model. *Performance Improvement Quarterly, 1*(2), 71-84.

Rosenberg, M. J. (1990, February). Performance technology: Working the system. *Training.*

Rossett, A. (1987). *Training needs assessment.* Englewood Cliffs, NJ: Educational Technology.

Rothwell, W. J., & Kazanas, H. L. (1998). *Mastering the instructional design process: A systematic approach.* San Francisco: Jossey-Bass.

Rummler, G. A. (1986). Organizational redesign. In M. Smith (Ed.), *Introduction to performance technology, Part 1.* Washington, DC: National Society for Performance and Instruction.

Rummler, G. A., & Brache, A. P. (1990). *Improving performance: How to manage the white space on the organization chart.* San Francisco: Jossey-Bass.

Samuelson, R. J. (1996, January 8). Great expectations. *Newsweek,* pp. 24-33.

Schaaf, M. (1986, October 24). Wants: Whether we need them or not. *Los Angeles Times,* Part V, p. 3.

Scholtes, P. R. (1988). *The team handbook.* Madison, WI: Joiner Associates.

Schwartz, P., & Kelly, K. (1996, August). The relentless contrarian. *Wired.*

Scriven, M. (1967). The methodology of evaluation. In R. Tyler, R. M. Gagne, & M. Scriven (Eds.), *Perspectives of curriculum evaluation* (AERA Monograph Series on Curriculum Evaluation). Chicago: Rand McNally.

Scriven, M. (1973). Goal free evaluation. In E. R. House (Ed.), *School evaluation: The politics and process.* Berkeley, CA: McCutchan.

Senge, P. M. (1990). *The fifth discipline: The art & practice of the learning organization.* New York: Doubleday-Currency.

Shanker, A. (1990, January). The end of the traditional model of schooling—and a proposal for using incentives to restructure public schools. *Phi Delta Kappan.*

Shewhart, W. A. (1931). *Economic control of quality of manufactured product.* New York: D. Van Nostrand.

Siskin, L. S. (1994). *Realms of knowledge: Academic departments in secondary schools.* Washington, DC: Fulmer.

Sleezer, C. M., & Gradous, D. B. (1998). Measurement challenges in evaluation and performance improvement. *Performance Improvement Quarterly, 11*(4), 62-75.

Sobel, I., & Kaufman, R. (1989). Toward a "hard" metric for educational utility. *Performance Improvement Quarterly, 2*(1).

Stakenas, R. G., & Mock, D. B. (1985). Context evaluation: The use of history in policy analysis. *Public Historian, 17*(3).

Stanley, T. J., & Danko, W. D. (1996). *The millionaire next door: The surprising secrets of America's wealthy.* Atlanta, GA: Longstreet.

Stettler, H. F. (1970). *Auditing principles* (3rd ed.). Englewood Cliffs, NJ: Prentice Hall.

Stevens, S. S. (1951). Mathematics, measurement, and psychophysics. In S. S. Stevens, *Handbook of experimental psychology.* New York: John Wiley.

Stolovitch, H. D., & Keeps, E. J. (1992). *Handbook of human performance technology: A comprehensive guide for analyzing and solving performance problems in organizations.* San Francisco: Jossey-Bass.

Suzaki, K. (1987). *The new manufacturing challenge: Techniques for continuous improvement.* New York: Free Press.

Swanson, R. A. (1994). *Analysis for improving performance.* San Francisco: Berrett-Koehler.

Swanson, R. A., & Gradous, D. (1988). *Performance at work: A systematic program for analyzing work behavior.* New York: John Wiley.

Sweetland, S. R. (1996, Fall). Human capital theory: Foundations of a field inquiry. *Review of Educational Research, 66*(3), 341-359.

Swiss, J. E. (1992, July/August). Adapting total quality management (TQM) to government. *Public Administration Review, 52*(4), 356-362.

The Talmud. Sayings of our fathers. Chapter 1, Verse 14.

Taylor, A., III. (1998, August 3). Jack Smith the man to fix GM? *Fortune,* pp. 86-92.

Toffler, A. (1970). *Future shock.* New York: Random House.

Toffler, A. (1980). *The third wave.* New York: Morrow

Toffler, A. (1990). *Powershift: Knowledge, wealth, and violence at the edge of the 21st century.* New York: Bantam.

Tosti, D. T. (1986). Feedback systems. In M. Smith (Ed.), *Introduction to performance technology, Part 1.* Washington, DC: National Society for Performance and Instruction.

Triner, D., Greenberry, A., & Watkins, R. (1996, November-December). Training needs assessment: A contradiction in terms? *Educational Technology, 36*(6), 51-55.

U.S. General Accounting Office. (1991, May). Management practices: U.S. companies improve performance through quality efforts (GAO/NSIAD Rep. No. 91-190). Washington, DC: Author.

U.S. General Accounting Office. (1997, June). *The Government Performance and Results Act: 1997 governmentwide implementation will be uneven* (GAO/GGD Rep. No. 97-109). Washington, DC: Author.

Van de Ven, A., & Delbecq, A. L. (1971, June). Nominal versus interacting group process for committee decision-making effectiveness. *Journal of the Academy of Management.*

Walton, M. (1986). *The Deming management method.* New York: Dodd, Mead.

Watkins, R., & Kaufman, R. (1996, November). An update on relating needs assessment and needs analysis. *Performance Improvement, 10*(2), 7-21.

Watkins, R., Leigh, D., Foshay, R., & Kaufman, R. (1998). Kirkpatrick plus: Evaluation and continuous improvement with a community focus. *Educational Technology Research and Development Journal, 46*(4), 90-96.

Watkins, R., Leigh, D., Platt, W., & Kaufman, R. (1998). Needs assessment: A digest, review, and comparison of needs assessment literature. *Performance Improvement, 37*(7), 40-53.

Watkins, R., Leigh, D., & Kaufman, R. (1998, September). Needs assessment: A digest, review, and comparison of needs assessment literature. *Performance Improvement, 37*(7), 40-53.

Watkins, R., Triner, D., & Kaufman, R. (1996, July). The death and resurrection of strategic planning: A review of Mintzberg's *The rise and fall of strategic planning. International Journal of Educational Reform, 5*(3), 390-393.

Wedman, J. F. & Graham, S. (1998). Introducing the concept of performance support using the performance pyramid. *Journal of Continuing Higher Education, 46*(3), 8-20.

Wedman, J. F., & Wedman, J. M. (1985). Changing instructional practices using a performance engineering model. *Performance & Instruction, 24*(8), 1-4.

West, J. (n.d.). *W. Edwards Deming: Prophet of quality.* Milwaukee, WI: American Society for Quality Control.

Wheatley, M. J. (1992). *Leadership and the new science: Learning about organization from an orderly universe.* San Francisco: Berrett-Koehler.

Wiesendanger, B. (1993, September-October). Deming's luster dims at Florida Power & Light: A case study. *Journal of Business Strategy, 14*(5), 60-61.

Wilkinson, D. (1989). Outputs and outcomes of vocational education programs: Measures in Australia. *Performance Improvement Quarterly, 2*(2).

Wilkinson, D., & Pedlar, M. (1995). Strategic thinking in public service. In B. Garratt (Ed.), *Developing strategic thought: Rediscovering the art of direction-giving.* London: McGraw-Hill.

Windham, D. (1975). The macro-planning of education: Why it fails, why it survives, and the alternatives. *Comparative Education Review.*

Witkin, B. R. (1984). *Assessing needs in educational and social programs.* San Francisco: Jossey-Bass.

Witkin, B. R. (1991). Setting priorities: Needs assessment in time of change. In R. V. Carlson & G. Awkerman (Eds.), *Educational planning: Concepts, strategies, and practices.* New York: Longman.

Witkin, B. R. (1994). Needs assessment since 1981: The state of the practice. *Evaluation Practice, 15*(1), 17-27.

Witkin, B. R., & Altschuld, J. W. (1995). *Planning and conducting needs assessments: A practical guide.* Thousand Oaks, CA: Sage.

Xerox Corporation. (1989). *Leadership through quality processes and tools review: Quality you can copy.* Rochester, NY: Multinational Customer & Service Education.

Zahn, D. A. (1988). Quality breakdowns: An opportunity in disguise. In *Forty-Second Annual Quality Congress Transactions* (pp. 56-62). Milwaukee, WI: American Society for Quality Control.

Zemke, R., & Bell, C. (1990, June). Service recovery. Doing it right the second time. *Training.*

Zemke, R., & Kramlinger, T. (1982). *Figuring things out: A trainer's guide to needs and task analysis.* Reading, MA: Addison-Wesley.

Index

About the Author

Roger Kaufman is Professor and Director, Office for Needs Assessment & Planning at Florida State University. He is also Research Professor of Engineering Management at Old Dominion University, Norfolk, Virginia. Before entering higher education, he was Assistant to the Vice President for Engineering as well as Assistant to the Vice President for Research at Douglas Aircraft Company.

His clients—working in the areas of strategic planning, quality management, needs assessment, and organizational improvement—include Andersen Consulting; Chase Manhattan Bank; Los Alamos National Laboratories; AT&T; Australian Public Service Commission; Florida Power & Light, Australian Department of Defence; Microsoft; New Zealand Treasury; Shell Oil Company, U.S. Department of Veterans Affairs; U.S. Coast Guard; Texas Instruments; Florida Governor's Office of Planning and Budget; Sun Microsystems; Bank of Boston (Argentina); Fireman's Fund Insurance; Milliken/Milliken University; MB&A (Argentina); American Airlines Group/Blue Cross of Texas/ISPI; New Zealand Army; Tricon; BellCanada; Wellington (New Zealand) City Council; Florida Department of Corrections; and U.S. Army Training Support Center, to name a few.

He is a Fellow of the American Psychological Association, a Fellow of the American Academy of School Psychology, and a Diplomate of the American Board of Professional Psychology. The International Society for Performance Improvement, an organization for which he once served as president, has awarded him its highest honor by naming him "Member for Life," and he is also recipient of its Thomas F. Gilbert Professional Achievement Award.

He has published 34 books and 180 articles on strategic planning, performance improvement, quality management and continuous improvement, needs assessment, management, and evaluation.